Learning to Love

Learning to Love

From Conflict to Lasting Harmony

Don and Martha Rosenthal

A Living Planet Book

Sterling Publishing Co., Inc.
New York

Library of Congress Cataloging-in-Publication Data Available

2 4 6 8 10 9 7 5 3 1

Published by Sterling Publishing Co., Inc.
387 Park Avenue South, New York, NY 10016
© 2006 by Don and Martha Rosenthal
Distributed in Canada by Sterling Publishing
c/o Canadian Manda Group, 165 Dufferin Street
Toronto, Ontario, Canada M6K 3H6
Distributed in the United Kingdom by GMC Distribution Services
Castle Place, 166 High Street, Lewes, East Sussex, England BN7 1XU
Distributed in Australia by Capricorn Link (Australia) Pty. Ltd.
P.O. Box 704, Windsor, NSW 2756, Australia

Designed by Nancy B. Field

Manufactured in the United States of America
All rights reserved

Sterling ISBN-13: 978-1-4027-3380-2
ISBN-10: 1-4027-3380-1

For information about custom editions, special sales, premium and
corporate purchases, please contact Sterling Special Sales
Department at 800-805-5489 or specialsales@sterlingpub.com.

To Aram

Acknowledgments

We wish to express our deepest gratitude to the following:

To the staff at Sterling Publishing Co. for their geniality and competence at every turn. Especially to Patty Gift, editor *par excellence*, who held the vision unfailingly and was a special pleasure to work with.

To Josh Horwitz, best and most indispensable of agents, for believing in us, taking up our cause, and ensuring that the book came to fruition.

To Simon and Stephen Pearce, for their encouragement and help with our earliest ventures in the publishing process.

To Joel Kramer, for all he taught us years ago, especially about yoga and "playing the edge."

To friends and supporters too numerous to name, but especially Margaret Boone, Reza Bundy, Jeff Cotton, Stewart Cubley, Bill Culp, Mary McIsaac, and Richard Miller, for serving as sacred and loving witnesses to our process over the years and speaking so eloquently on our behalf.

Martha would also like to express her unending gratitude to Paramahansa Yogananda for awakening her deep love of God, through which she has been able to love Don and others in her life more fully.

To our especially dear friends and colleagues, Rich and Antra Borofsky, for their sustained love and support, and for all they have taught us about loving. Also to Rich for his wonderfully eloquent and generous Foreword.

To long-time cherished friends and companions Dan Breslaw and Judy Tharinger, for their loyal friendship throughout the years, and for seeing the value of our work from the beginning and helping make it known. Also to Dan for his encouragement, his editorial finesse in helping us hone our thoughts, and his devoted and unflagging assistance at every level, well beyond the call.

And finally, to the many, many couples we have worked with over the years, whose honest effort and willingness to open their hearts have never ceased to inspire us, and from whom we have learned so very, very much.

Contents

"For one human being to love another: that is perhaps the most difficult of all our tasks, the ultimate, the last test and proof, the work for which all other work is but preparation."

—*Rainer Maria Rilke*

"Whenever your relationship is not working, whenever it brings out the 'madness' in you and in your partner, be glad. What was unconscious is being brought up to the light. It is an opportunity for salvation."

—*Eckhart Tolle*

Foreword

by Richard Borofsky, Ed.D.

Near the end of a dirt road in rural Vermont is a most unusual laboratory. Housed in a red clapboard cape cottage, this laboratory has no scientific instruments, computers, animals in cages, or scientists in white lab coats. There are only two researchers here—a man and a woman, who have spent over thirty years together investigating with great dedication a single question: How can one cultivate an open heart in the context of a long-term committed intimacy? Their names are Don and Martha Rosenthal, and the book you're holding is the fruit of their inquiry.

My wife Antra and I have been frequent visitors to this laboratory, and have come to know these two researchers well—first professionally (we're couples therapists and workshop leaders ourselves) and later through our deepening friendship. And it has been an extraordinary friendship indeed. The four of us have worked together, shared each other's hospitality, walked and meditated together in every kind of weather and season, talked shop, cooked meals, laughed a lot, and confided to each other everything from our smallest anxieties to our deepest spiritual yearnings. Everything we have come to know about Don and Martha has increased our affection for them personally and our profound respect for their teaching. So, it is a great pleasure and honor for me to be able to introduce you to my dear friends and this wonderful book.

What you are about to read is a distillation of what Don and Martha have learned from their joint investigation of what it means to cultivate an open heart. As you will see, *Learning to Love* is both practical and inspirational. It is quite realistic about the many difficulties, limitations, and pitfalls of intimate relationship without being discouraging. It is enormously hopeful about the possibility of transforming even the most damaged relationships, yet it is never naïve or simplistic. In a word, it is balanced. *Learning to Love* successfully integrates both psychological and spiritual perspectives on intimate relationship without falling into the mistakes or limitations of either.

Learning to Love also navigates quite skillfully the many dichotomies on which couples often founder—dichotomies such as freedom and commitment, honesty and compassion, safety and risk-taking, change and acceptance. All these apparent polarities are resolved here quite elegantly by the understanding that true love has no opposite. It includes everything—discomfort, pain, anger, resentment, despair—all the troubles that at one time or another afflict every serious relationship. In an authentically open-hearted relationship there is room for all of it.

This is what makes Don and Martha so successful in their work with couples—even those who are in dire straits, believing there is no way to resolve their conflicts. As *Learning to Love* makes clear, when we are in the presence of an open heart, conflict is readily resolved. Problems begin to dissolve (as opposed to being solved), and genuine transformation is possible. Personal and interpersonal difficulties can become a vehicle for deeper intimacy, while fear, hurt, and shame are composted into a fertile soil where love can grow again. This is what Martha and Don are able to accomplish in their work, because theirs is a love inclusive enough to embrace the whole human condition.

This open-heartedness is made possible through the practice of mindfulness—the ability to be aware of how we are with each other moment to moment. Like direct, unfiltered sunlight, awareness makes love grow. It illuminates and animates the best in us. When we are aware, paying attention to whatever is happening right now, we are more able to make loving choices—most importantly, the choice to keep our hearts open. More than anything else, it is making this choice, over and over again, that sustains and deepens our relationships.

In effect, what Martha and Don offer us here is a new form of meditation practice—a kind of mindfulness *à deux*—that helps couples learn how to be present and attentive *while* they are relating. Whereas mindfulness has traditionally been practiced alone on a meditation cushion with eyes closed, *Learning to Love* shows couples how they can be mindful together while they are talking and listening, even when they are hurting, frightened or angry. Whereas mindfulness has traditionally focused on cultivating an aloof detachment from all desires or preferences, this approach enables us to be more passionately and compassionately involved.

To be sure, becoming more mindful requires discipline and commitment. It is an art that can be practiced for a lifetime. However, years of training or formal meditation practice are not required. This is a mindfulness that makes it possible for us to open our hearts to each other right now—*no matter what is going on between us*. This choice, which the authors tell us can be made whenever we are self-aware, is what this book is all about. Through lucid instructions, explanations, and anecdotes, Don and Martha show us what it means to keep our hearts open in every circumstance life offers— not only when we are feeling loving, but even in our most difficult and painful moments together. Their basic assumption—which radically challenges all our habitual defenses and rationalizations— is that "there's never a good reason to keep the heart closed."

This is a bold and inspiring vision—the possibility of relating to each other open-heartedly under *any* conditions. Yet far from being idealistic or unattainable, this vision is wholly practicable. It is grounded in years of personal experience. In clear, jargon-free language the book shows us what this vision looks like in the real world, in real time. It shows us how any couple, no matter what their difficulties, background, or education, can make it a palpable reality. The only requirement is that we be willing to become apprentices to love, open to learning from whatever happens between us.

Novelist Katherine Anne Porter once wrote: "Love must be learned and learned again and again; there is no end to it." The Rosenthals know this well. Their book is all about learning to love, and developing the skills and attitudes that make this learning a lifelong process. Their main qualification for writing on this subject is that they—like all good teachers—are themselves dedicated students. One senses this dedication throughout, as well as their curiosity, humility, and wisdom. Because they are living their own teachings, they are inspiring models for those of us wishing to enlarge our own capacity for giving and receiving love.

I hope you will be inspired by these teachings as much as Antra and I have been. May they inspire you to create a laboratory of love in your own home, and to devote yourself passionately to the noble and practical art of unconditional loving.

Cambridge, Massachusetts
November, 2005

Richard Borofsky, Ed.D., is a clinical psychologist, formerly codirector of the Boston Gestalt Institute, and a former instructor at the Harvard Medical School. He and his wife, Antra, are founders and directors of the Center for the Study of Relationship in Cambridge, Massachusetts.

Introduction

Martha and I began our relationship in a small, spartan cabin in the Kachemak wilderness area in South Central Alaska. There were no roads; once a month, we had to take a boat about eight miles to the nearest town for supplies. Our life was simple. We gathered wood, took walks, and practiced yoga. We sat in stillness by the window and watched it get light and then dark. In the plentiful northern winter darkness, we had long, deep talks by kerosene light. Peacefulness arose as we followed ancient rhythms, attempting to come upon simplicity and balance after years of stressful living. With no outside pressures, we found ourselves getting along quite well for the first few years. Fights and unpleasant exchanges were alien to us, and in their absence, we thought we had attained something special. In fact, our unusual lifestyle had allowed us to fabricate an unrealistically positive image of our relationship.

After five years of living this way, we realized it was time for a dramatic change. A sameness had crept into our rhythms, and with a lack of newness, the quiet life began feeling more like stagnation than serenity. It was time to try something different. We ended up in a small coastal village in Northern California, where we gradually entered into a more traditional (relatively speaking—it was still California!) lifestyle.

All of a sudden the precious peace we had so carefully crafted together was shattered. In the abrupt influx of new people, ideas, experiences, and stresses, we found ourselves not only noticing flaws in each other, but becoming increasingly disturbed by what we saw. As a result, over time, each of us closed down to the other emotionally and sexually. Within two years we hit bottom. Many a simple exchange erupted into a painful and seemingly pointless fight. The kindness and tenderness were gone. Neither of us felt emotionally safe with the other, and the mutual trust had evaporated. Something felt terribly wrong. Where had the love gone? How did we get here?

Today, almost thirty years later, we still observe friends and acquaintances reliving problems that are very similar to ours. A truly flowering intimacy is apparently most elusive. Even intelligent people with integrity and goodwill are finding that their education and experience have not taught them enough to keep intimacy flourishing. Those who take their spiritual lives seriously are also not immune from the sometimes breathtaking difficulties of being intimate. Couples of every persuasion, from the most traditional to the most "New Age," have the same difficulty feeling and expressing the love they originally felt. Others, alone and scarred from the battlefield of relationship, seriously wonder if such an ongoing bond is even possible.

Martha and I survived our crisis. In so doing, we found a depth of connection we never could have imagined. We've gone through many moments of joyous discovery and have committed many a painful blunder. In confronting our difficulties, we have made full use of the meditative pursuits we assimilated in our cabin days, as well as Eastern and Western spiritual teachings, Western psychology, and a great deal of groping blindly. Although we still have difficult moments occasionally, we are deeply grateful for the love we now experience together, and we'd like to share with you in the following pages that which has made it possible.

—*Don*

As Don's account makes clear, the course of our lives has taken us to some unexpected places. When the two of us embarked on our path together some thirty-five years ago, we hadn't the remotest idea what we were getting into. Like many other couples, we began with a romantic, somewhat naïve vision. We were in love. What's more, we were surrounded by glorious mountains and glaciers, with plenty of time to enjoy the scenery. In our little cabin on the shore of Kachemak Bay, it was easy to imagine our life of peace and simplicity going on forever. It felt like we had attained a level of bliss that would sustain us the rest of our lives.

But as Don says, it all began to fall apart after a while, despite our idyllic surroundings; and our move to the busy world of California tested the relationship in ways we'd never dreamed. We had virtually no money, and we had to take on unfulfilling meager-paying jobs to sustain ourselves. We moved around in a succession of group living situations that involved all sorts of stresses. And in the midst of all this chaos, we found ourselves doing something we never imagined we would do. We began to argue. We argued over money, over household chores, over different levels of tidiness, over how much attention we were giving each other. Sometimes we would argue over seemingly nothing, just out of irritability. It became shockingly clear that our relationship was afflicted with all the same problems that the people around us were having—people we used to feel superior to. At a certain point, I realized, Oh my gosh, I'm not who I thought I was, and Don's not who I thought he was. And I haven't a clue how to deal with it. It was like the first day of kindergarten, not knowing where you're supposed to hang your coat.

Well, here we are, having been in school a long time now. All the important lessons, we've found, have to do with learning to love more unconditionally. There was no way of knowing at the outset how demanding the curriculum would be—how much stamina and focus it would take to work through the obstacles, and how deeply those hindrances would turn out to be imbedded in our innermost selves. Yet I can't imagine learning so much about myself in any other way. It took that deep involvement with another human being to bring out my hidden darkness and expose it to the light.

Fortunately, my relationship with Don also brought to light the possiblity of moving into my eternal Self—the part of me that's willing to sacrifice the demands of my ego and seek fulfillment on a vaster scale. Being tossed into the trials of relationship is what forced me to tap into that deeper Source of Love. Had we known the extent of the difficulties, we might never have started on this path. Yet having done so, and having experienced many of the true joys of intimacy, we feel supremely blessed.

It's not that we've left our old selves completely behind. We occasionally encounter some of the old issues: money, household chores, messes that have to be cleaned up. We even have some new ones: long-range health concerns and financial security. But we do not often have discord, and certainly not in the same way. When we do express our differences, we're able to do it within a context of underlying love and good will. There's a spaciousness surrounding our disagreements that comes from the reassuring presence of love.

The one thing I would want every reader of this book to know is that no matter what your relationship is like now, you can have this loving presence in your lives. However great your doubts and uncertainties, however dark or littered with obstacles the way may seem, there is a vastness holding you, a love within you that is larger than your problems. If you allow yourself to receive it, it will prove more powerful than all the negativity. Underneath all the obstacles in your relationship lie a richness and joy almost beyond imagining.

In the following pages, we've tried to summarize all that we've learned from our many ups and downs. We're grateful for the opportunity to share it with you. May our blessings go with you as you walk the path.

—*Martha*

PART I:

Working Together

A successful intimacy requires the development of wisdom and skill at two levels. First, the partners must be able to bring clarity and kindness to their communication even when—most particularly when—difficult feelings are present. Second, the individual partners must learn to release those difficult feelings within themselves by looking deeply into their origin in the depth of the mind. Although these two noble tasks are intimately related, we've organized the chapters of this book around the division between the interpersonal and the intrapersonal, the art of communication and the journey of self-awareness. Both are necessary for relationship to flourish.

We begin by shining a light on mutual interaction. In the first seven chapters of Part I, we examine the dynamics of the couple relationship from a number of different angles. Chapter 1 presents an overview of what generally goes wrong in relationships and addresses the potential value of using conflict wisely. Chapters 2 and 3 discuss listening and asking for change, respectively, and offer some fundamental techniques for communicating effectively around thorny issues. Chapters 4 and 5 focus on the healthy exchange of energy that makes intimacy possible, and how to nurture it. Finally, Chapters 6 and 7 explore in some detail anger and pain, which for most couples are the greatest obstacles to harmonious interaction.

CHAPTER 1

What Goes Wrong

What Holds Relationships Together?

What is the force that holds couples together? In earlier days it was mutual dependence, economic necessity, and social or religious pressure. Most married couples remained together for a lifetime, although few were able to reach across the formidable barriers of traditional male and female role models to make a genuine connection. In fact, few had any vision of what true intimacy might look like.

The 1960s and '70s brought major changes to our culture. The women's movement, the sexual revolution, and the abandonment by many of traditional religious thinking demolished in great part the notion that couples should stay together through difficult times. As a society, we searched desperately for a new purpose in being together. Many hoped to find it in the sexual and emotional gratification that mark the early phase of romance.

Most of us, as we enter into intimacy, feel an incompleteness in our being. It is tempting to regard intimacy as a means to fill this vast emptiness. We hope to receive uninterrupted positive attention and a continually passionate and exciting sexual experience. What even allows us to believe in such a patent impossibility is the presence of these qualities for a brief period during the early romantic phase of the relationship. Thus encouraged, we set up an image in our mind of a relationship whose continual positive and passionate qualities keep us from experiencing our loneliness. Our union is now held together by the hope for uninterrupted gratification.

This unrealistic desire leads to inevitable disillusionment. Anyone who enters into intimacy with the purpose of constant gratification is embarking on a path of pain. Nobody is capable of keeping us perpetually satisfied; nobody else can rescue us from our demons. Should we fall into the common trap of thinking so, the futility of our arrangement will quickly become apparent. Each will begin to resent the other for not fulfilling their impossible task. A new phase of relationship begins in which both partners experience a growing negativity that they are sorely unequipped to handle.

Unworkable Strategies

Living with another person brings us face-to-face with our deepest layers of inner disturbance, which date back to childhood. These disturbances are manifested in mental habits that create illusions and close the heart, interfering with feeling and expressing love. Nothing reveals these inadequacies as forcefully as intimacy.

For most of us, these habits bring hurt, anger, and other painful feelings as an inevitable accompaniment to intimacy. Though the feelings are inevitable, how we respond to them determines whether they erode the foundations of love and trust, or become the raw materials for greater understanding and compassion.

Most of us have not developed the special skills needed to respond wisely to the powerful negative feelings that intimacy awakens. When conflicts arise, we tend to react primarily from conditioning and habit.

In the early years, we develop certain survival strategies that help us respond to the difficulties of our family life. These methods of coping become programmed deep into our consciousness. They may control our behavior over a lifetime, unless they are recognized and released through understanding.

Although many types of survival strategy abound, they can be broken down into three traditional forms. You may recognize one or more of these styles as your own.

Niceness—Do you put on a pleasant face, and attempt to find love by transcending or denying negativity? Those who employ this strategy avoid conflict by making peace at all costs. In order not to create disturbance, they are willing to sacrifice their integrity. Those who favor "niceness" need to become familiar with the ways they deny their truth. Their work is to embrace uncomfortable feelings as an acceptable part of life. It may, for example, require courage to express anger, and wisdom to do so at the right moment and in the right spirit.

Withdrawal—Do you withdraw behind an emotional barrier and attempt to find peace by not allowing pain into your conscious awareness? Men in particular admire and emulate the stoic hero of the Western—the classic example of one who puts his feelings aside because it seems safer not to be in touch with them. An emotional numbness, or loss of passion, is the result.

Those who withdraw from feeling must learn how to move their energy, perhaps through guided expression of anger or pain. They, too, require the courage to acknowledge their feelings and learn that it is safe to express them.

Aggressive behavior—Do you feel a sense of power and control when you are being aggressive? If you employ this approach, you tend to lash out at your partner, continually finding fault, picking fights, and blaming the other for all that isn't right. The result is weariness from so much emotional turmoil and guilt for being such a difficult partner. In addition, one's mate tends to close down out of self-protection, and a loss of trust results.

Those who explode in blame and anger need to find alternative, less harmful outlets for their emotional intensity. They will also benefit from fully questioning the beliefs that lead them to blame others for their own pain.

Niceness, withdrawal, and aggressive behavior are unsatisfactory because they all avoid dealing directly with difficult feelings. Pretending everything is okay, hiding behind a wall, or lashing out are painfully ineffective ways of communicating. They inevitably fail to bring resolution. But we are faced with a difficult challenge: Our strategies are so deeply ingrained that they often remain with us for a lifetime, unless we work to replace them with new ways of coping. Only those who are able to transcend their strategies will have an opportunity to experience an intimacy that flourishes over time. Much of this book deals with the releasing of these habitual and inadequate ways of responding to conflict and pain.

The Downward Spiral:
How Relationships Fall Apart

Through the years, we have worked with hundreds of couples who, like us, originally perceived the purpose of their relationship to be mutual gratification. Eventually one party would fail to gratify and their partner would resent them, since they were not fulfilling the function they had been assigned. The partner would express their resentment unskillfully, and the painful downward spiral would begin its inevitable course.

Whenever we perceive our partner to be looking unkindly on us, unless we are extremely alert, we react. We close down, defend ourselves, and even go on the offensive. A variety of negative thoughts and emotions may arise at this point: hurt, anger, anxiety, judgment, resentment, confusion . . . anything but love.

If our purpose in being intimate is merely to feel good, this unpleasantness is seen as an annoying and regrettable obstacle to be pushed away or overcome. If we believe our partner's role is to make us comfortable or whole, then whenever they are not fulfilling this function, we resent them. In so doing, we aren't helping them feel comfortable or whole, and the resentment swiftly becomes mutual. Negative feelings start to feed on themselves. As imperfections arise, each partner begins to resent the other for not being the perfect, radiant, loving person whom they experienced at the beginning.

Traits that were initially admired may now seem less attractive. The pristine honesty for which we once esteemed our partner is now seen as a blunt and tactless disregard for our feelings. Their childlike spontaneity has become a juvenile emotional indulgence. Their rocklike steadiness feels more like drab predictability, a lack of passion and vitality.

This change in perception leads to a loss of affection. The sweet little gestures that so naturally accompanied the romantic stage wither away. The tone of voice begins to acquire an edge. A once-exciting sexuality takes on a mechanical quality. As the downward spiral deepens, fights or withdrawal become more frequent and the kindness begins to dissipate. As each feels more misunderstood, it becomes increasingly difficult to see what it was in their partner that initially attracted them.

Every loveless act in one partner generates a negative reaction in the other. The fear of losing what was so precious increases mutual fear. Guilt, too, is generated by this process. Each partner, observing themselves becoming more difficult to be around, likes themselves less and less in the presence of the other. The increasing guilt intensifies the discomfort level in the relationship and may lead to further hostility or avoidance. Now the classic downward spiral is in full force.

Since our education has taught us virtually nothing about this painful but prevalent phenomenon, we are totally unprepared to respond when it arises. We find ourselves getting drawn into a process that feels out of our control, as the dream begins to crumble.

Left to run its course, the downward spiral results either in the relationship blowing apart or in a lifetime permeated with resentment. Couples who remain together in the midst of such bitterness end up quarreling endlessly or putting an emotional callus around their negativity. A common result is a relationship without joy or passion, one that's essentially dead. If the original purpose was mutual gratification, the inevitable outcome is disillusion. Few couples escape these painful consequences.

To arrest this downward spiral it is necessary to learn a more effective response when our partner is not pleasing us. Waiting for the change to come from another is a fruitless endeavor; the responsibility for change has to come from oneself. But if you have tried to alter the way you respond to negativity, you well know that it is no easy task.

In addition to our personal strategies for dealing with conflict, our culture has provided us with two approaches: one psychologically based, the other spiritually. Each of these approaches contains an important truth, yet each is fatally flawed. It will be helpful to look more closely at why these common ways of responding to difficulty in intimacy are problematic.

The Psychological Mistake

We call the first ineffective strategy "the Psychological Mistake." It originates from our need to accept ourselves the way we are, the need to escape denial. We cannot push away our self-centeredness, resentment, or other undesirable feelings and change them simply by an act of will. In fact, no internal or external manipulation, however subtle, can bring fundamental change.

This perspective emphasizes the limitation of living according to "shoulds." When we find ourselves getting angry or resentful toward our partner, we refuse to suppress these feelings. We are encouraged to get angry, to cry, to relive old hurts, and to express our frustration with our partner.

However, this approach is flawed by its lack of vision. There is little interest in going beyond these negative feelings; in fact, spiritual aspirations are seen as an escape from the real world. The Psychological Mistake unquestioningly assumes that our partner's negative behavior is an actual threat, rather than a perceived one. Therefore our unloving feelings and defensiveness are fully justified.

At its worst, the Psychological Mistake encourages indulgence of negative feelings and righteous judgment toward the imperfections of one's partner. It is possible to spend years in therapy honing one's blaming apparatus. We become highly skillful at identifying what doesn't feel good, getting in touch with and giving full expression to anger and hurt. In fact, we may enjoy this indulgence on a regular and frequent basis.

The problem with this approach is that we can spend a lifetime luxuriating in the pleasure of negative feelings, and never come to the end of it. We are tempted to lay our difficulties at the feet of others, to enjoy the role of victim, and to deny our own contribution as adults to the way we feel. We fail to call into question the hidden attitudes that give rise to our negative feelings and perpetuate them.

Perhaps more important, this indulgence strengthens and solidifies some profoundly mistaken notions that lie at the root of our pain. By blaming others for our suffering and remaining complacent about our own responsibility, we fail to investigate the real purpose of our distress. The uncomfortable outcome is a relationship where unexamined blaming of the other becomes a way of life. Therefore, the Psychological Mistake keeps us feeling powerless, afraid, and resentful of the people we believe responsible for our pain. Something of profound importance is missing here.

The Spiritual Mistake

What is missing from the Psychological Mistake can be found in its antithesis, the Spiritual Mistake, although this perspective too has its limitations. The virtue of this approach lies in seeing the true need to go beyond the petty concerns of the daily mind; to transcend self-centeredness, anger, and violence.

Deep in our being lurks a sense that we have the right and the capability to experience love, peace, and joy in our lifetime. We often ask ourselves, Why remain content with the gray world of guilt and fear, or with the superficial pleasures with which we escape our pain? Our discontent with the experience of life is telling us that something very real needs to be honored. It inspires us to live by a loftier vision. We don't have to live our lives in the prison of fear that we have crafted for ourselves. Fundamental change *is* possible.

Those who hold this vision of going beyond the prison of daily life try very hard to live up to certain ideals: forgiveness, a positive attitude, acceptance of one's partner "just as they are." All the spiritual traditions tell us we should obey the Golden Rule. We should forgive others, and be charitable and kind even to those who are unkind to us. This perfect state is in deep contrast with our present imperfection; yet we are exhorted to make an effort, gross or subtle, to realize it. If, at present, our hearts are closed, if we are unforgiving, angry, agitated, or self-centered, we are asked to envision a state—always in the future—in which our hearts are open and we are forgiving, peaceful, quiet of mind, loving. We make a supreme effort to have good thoughts and emotions, as well as right actions. We feel virtuous if we succeed; pathetic or sinful if we fail. As an inducement to make this shift, rewards and punishments are sometimes offered, in this life or the next.

A major difficulty with this approach is that we want so much to be "good," to transcend our humanness, that we are tempted to deny the darker aspects of our emotional reality. For example, many of us as children were told that big boys (or girls) don't cry. Our sadness was denied, but not dispelled. But what is not first accepted cannot be transformed. We can never get rid of a feeling by denying or resisting it; by saying that we shouldn't have it. Although we may try to hide the less savory facets of our inner life, they do not disappear, but remain to haunt us from deep within.

The attempt to live up to spiritual ideals presents another common difficulty. To the extent that we take our spiritual progress seriously, we harbor fear, often unconscious, that we won't succeed in our transformation. This fear gives rise to an act of harsh self-judgment every time we fail to live up to our ideal. And this lack of charity toward ourselves will often cause us to close our hearts to others—to those who, like us, are not able to attain our ideal of spiritual perfection.

Without accepting our human imperfections, we end up judging them when they arise in ourselves or in others. But the very act of judgment is another act of violence, an example of the thing we are judging. To achieve a peaceful and loving end, we employ a means that is repressive and unkind. When we deny our humanness in the interest of transcending it, we far too often foster those very qualities of separation, closed-heartedness, and self-centeredness that we find so distasteful.

This may help explain why, after so many thousands of years of high-minded teachings, we seem largely unable to live up to them, especially with the person we claim to love most in the world. How many of us, when our partner is upset with us, are actually able to put into practice the great and inspiring principle of responding to negativity with love? Anyone who has tried will acknowledge that it is far easier to appreciate the beauty of this teaching from a safe distance than actually to live by it.

Denial is the end product of making certain feelings unacceptable. The Spiritual Mistake breeds relationships filled with indirect expressions of negativity, seriously impeding honest communication.

After Martha and I reached our lowest point, we tried everything we could, falling frequently into one or the other of these mistakes. Sometimes we became experts at the righteous expression of negativity. Other times we tried heroically to relate from a more enlightened perspective, pretending to an equanimity we did not feel. Of course, neither helped. We seemed so thoroughly unable to give each other what we thought we wanted that we came very close to ending our relationship.

But something kept us going. Perhaps it was our shared interest in finding a path that would allow ample expression of all our feelings, even the most negative, while at the same time preserving a loving space in which both of us felt safe. We wanted to bring together heaven and earth, as it were, holding to the vision in the midst of chaos. Sometimes it felt like we were walking along a narrow ridge with a precipice on each side. After struggling for years, with many victories and setbacks, we have come to see that there is another way of responding to difficult feelings that neither represses nor indulges them, but allows them to be transformed into something higher.

A New Purpose in Being Together

We come back now to the quest for a new purpose that will succeed in holding couples together. An approach is needed that will allow couples to go through hurt, anger, fear, confusion, and conflict, and somehow manage to emerge with their relationship not only intact, but more deeply alive.

What can hold couples lovingly together is a shared vision of relationship as a spiritual path. This vision will bring together what is best from both the psychological and the spiritual approaches. Much of this book is an elaboration of what this means in actual practice.

The process involves a fundamental shift in the relationship's center of gravity. No longer is our purpose in being together simply the serving of our individual needs. Our relationship is no longer a bargain of convenience. Rather, our joint purpose is to find the truth of who we really are by bringing compassion, awareness, and honesty into every aspect of our relationship and our daily life. In discovering together what blocks our love, we open ourselves to higher possibilities. Instead of being antagonists in a power struggle, we become allies in a journey of exploration. Instead of struggling against each other in conflict, the two of us become allies in a common effort to eliminate old patterns of fear, blame, and unconsciousness. We join forces in overcoming the habits that engender disharmony at the physical, emotional, mental, and spiritual levels. Whichever one of us is more aware in the moment can lead the way. If our light goes out, we will temporarily borrow our partner's, and vice versa. The old struggle tore us apart, but the new struggle will strengthen our bond.

In pursuit of this quest we learn that change comes not through effort or resistance but through understanding. We learn to hone our awareness when we would normally be mechanical; to open our heart when we would usually be judgmental. We learn to look upon all anger, hurt, and fear-based behavior—our own and our partner's—as a cry for healing rather than as a threat to our safety or a reflection of our unworthiness. We learn a radically new way of communicating in which we release defensiveness in the interest of our true safety. We create an emotionally secure environment in which we facilitate the healing of old wounds. We do all this because we have embraced a spiritual vision that aspires to something better and nobler, yet has room for our imperfections. This is a profound and significant challenge. Our parents, schools, society, and religions have not adequately prepared us for it.

The Right Use of Difficulty

A great mass of fear lurks in the human consciousness. Each of us has taken on our own piece of it to process and release. Some of us have chosen a partner to help us discover where our understanding is incomplete.

It is hard to understand how there can be negative energy between you and your partner without there being anything wrong, or anyone to blame. When a relationship becomes a spiritual path, we are no longer interested in blaming our partner if things don't feel comfortable. Being comfortable is no longer our goal. Instead, our purpose is to help each other unearth our essence and work through anything that might be blocking its full expression.

This gives us a new perspective on our conflicts. All the difficulties between us can now be used to reach our new goal. The troublesome feelings are feedback that point, if we know how to look, to those places in us that are in need of light, clarity, or reenvisioning.

We sense that at some level, we have asked for these difficulties as a teaching to show us our obstacles. Therefore, deep in our hearts we are grateful to each other for those trials that help us see the truth about ourselves. Knowing ourselves frees us from the illusion that has kept us in a state of pain and conflict.

Pain as Feedback

How then do we begin to change our attitude toward uncomfortable feelings? The use of pain as feedback is perhaps easiest to understand at the physical level. Hangovers taught me a great deal

in my heavy-drinking days; in fact, they kept me from fully succumbing to alcoholism at a relatively early age. If I have a terrible
headache every Sunday morning, I can regard this as a piece of
feedback directing me to look at what I am putting into my system
every Saturday night. A hangover is a direct, specific, nonverbal
message, a reaction from my body. It is an invitation to investigate
where the toxins are coming from.

But toxins can assume many forms. Psychological toxins, for
example, can be any values, beliefs, and attitudes that are not in harmony with the way our minds were meant to function.

It has been said, "The truth will set you free; but first it will make
you miserable." Psychological toxins, like hangovers, give rise to a
suffering that asks something of me. Just as the physical discomfort
of my hangover is an invitation to investigate on the physical plane,
the mental discomfort in my relationship invites me to investigate
on the psychological plane.

A typical psychological toxin might be the belief that when my
partner expresses anger, I am in danger. But what if my discomfort
arises not from their behavior, but from the fact that I am regarding it
through a powerful distorting lens? What if I were to take all the energy
I have been using to blame my partner, and use it to explore how my
mind suffers because of its *interpretation* of my partner's anger?

It takes courage to face yourself, to look unflinchingly upon the
attitudes and behaviors that compromise your integrity. It takes real
clarity to see the ways you compress your experience of yourself,
restrict your creativity, and diminish your value in your own eyes. As
imperfections and insecurities are shared, they become undone, and
the openness that evolves from such sharing has a vitality and a truth
that strengthens the relationship. In this process lies true intimacy.

The Value of Conflict

There is nothing that can't be used to deepen your intimacy.
Relationship is not meant to be played out only harmoniously in
the key of C major; there are sharps, flats, dissonant notes that

enrich the music you make together. An intimate relationship does not fear conflict, but uses it to uncover new depths, to open up a deeper sharing. Conflict is not something to avoid, for in it lies the potential for concentrated learning. Conflict is a way station along the path where differences are fully appreciated and accepted.

Rick and Sally came to one of our weekends for couples harboring a deep fear of conflict. Rick was a landscape contractor who also led men's workshops. Sally was a former teacher now raising a family, as well as doing a lot of volunteer work in the school and the community. Both were highly articulate and seemed competent and practical; their very appearance (Rick sporting a ponytail, baseball cap, and work clothes; Sally with straight hair and a long skirt, looking every bit the down-to-earth country woman) bespoke a relaxed amiability that put others at ease. Theirs looked to be the picture of a well-functioning marriage; one that included a large circle of friends, a strong presence in the community, and an ability to make things happen for themselves and for others.

Nothing we learned about Rick and Sally that weekend contradicted any of these impressions, but during the course of the workshop, some other aspects of the picture began to emerge. Their communication revealed a deep dissatisfaction—one that, judging from their tentativeness in talking about it, had rarely been expressed.

For example, Rick, after some difficulty in coming up with anything he considered a problem in the relationship (a common thing, especially for men), finally launched into something he was careful to label "trivial." He said that when he came home frustrated or discouraged by the day's events, Sally's response was usually sympathetic. She would quickly find out what was bothering Rick, question him about it, and take up the problem with gusto. As Rick groused about his difficulties, she would offer all kinds of constructive suggestions. If Rick was having a problem with a guy on his crew, she would have advice on how to deal with it. If he was overstressed from trying to combine job estimates with getting the kids to Little League games in the evening, she would offer to arrange carpooling, or propose rescheduling the estimates for the weekend.

On one level, Rick's response to all this was gratitude. How wonderful to have a wife who takes such an interest in your problems and tries to help you solve them. Indeed, Rick admitted, Sally's suggestions were often really good. However, on another level, he found himself experiencing deep frustration and resentment. He wasn't sure why. As he spoke, his voice began to rise. Finally, what he really wanted from Sally came to him: "I wish sometimes you'd just shut up and listen!"

We were all a little surprised by his vehemence, though as he went on, it began to make sense. More than anything, Rick wanted Sally to understand how frustrated or angry he felt, *before* telling him what to do about it.

"How can I even think about what to do when I'm feeling that way?" he asked. "When you jump in and start trying to fix things, it just about drives me crazy." Because Rick had never expressed this feeling (partly because he was so ashamed of his own ingratitude), he was quite charged over the issue. When his resentment erupted, it was with considerable anger.

Sally was taken aback. She had been completely unaware of how this dynamic was affecting Rick. The fact that she was able to hear and understand all this without getting defensive seemed to soften his anger; his face had a new look. "I never thought I'd be able to tell you this and be heard," he said. Then he hugged her.

Sally, later in the same session, brought up an issue that had a striking symmetry to Rick's. She had been asked to be the head of the board of her local parent-cooperative preschool, which felt like a great honor. Nevertheless, it was a demanding commitment and she was not totally sure whether she could do it, given her other activities. Naturally, she conveyed her dilemma to Rick. He reacted swiftly: "My God, Sally, you can't be serious. Both of us are already totally maxed out and our finances are stretched. You're at your limit. Do you really want to take on a whole new job that pays zip? Do yourself a favor, tell them to get someone else."

Even though Rick was ostensibly displaying concern for her well-being, something didn't feel right to Sally. Something in Rick's words, she confessed, had deeply hurt her feelings. As she talked about it in the group, she began to cry. She became aware of a deep sadness, and a feeling of worthlessness. Sally continued to discuss her feeling and it became clear.

Rather than first acknowledging the pride and pleasure she had felt in being asked to be on the board, Rick had rushed in with rather harsh advice, based more on fear than on understanding. Just being asked had meant a great deal to her and made her feel wanted and accepted by people she cared about. Whether or not she could handle the commitment, there was a part of her that deeply desired to say yes. By dismissing this entirely, Rick was in effect telling her that none of these feelings mattered. Her joy at being appreciated had been utterly shattered by the one person by whom she most wanted to feel valued. "Weren't you even glad for me?" she said through her tears. "Weren't you proud of me? Didn't you understand how much I wanted to do this?"

Rick had no idea how he'd been affecting her, but by the time she was done, he found it easy to see the reason for her tears. He was made to see his insensitivity just as Sally had been made to see hers.

In subsequent sessions that weekend, Rick and Sally brought up several more of these ostensibly minor issues. They progressed as through a funnel, with old upsets coming to light. They began to realize how much had remained unspoken over the years, and what the price for that silence had been.

We were struck by how remarkably similar their feelings were. Each one wanted more from the other. Each one experienced the other's behavior, no matter how positive-seeming, as an obstacle to intimacy. Each one craved a degree of closeness that they were afraid to ask for; their lack of intimacy was veiled by the superficial harmony of the relationship. In fact, the need to maintain peace at all costs was becoming a kind of tyranny. Where there is no room for creative dissonance, no space to share difficult feelings, there is a lack of trust; and where trust is lacking, love cannot fully flourish. The task that

Rick and Sally saw for themselves by the end of the workshop was quite different from the one they had pictured at the start. It was not to iron out the few remaining wrinkles in a basically smooth-running partnership. Keeping the surface unruffled was, in fact, troubling the depths. Rather, the task was to allow dissatisfaction, to allow disruption, to allow disharmony to occur. In a sense, it was to create a larger harmony where there would be room for disharmony. It meant speaking one's mind when something didn't feel right, and encouraging one's partner to do the same. It meant having the courage to take the risk of not being "nice." It was an important revelation for Rick and Sally that all this could be done without shaking the underpinnings of their relationship, or impairing their ability to function well together. They came to the workshop feeling like they had to have it together; they left feeling a huge relief that their intimacy did not depend on superficial harmony.

Risk-taking Versus Safety

It will often seem risky to allow unsavory aspects of yourself to be seen by your partner. Every true intimacy must confront this dilemma. One option involves venturing forth into new and possibly frightening territory: being honest in potentially painful areas. The other option is to respect a natural timing, to refrain from forcing things, to create an emotional climate that feels truly safe. A healthy relationship needs to integrate and balance these opposites.

If you take too many risks, you may have more conflict than the relationship can handle. There is a temptation to disregard the other's vulnerability. One does not feel safe in this relationship. Too much risk-taking subverts the very exploratory climate it means to foster.

On the other hand, everyone feels uncomfortable sharing certain personal feelings with their partner. To stay entirely away from these difficult issues leads to an overemphasis on safety and creates an environment so predictable that the relationship becomes dull from want of growth, like Rick and Sally's. If you find yourself in a relationship that has become stale, perhaps you need to take more risks.

• • •

Most people have a tendency toward either risk-taking or safety. Those who naturally enjoy risk-taking may sometimes regard their partner, if they are not similarly constituted, as too nice, too careful, or just plain cowardly. Those who lean toward safety may regard someone who's more adventuresome as pushy, aggressive, or insensitive. It's easy to fall into an extreme and to look with disfavor upon one's opposite, but it's far more useful to understand the virtue in that opposite, especially when it brings balance to the relationship.

Risk-taking has its virtues, offering excitement and growth. All of us have a tendency to stay within the relatively comfortable limits of our personality, with its known repertoire of feelings and expressions. Limits vary from person to person and change as we go through life, but we all share the feeling of danger as we approach our personal edge. Taking risks means daring to explore the outer limits of our rage, our tears, our terror, our emotional black holes. To approach our edge, some of us require but a suggestion, while others may need a more concerted and skillful nudging. But for all of us, the value of exploring the unknown lies in the newness it brings into our lives.

Safety means security, and this is especially important when we're feeling vulnerable. When we feel safe, we know we won't be attacked or judged, but honored and respected. Particularly for those of us who are by nature more cautious, this feeling of safety is a crucial ingredient in the willingness to venture beyond the known. Therefore, safety balances risk-taking.

Seeking the Treasure

A game that is often played at children's parties involves children searching for a hidden treasure. Someone plays the piano, and as the children get closer to the treasure, the piano gets louder; as they get farther away, the piano gets softer.

In an intimate relationship consecrated to a spiritual goal, there is a treasure that's shared by both parties: the fulfillment of love in its most perfect expression. As partners move together through the ups and downs of daily life, a great Piano Player offers encouragement and guidance for attaining this treasure.

As the partners open their hearts, when they are more loving and forgiving, the Universe plays the music louder, and they feel more alive, happy, and fulfilled. As their hearts close, when they are attacking and blaming each other, the Universe lets them know they are on the wrong track. Their thoughts darken, they become more uncomfortable, they have less energy. Even their bodies lose vitality and health. They have lost their way.

If one's hearing is blocked to the harmony of their relationship, one's partner may be able to catch the strains clearly. Whoever has the better hearing at the moment can prevail, and the leadership can be handed back and forth. What could be simpler?

One of the great fruits of this work comes when you experience your partner acting in an unloving way, and you watch yourself respond for the first time with compassion instead of hurt or anger. It's a lovely experience, one that feels deeply good to the core. The music has just gotten a bit louder. Such experiences can turn a stuck or dull relationship into one that's passionate, alive, and creative.

To listen closely to this music brings a kind of exhilaration into one's life. A new quality is introduced to the relationship, as one begins to let go of old conditioning that closes the heart.Then all the imperfections can be used as compost to enrich the soil of intimacy. The most difficult times are now seen as blessings in disguise. The alliance becomes a sacred vehicle for helping each other come into the fullness of our being.

Thoughts from Martha

I feel it's important to begin this work with a message of hope for those who may not be feeling much hope. In our years of offering couples retreats, Don and I have seen many relationships in dire straits. It's not unusual for half the couples at a workshop to be questioning whether they want to remain together. We see couples who are barely on speaking terms, ones whose marriages have been rocked by affairs, ones who can't stop creating misery for their children, ones utterly deadlocked over the basic issues of their lives. And yet, no matter how bad it is, Don and I always reassure them that they have the power to change it all. It takes willingness and persistent focus, but it can be done. In a surprising number of cases, these couples leave with an understanding that allows them to let in a little light and hope, enough to begin creating a new relationship.

People in a desperate state are often the last to know the true potential of their relationships. Their opinions on the subject simply aren't trustworthy. Oftentimes they've already made up their minds that the relationships can't work, which becomes a self-fulfilling prophecy if not challenged. We tell them that from our experience, they do have reason to hope. Not only have we been hopeless ourselves, but we have seen many others come back from the same darkness. This is a message worth hearing, no matter how bleak things look.

Taking a workshop by itself could never be a panacea, but it's a beginning. We don't try to convince people with arguments that they can change. We try to show them ways of dealing with the most difficult problems, to give them an experience that proves even the knottiest long-term issues are workable.

Usually the key is a shift in attitude. We often meet with couples who describe the painful situation in their relationship as if it were either their partner's fault or something that just happened to both of them. Each is encouraged to ask, "What's going on between us now, and what is my role in creating our pain?" Those who are willing to do this have to examine some of their deepest assumptions, such as: "I would never do what my partner is doing," "I could never love someone who's behaving thus," or "My partner is responsible for my pain." They see how the mind closes the heart, and how readily they can undo a decision made from a place of illusion. These are the people most likely to emerge from the dark tunnel, to leave the workshop with a reference point for finding their love. Once couples experience even a small part of this, they can no longer maintain the fiction that their situation is hopeless.

We don't say every intimacy needs to continue. Keeping people together for its own sake is not our interest. Some may be so far down the path of resentment that they can no longer find the embers of their love. But if the embers can be located, they can be fanned. Yes, it takes time and dedication, especially after toxicity has built up. It means developing the willingness to open the heart in the midst of all the cumulative hurt and anger that usually prevail. Over time, this capacity can be reinforced in many ways: books and tapes, friends, conscious intention, prayer and affirmations—whatever helps us remember the essentials. For those willing to try, the effort generally makes a difference. But it's surprising how many people come to us with no idea of how different it could be. When couples emerge from the darkness of their crisis—and many have, including us—they often come to see it as a blessing in disguise.

A painful experience points to what isn't working. When the pain becomes intense enough, it gets everybody's attention. If partners can use their distress to move from judgment to empathy, from blaming each other to acknowledging their own role in the difficulty, they have a tremendous opportunity for new life and a new relationship.

It's heartwarming to have met so many couples willing to accept this challenge, to step onto a new and extraordinary path. The choice is an adventurous one, but its rewards are sure. This message of hope is one based on personal experience, and my greatest wish is that it be heard by all.

CHAPTER 2

Openhearted Listening

What Does "Being Safe" Mean for Your Partner?

Nothing is more important to intimacy than a feeling of mutual safety. Have you ever asked yourself what makes you feel safe in a relationship? If you begin to explore this in your daily life, you will probably find that your partner contributes to your feeling of safety in several ways:

- They have room for you to feel whatever you are feeling and are not threatened by it.
- They do not judge you, or believe that they know best what you should think, feel, or do.
- They honor the path you have chosen and wish you well on your journey.
- They care about your inner life enough to want to understand it fully.
- They let you feel the fullness of their empathy.

When your partner's responses arise from fear, they do not contribute to your feeling of safety. When their responses arise from love, they will help you to feel safe.

Here is one of the greatest challenges of intimacy. We all want a relationship in which we can communicate our feelings if we're upset by our partner's behavior. If this is not possible, a reservoir of frustration and anger builds, and we end up resenting each other. Unfortunately, most intimate relationships end up in this place much of the time.

If you are like most couples, when you express a negative feeling, it will usually be perceived by your partner as a threat. Out of their own fear, they will typically respond by getting defensive, and you won't be heard. Here are some of the most frequently employed defenses:

- putting up an emotional barrier and becoming cold, distant or sullen
- going on the attack and accusing you of faults equivalent to or worse than theirs
- explaining or justifying their behavior
- informing you that you are overreacting
- trying to fix things—explaining how you should regard the situation or what you should do
- becoming so emotional that they switch the focus from your issue to their feelings
- dismissing your feelings with humor or sarcasm
- pretending to listen, saying all the right things, and then proceeding in the same unconscious fashion

None of these responses brings resolution or facilitates healing, because your partner has tuned out to what is really going on for you.

Fortunately there is an alternative response, which brings about the desired communication by creating an atmosphere of emotional safety. We call it Openhearted Listening. It could be described as a kind of emotional yoga.

Just as yoga postures are refined tools that help open up tight places in the body, Openhearted Listening is an equally effective tool for opening up tight places in the heart. This process will quickly reveal where the heart is closed, and show you specifically how to work with it.

This special sort of listening can be used when one (or both) of you is feeling upset, hurt, sad, frustrated, angry, confused, afraid—in short, whenever the feeling of love and peace has departed. The tool is useful if you sense you're about to have an argument, or if one of you is starting to get defensive. It can be employed when you feel you are not being heard, or if you are going to communicate something that, from past experience, you feel your partner is unlikely to listen to.

What Is Listening with an Open Heart?

Openhearted Listening replaces defensiveness as a way of responding to our partner's feelings. It allows us to show our partner that we are more interested in understanding their reality than in being right. If we succeed, we allow our partner to experience not only our ability to see the circumstances through their eyes, but also our empathy for and validation of their feelings. Great healing results for both parties.

Openhearted Listening is divided into two parts. The first is called "mirroring." Our partner begins by telling us about some event that has upset them and how they felt about it. We then repeat what they said back to them in our own words, including as much as we can remember, and giving special importance to describing our partner's feelings with accuracy. If their story gets too long, we may always stop them to repeat what they have said up to that point.

It's perfectly natural not to get it right the first time. If we're not exact, or leave something out, our partner lets us know the part that was inaccurate or missing. We retell this new part, going back and forth with the process until our partner feels that we have accurately reflected the content.

Here's an example of how one couple, Jennifer and Michael, brought greater clarity to their communication through mirroring. Michael, a carpenter, had a casual appearance and a pleasant manner. Jennifer, whose work was tending their two young children, appeared more high-strung and sensitive.

Michael: We both know I'm dissatisfied with my work, and that I want to get a better job, maybe go back to school. But I don't like to move too quickly on things like that. I want to wait until the timing feels right to *me.* Last night you came into the living room—I was just sitting there reading—and attacked me about not moving ahead faster. You often criticize me for this. It makes me feel like I'm expected to change overnight. I may not seem like a very motivated person, but I'm working on it. It really pisses me off when you nag me like that, especially when I'm down like I was last night. You seem to be saying that you work on your issues and I don't. That makes me feel inadequate.

Jennifer (attempting to mirror): You are angry because you feel that the way I communicate makes it seem like you're wrong. And you assume that because of my response, I think it's your fault.

At this point, we told Jennifer that she had changed the meaning of Michael's words on her own behalf when she said "you assume that," a phrase we discourage in mirroring, because it implies that you *think* something is a certain way, but I know it isn't really so. In addition, she had generalized, leaving out many of the specifics. She needed to convey in more detail just what she does to trigger Michael's feelings. She tried again.

Jennifer: When I criticize and blame you for not moving faster at finding new work or going back to school, you get angry at me. You want me to know that you are also discontent with the situation, but your rhythms are different from mine. You move more slowly. The way I come off makes you feel as though I am saying, "I work on my issues and you don't." When I do this you feel inferior.

Michael: That's better, but what I said was "inadequate," not "inferior."

Jennifer: When I lambaste you for going too slow and imply that I've got it together, you feel inadequate.

Michael: That's right. But you left out the part about your doing it when I am feeling down.

Jennifer: One of the things that makes you feel so inadequate is that I come to you when you are feeling really bad and make it worse by attacking you.

Michael: Yes. You've got it. Oh, and there's one more thing. When you do it, I don't feel any love coming from you.

Jennifer: In addition to feeling angry at me and feeling inadequate, you also feel that when I come to you this way, you don't feel my love. Is that it?

Michael: That's it. I think you've mirrored me.

After we correctly mirror our partner's original communication, it's not uncommon for another level of intimacy to appear. Being truly heard, often for the first time, can be sufficient to create a new level of safety. Now it may be possible for deeper layers of feelings to emerge. Sometimes the original communication is seen as a piece of a much more expansive concern. The particular incident may reveal unexpected connections to other events, both within the relationship and from the past. In such cases it's good to thank your partner for the correct mirroring they did, but then to let them know that there's more. Revealing explorations are possible if both of you are willing to follow the feelings wherever they lead.

Validation

Although mirroring is important, it is just a prelude. When it's complete, we move on to validation, the place of greatest movement and healing. To validate your partner's feelings is to show them—verbally and nonverbally—that their feelings make sense to you. They are not crazy, exaggerated, or inappropriate. Although they may not be what you would feel, you can imagine a person having such feelings under such circumstances.

It is important to convey that you understand the connection between your actions and their feelings. It is not that your actions *caused* your partner's feelings, for this would mistakenly absolve your partner from the significant role they play in creating them. You communicate, rather, that it makes sense to you that, given your role in the exchange, your partner could feel this way.

The quickest way to learn about validation is to have someone actually validate your feelings, and discover the inner release that follows. It is hard to describe the nature of this experience if you have not undergone it. You will notice a shift in the quality of energy between you and your partner. The feeling may be something like, "Ahh, she finally gets it!" If you don't have this release, you may need to tell your partner, "Sorry, I don't feel validated yet." It's okay to have high standards. When your partner attempts to validate you, check in deeply and honestly with yourself to see if you feel truly validated. It is perfectly acceptable not to feel validated even when you appreciate the sincere efforts of your partner.

Sometimes you may feel almost validated, sort of like finding a piece in a jigsaw puzzle that almost fits. Don't settle for almost, because that last bit of work that allows the piece to fit perfectly is the most important part. See if you can get in touch with what was missing from your partner's attempt, and communicate it to them. Maybe you have this feeling because your partner's heart is still a bit closed. Perhaps they were subtly holding on to a feeling of being right, which got transmitted nonverbally and blocked the validation. You might say to your partner on such occasions, "I could tell you were trying, which I really appreciate, *and* I still didn't feel fully validated. It felt like you were holding back a little. Is that true?" In this process there is no blame.

The feeling of wanting to hold back, experienced at some point by all who embark on this process, is the most common obstacle to complete validation. The ego proclaims that if I validate your feelings, then mine are invalid, which to the ego is unacceptable. Therefore my only protection is to hold on to the notion of being right. This deeply rooted misunderstanding is not always easy to release. Yet validation depends on disengaging from this false idea, since my partner will not feel truly validated if I am holding on even slightly to the notion that I am right and my partner is wrong.

Tell yourself: No matter how skillful my words, you won't experience validation if my heart is closed to you, if I am judging you, if I think you are crazy, oversensitive, or unworthy for having the feelings you have. If I have such an attitude, I am being asked to go deeper into myself and transcend the belief that my partner shouldn't feel what they feel.

What can help greatly in such a circumstance is getting in touch with something from a past experience that resembles this situation. If my partner is feeling hurt because I made a decision without consulting them, I attempt to recall if there was ever a case in which I felt similarly upset because I was left out of a decision-making process. If my partner is angry because I failed to keep an agreement, I think back to a time when someone else's lack of dependability triggered my own anger. There is an art to locating such a place within oneself. Sometimes, if I'm unable to find a comparable experience, I try scanning my memory for something sufficiently similar that will allow me to relate to my partner's feelings. If this proves beyond my capacity, imagination may serve, as it did in the following session.

An Example: Out with the Boys

Paul and Gloria needed to deal with one small problem in an otherwise smooth relationship. Paul, a handsome doctor in his fifties, worked and played hard. He was an avid golfer, skier, and tennis player. He also enjoyed time out with his men friends, often going to bars for hours after his sporting events, and putting down quite a few beers. To him this was a natural reward for his focused and highly responsible work.

The problem lay, he felt, with Gloria. He had met her several years earlier, when she became a nurse at the hospital. They fell madly in love, and Paul left an unhappy marriage to be with Gloria. She was a slim, attractive woman in her early forties, with an air of quiet self-confidence. Although Paul had gone through many relationships, she had given him the gift of his first real intimacy. He loved her now as much as when they first became involved. However, Gloria, who seemed so accepting of Paul's imperfections, was unable to be supportive of his time out with the boys.

Paul wanted to go out with his friends several times a week, and he wanted Gloria's blessing. He was trying hard to adopt a reasonable tone. "Look, you've been really good to me, and also good for me. I know I'm sometimes hard to be around, and you really do a great job putting up with me. So I can't understand why you're making this one thing so difficult for me. There's really no harm in my going out and having a couple of beers with my friends. I work really hard, and I deserve to relax. My ex was really uptight about this and used to give me a hard time. I ended up lying to her and then feeling guilty as hell. I really don't want a repeat. I can't understand why you won't just relax and let me have fun. After all, I haven't gotten in the way of your hanging out with your women friends. It just doesn't seem fair."

Gloria listened without interrupting. When he was finished she seemed uneasy. "I've never been able to get through to you why I'm so uncomfortable when you go out drinking, but I guess this is the time to do it." She took a deep breath. "You know that time last fall when you had finished playing in the tournament and I was going to meet you later at the bar?"

Paul nodded. "Well," she went on, "I was maybe a half hour late, and when I showed up, you'd obviously had a few. I could tolerate that, but then that waitress in the very short skirt came by and you reached out to grab her. I was mortified."

"Aw, come on, you're exaggerating," Paul replied. "I was just flirting a little. It's just what men like to do, there's no harm in it. I think you're making a mountain out of a molehill."

Gloria stood her ground. "I understand men like to flirt, and I don't mind innocent flirting. I've even been known to do a bit of that myself. But you stepped over the line. You were totally inappropriate, and I was really uncomfortable. In fact, I was downright scared for what this might mean in the future. I picture you going out drinking and one day ending up in bed with someone."

Paul was beginning to get angry. "I was *not* being inappropriate. The trouble with you is you're just too sensitive. There wasn't anything to be afraid of. Look, it was nothing, why can't you just take my word for it?"

Gloria looked heavenward with an expression that said, What's the use? She seemed to have lost all hope, and added, "This happens every time I try to tell you how you make me feel. You just don't listen."

After they were instructed in the art of listening, Paul agreed, a bit reluctantly, to hear Gloria out. After she spoke, he was able to mirror back what she had said. However, when it came time to validate her discomfort, Paul balked.

"I just don't know how to validate her fear. I can't do it, because I can't relate to it. I really don't understand why she was so upset. Maybe I'm just not cut out for this kind of process."

"Hang in there, Paul," I answered. "It's okay that you haven't been able to validate; in fact it's often the case with people who are learning the process. Would you be willing to use your imagination for a moment?"

Paul let out an annoyed sigh. "I guess so."

"Close your eyes and picture this. You meet up with Gloria at a bar. She's been there for a while before you arrived, and had maybe four or five drinks with her friends. She's dressed in a sexy outfit, exuding her allure and enjoying it. A handsome young waiter in tight pants comes to see if she wants another drink. She looks him over slowly, letting her glance rest on his pelvis. She reaches out and runs her hand languorously down his leg, and orders her next drink in a sexy voice. You can tell she would never do this without alcohol.

"Now check in for a minute and see how you feel. See how the thought of Gloria going out and drinking with her friends feels to you now."

Paul kept his eyes closed and paused for a long time. " Okay, I get it." He looked at Gloria with a slight smile and took her hands. "Gloria, I understand now why you were afraid when you saw me flirting in the bar. I can see why you'd think that if I was coming on so strong on this one occasion, the next time it might really lead somewhere, if you weren't there and if I'd had a few more drinks under my belt. When I pictured you doing the same thing, it didn't feel good at all. I get it."

Gloria was validated. Of course, the issue had not been completely resolved; but any further discussion would now take place at an entirely different level of understanding.

When the need to be right is replaced by the desire to understand, it is usually possible to find some way of getting inside your partner's feelings. There may be the temptation to assume that your partner's experience is simply too different from anything in your own past for you to be able to grasp it. Before you succumb to this notion, consider the likelihood that our similarities may outweigh our differences. We all have experienced the basic human emotions of hurt, sadness, fear, frustration, and anger. In the act of finding some feeling in yourself that resembles your partner's upset, you may be graced with a valuable insight or a moment of opening.

This does not in any way mean that you must agree with your partner's assessment of the situation. It does not mean that you have to make yourself be wrong or guilty for your feelings. It does not mean that your partner is good and you are bad, or that you have to change your behavior or give something up. It often does, however, bring you a more enlightened perspective on some of your unconscious behavior patterns, which might then make you want to take a closer look.

An example might help make this clear. Say you have two children who are having a difficult time with each other. The older child wants to spend some time alone with a visiting friend. She finds her younger brother's unwanted intrusion a nuisance and tells him to leave her alone. The brother feels hurt at being left out and keeps trying to include himself, only to be rebuffed. They come to you, each upset and blaming the other. To create a safe environment for each one does not involve making one of them think they're wrong, or denying their feelings. They are both right. The older child deserves freedom from intrusion, while the younger one's pain at the exclusion is perfectly understandable. It is easy to validate the feelings of both. This is the spirit to keep in your heart as you are exploring what it means to validate your partner. Both your feelings are valid; it's just that yours are temporarily on hold.

Hints for Successful Validation

It's natural at first to experience some obstacles on the way to successful validation. Success will increase with practice. As you're learning to work things through with your partner, it helps to keep in mind several key points.

Be specific. Instead of, "I can see how you didn't like it when I did that," say, "I can understand your feeling of hurt and abandonment when I made another appointment, after agreeing to spend Saturday afternoon with you."

Be direct. Instead of, "When you feel ignored by me . . ." try, "When I turn away from you . . ." It's important to describe the behavior clearly that's triggered your partner's feelings.

Be precise. There's a distinction between "I understand *that* you feel angry when I keep interrupting you," and "I understand *how* my continual interruptions *would* make you angry." "I understand that" is more mirroring than validation. It doesn't convey your empathy for the feeling, how it might make sense to you. "I understand how" conveys a true validation.

Be attentive. Pay attention to nonverbal messages. Be conscious of how close you sit (many couples sit too far away from each other; but check the distance with your partner to make sure you're both comfortable with it). Consider if holding hands feels right. Face each other and make eye contact. Pay attention to the message conveyed in your tone of voice, as well as in the look in your eyes, or your body language. Observe how crossed arms convey a message of defensiveness. Have you let go of being right?

Be aware. Try to understand your partner's feeling and the level of intensity. Sometimes you may get the feeling right, but not know just how intense it was for your mate. It is hard to convey an understanding of a fervent feeling using a casual tone.

Be persistent. Many situations require several attempts before the validation is successful. Don't let seeming failure get you down; the last arduous 5 percent is worth the struggle, and has within it the potential for learning of great depth.

Of course, it is the nature of this process that you, too, will have a chance to be validated. Both partners have equal responsibility to listen with an open heart. In actual practice, if your partner feels heard and validated, they will be far more motivated to make the necessary effort for you. It is especially true here that you get back what you put out.

What If I'm Being Unfairly Attacked?

Many have wondered whether they have an obligation to continue with Openhearted Listening if they perceive their partner is using it repeatedly to attack them unfairly.

Willy and Julia had learned Openhearted Listening at one of the workshops. They had abandoned academic careers in their mid-forties for a more down-to-earth life in Vermont. Both of them seemed quite in touch with their feelings and willing to express them. Following the workshop, they had practiced listening to each other and seemed to be doing well. But one day they showed up looking somewhat unhappy. They had been going around in circles over the same issue for some time.

Julia began: "I feel absolutely stymied! You agree to listen with an open heart, but the minute I express any kind of negative feeling, you close down and refuse to continue. I can't say anything to you!"

Willy took offense. "That's not fair. You know I'm perfectly willing to listen as long as you're not indulging in it as an excuse to dump all over me. I'm happy to listen to your feelings, but you don't just tell me how you're feeling. You tell me what's wrong with *me*. You blame me, assault me, make me into a villain. There's nothing that says I have to sit there and take that kind of abuse."

Julia appeared extremely frustrated. "Look, I know I sometimes lose it. There have been occasional times where I've attacked you the way you're describing. But I've been working really hard trying to communicate more clearly without blaming you." Her anger became mixed with tears, as she cried out, "You never acknowledge me for all the work I've done! I don't always come at you with attack and blame. I honestly think that most of the time I'm just stating how I feel. But if I show just a hint of annoyance, you close right down and claim that I haven't presented it right, for God's sake! I have to be some kind of perfect saint, without any negative feelings, for you to even listen."

"I don't think you see yourself very clearly," Willy retorted. "You may think you come across objective and clean, but I wish you could see a tape of yourself. You'd see how much you're attacking me. If you were as fair as you claim to be, I wouldn't have any problem listening." He pleaded, "I shouldn't have to put up with verbal abuse in doing this, should I?"

Julia, with tears in her eyes, responded, "Do I have to have my act totally together for you to listen? Is just being a little bit mad considered abuse? Don't I get a certain amount of latitude in my feelings? Isn't the whole point of this that you hear your partner even when they're upset? Even very upset?"

This was a complex issue. On the one hand we want to create an environment where all feelings are permissible, where it's acceptable to be human. The listener should not hold up exalted standards of emotional purity for their partner to express themselves and be heard.

On the other hand, there are ways of misusing Openhearted Listening. With a captive audience, one may dump their negativity on their partner in a hostile and sometimes even unfair manner.

Neither Willy nor Julia was wrong. There was simply work to be done on both sides. Intimacy requires that you learn to stretch in two directions. First, you discover how to be present for all of your partner's feelings without getting caught up in how unfair they may seem to be. It is difficult to listen when you think you are being unfairly assaulted, but it is well worth learning the art of non-defensiveness. Your partner's negative feelings can be seen as outpourings of a hurt child rather than evidence of your inadequacy. Let go of the need to make sense of your partner's emotions.

However, when you are in the role of the speaker, you also have a task. You need to take responsibility for the way you express your emotions. When you give your partner feedback, watch carefully for the assumption that they are responsible for *causing* your negative feelings. If you harbor such a belief, you're likely to look without compassion at your partner's imperfections. You'll tend to expend a fair amount of energy blaming them for not being sufficiently loving or supportive. You have a critical role in the creation of your own emotional state.

Many of us expect the impossible from our partner. Not having received the wise, mature love we needed as children, we expect our partner to do for us what our parents couldn't do: to fill our emptiness by always being loving and supportive, always being sympathetic to our feelings. We have forgotten that the only source where we can find the unconditional love that will heal us is within.

When we are driven by unrealistic demands, we can become intoxicated by Openhearted Listening, making it a tool of our confusion. Now that our partner is finally listening without defense, it is tempting to begin unloading our backlog of negative feelings. Instead of bringing understanding and compassion, an originally loving tool can create greater separation, blame, and conflict. In such an atmosphere, our partner will soon come to associate Openhearted Listening with being continually dumped on, and will likely find excuses to avoid it.

If things aren't going well, ask yourself these questions:

Is it a two-way communication? When one party dominates by doing most of the asking, something has gotten off balance and needs correction. To receive the full benefit, both parties need to experience the process in both directions.

Are you doing it too often? We have grounds for caution if we employ Openhearted Listening to continually point out to our partner the ways they fall short of our lofty standards. Space is needed to acknowledge each other's virtues and to enjoy life together without endless processing.

Are both parties taking responsibility for their negative feelings? Instead of, "You're always scaring the hell out of me with those childish outbursts of yours," try instead, "When you lose your temper that way, I feel afraid." If we find ourselves assuming the role of the injured, innocent victim more often than questioning the significance of our own role, perhaps fear has gotten hold of a loving tool and has begun to misuse it.

Commitment to Listen

Openhearted Listening is fully effective only when you make a commitment to do it any time it is requested (or as soon as it is possible). Without such a commitment, you will be embarking on a halfhearted journey, severely limiting yourself by backing away from the very moments that require your most dedicated courage and attention.

Commitments have no meaning when things come easily. If your life unfolded without challenge or obstacle, you would not need commitment. Commitment helps you respond with a deeper purpose during difficult times. It's a discipline in the face of what your fear would always like you to do, which is to escape discomfort. Commitment is your ally against the temptation to take the easy road; to indulge in the immediate gratification of being right. The more intense the temptation, the stronger your commitment needs to be.

Fasting has taught me much about responding to temptation. Whenever I decide to fast, I always get ravenously hungry at some point, especially in the first couple of days. On many occasions, I am able to say no to my craving, stay on track, and continue the fast. But other times, as soon as I get really hungry I give in, rationalizing to myself that this wasn't really the right time to fast. The difference is that in the first situation, whether I knew it or not, I had the natural discipline that arises out of a true commitment. Successful fasting entails taking into account the strength of the hunger you will likely feel, and greeting it with a resolve of equal power.

In order to accomplish any goal, you have to take fully into account the strength of the force that resists it, called by the Russian teacher G. I. Gurdjieff "second force." When you commit to doing Openhearted Listening, it is necessary to acknowledge the power of second force: the profound temptation to get defensive when your partner's annoying behavior elicits a strong negative reaction from you. Your partner will accuse you unfairly, look at you a certain way, or employ a certain tone, and every ounce of your being will crave to defend yourself, attack them, or just give up. When they express their hurt and fear, you will be tempted time and again to pull back or to attack. Fear will assert that you can't be present and open for your partner. Only the strength of your commitment will help you meet and overcome the second force.

If your child or someone you deeply care for got severely ill, and you had to climb a mountain at night in the rain to get the only available medicine, would you not find the energy to do it? There is no question in your mind, it wouldn't even occur to you not to, even if you were tired, sick, or not in the mood. When you make a strong commitment from your heart, you have aligned yourself with something deeper than your own personal needs. Strength and power are available far beyond what the limited mind thinks possible.

Sometimes the struggle can be extremely wearisome. At those moments you need to go within and reach for a place that you may not even know existed. Commitment reminds you that it is worth the effort to take the more difficult path. The more resistance you have, the more likely that you will learn something of inestimable value by struggling with your deeply rooted tendency to close down. For those warriors who embark on this path, the rewards will be beyond anything they could imagine.

Does Openhearted Listening
Eliminate Useful Dialogue?

Some people experience a reluctance to have one-way-at-a-time communication, afraid that this inhibits useful dialogue. Of course, real two-way dialogue is indispensable. But the quality of communication is limited when one or both parties aren't truly heard. If dialogue is attempted without this understanding, it is likely to result in mutual blame, and a great expenditure of energy in a futile attempt to be understood.

Greg and Tanya came to one of our couples' weekends, stuck in a conflict about his single incidence of infidelity many years ago. Greg had been contrite, acknowledging that it was a serious mistake, and promising never to repeat it. Nevertheless, Tanya was unable to forgive him. She was convinced that Greg hadn't fully understood how deeply betrayed she had felt. Whenever a major fight erupted, Tanya would bring up his infidelity and confront him with it.

Greg would defend himself, saying, "Look, how many times can I apologize? The past is over. Why can't we just let it go and start living in the present?"

Every time the issue was brought up, there was an unsatisfying, stuck feeling to the dialogue. Greg felt unfairly attacked for something that was past and gone, something for which he had apologized. Tanya felt frustrated in not being able to release powerful feelings that had never been fully heard.

Two errors are common when past mistakes cast their shadow over the present. Tanya would be tempted toward the first: to attack one's partner for their mistake, enjoying the feeling of being the righteous, wounded party. Greg would find it enticing to make the second mistake: to desire prematurely to let go of the past and move on, overlooking the importance of having patience with painful, unresolved old wounds. In truth, the past is neither to be indulged nor dismissed but learned from.

What was to be done? After we showed them how to listen with an open heart, Tanya asked Greg to do so while she explored the depth of her feelings. It was hard for Greg not to be defensive, but he made a supreme effort to listen and validate, for which Tanya acknowledged him. It helped Tanya to remember that while her partner had made a grave mistake, he was not a bad person.

She did not feel complete enough on this one occasion to release her feelings totally. But because she appreciated Greg's new effort to enter into her feelings, Tanya agreed to avoid using the incident against him. Greg acknowledged that her feelings were valid, and gave her permission to have them for as long as she needed to. They both agreed that it would be valuable to explore the feelings further at a later time; meanwhile they would wait for the trust level to improve by practicing listening with other issues.

To justify and take advantage of negative feelings is indeed a temptation. But Tanya realized that any pleasure she may have derived from dwelling permanently in the role of innocent victim wasn't worth the cost. Her willingness to forego blame was the key, even though she had not yet been able to release her feelings of anger. With the help of Greg's new capacity to hear and validate, Tanya was able over time to forgive her partner completely.

It's clear that the one-way-at-a time principle is essential for a certain depth of communication. I must be wholeheartedly present for my partner in order to hear their reality. If I'm planning my response, or clinging to my own point of view, the ability to hear and validate my partner will be seriously impaired. It is partly for this reason that we discourage using Openhearted Listening in a back-and forth way. If I have been validated by my partner, and have felt the deep satisfaction that comes from it, and then my partner immediately asks to be heard on the same issue, it is easy to see how the feeling of validation can be undermined or lessened.

Martha and I like to observe what we sometimes call the "twenty-four-hour rule," though it is not really based on the clock. It says that if one of us has validated the other on a charged issue, but, despite understanding and accepting the other's feelings, we still have feelings of our own around the same issue that need to be heard, we wait a suitable amount of time—generally till the next day—before asking for Openhearted Listening. This helps keep the process pure, and avoids having it shade subtly into a debate. (I should add that such a reversal of roles is rarely necessary. Usually when I validate Martha's point of view—i.e., when I have truly understood it—any need I had to state my own case miraculously vanishes. Such is the power of non-defensiveness.)

Openhearted Conversation

Although the principle of focusing only on one partner's reality at a time is the basis of Openhearted Listening, we've also developed a structure that allows partners to talk about charged issues in a more conversational way. As already suggested, a two-way conversation always has the potential for degenerating into an argument. If I hear and validate your perspective and then come back to you immediately with my own, I risk falling into a defensive posture: My perspective contradicts or refutes yours. This is not at all what we wish to achieve; our interest is in non-defensiveness. For this reason, Openhearted Conversation adds an extra challenge to openhearted communication. In a sense, it violates the twenty-four-hour rule, which says that we don't follow validation by coming right back with our own point of view. Nonetheless, under the right circum-stances, when practiced with diligence, respect, and an extra layer of caution, we have found the process quite valuable in exploring areas of disagreement, or when an important decision is required.

In a sense, Openhearted Conversation can be thought of as Openhearted Listening that goes both ways. It works as long as the spirit of Openhearted Listening is maintained. Each partner, as they listen to the other's perspective, needs to relinquish defensiveness in the same way they would when doing Openhearted Listening. As they state their own perspective, each one needs to avoid critiquing the other's, or slipping into an argumentative tone. To be effective, the conversation needs to be conducted by the two partners as allies.

The format is as follows: Partner A begins by speaking briefly on the matter at hand, emphasizing what they would like to see happen (not what they find objectionable in the other). Before responding with their own view, Partner B goes through a step called "joining." This joining may be a brief gesture, but it is the most significant part of the process.

Joining is a recognition of mutuality. It often includes an acknowledgment of shared desire, reaching out beyond disagree-ment to the place where both partners are in accord; where they want at bottom the same thing. It affirms their status as allies. For example, if two parents disagree about how to handle their chil-dren, one might join by saying, "I feel the same as you. We both want to raise children who feel good about themselves." The core statement underlying joining is: "I want what you want." There is always a level at which desires are shared; the trick is to find it.

Joining can also be an expression of understanding; validating a partner's concern, desire, or feeling. If the disagreement is about money, this kind of joining is manifested in statements such as: "I understand why you'd be afraid this might put us over the edge financially," or, "I can certainly see why you want to feel secure about our finances, and why you would feel troubled when our bank account gets this low."

After joining, B goes on to express their own view, again emphasizing what they would like to see happen. "We both want thus and so . . . here's how I see this happening." Focusing on what is desired puts out an energy more likely to elicit a positive response. It also offers one's partner something to join with. It is best if one avoids dogmatic or rigid scenarios, such as: "This is the only way I see this working." Instead, one can say: "Here's one possible way this could work." When B has stated their perspective, the conversation shifts back to A, who similarly joins and responds. The two continue to go back and forth, always joining to begin their response. They continue until they have reached some kind of accord. This does not necessarily mean a precise or comprehensive solution to the problem—indeed that will often not be possible in so limited a time. But the dialogue can produce a more harmonious atmosphere in which each partner can better understand the feelings behind the other's desires.

The principles of Openhearted Conversation, based on the golden key of joining, can be applied to many areas of life—business, friendship, family, work—anywhere conflict may arise and good communication can help to prevent or defuse it. A key concept is: "For this to work for me, it has to work for you, too." How deeply comforting it is to hear such words! With that kind of attitude, long-term opponents become instant allies who are more likely to create a mutually satisfying solution, or even a miracle.

Does Openhearted Listening Destroy Freedom?

Some might wonder if Openhearted Listening could destroy freedom and spontaneity in the relationship.

It's a strange notion to think that freedom means doing what I want to do in the moment. For example, if I make a commitment to exercise every day for the next week, this logic suggests that by forcing myself to exercise, I'm sacrificing my freedom and spontaneity. The implication is that I wish to retain the "freedom" to follow the whims of my cravings, addictions, and desire for immediate gratification. But being a slave to my cravings, whether for drugs, laziness, or indulging my ego, could scarcely be called freedom. This kind of freedom is actually the freedom of a machine—a spontaneity based on limited conditioning or addictions.

To break my old physical or mental reactive patterns, I create disciplines. These structures seem to limit my spontaneity, since they are often conceived as a way to force myself to do what I would rather avoid. But discipline is what arises naturally when I allow my behavior to be determined by my deeper wisdom, rather than by my desire for immediate gratification. In order to have true spontaneity, it is necessary first to interrupt the old reactive behavior. Discipline opens the door to real freedom, since I am now acting instead of reacting. Just as a commitment to exercise replaces a sedentary lifestyle, a discipline such as Openhearted Listening breaks the old habit of responding in a mechanical fashion to my partner.

But Will Their Behavior Change?

We are often told that Openhearted Listening sounds good in theory, but has no value if your partner validates your feeling and then keeps right on doing the same old thing.

Although there are no guarantees, we can offer encouragement to those with this concern. Martha and I found that as we listened to each other hundreds of times over the years, we became more finely tuned to each other's reality. We started catching ourselves far more often as we were about to behave unskillfully toward each other. We perceived connections between seemingly unrelated events, as unconscious patterns began to reveal themselves. It was neither our partner's complaints nor their demands that led to alterations in our behavior, but rather our greater awareness of ourselves.

Change takes time. Deeply ingrained behavior patterns are not so easy to alter. If you are in the habit, for example, of speaking to your partner with a sharp edge in your voice when they irritate you, watch how easy it is to fall into that unconscious pattern, even if you sincerely want to break the habit. Remember, it is just as difficult for your partner to overcome their own long-term patterns of unconscious behavior as it is for you.

Even if negative behavior persists for a while, you may notice that your partner sometimes remembers and behaves differently. Be gracious when your partner forgets, encourage them lovingly when they succeed. If a problem persists, at least you have created an environment that is more conducive to a creative solution. Your faith in your partner's capacity to change will, in itself, help them to change.

A Day of Grace: Another Level of Commitment

Here is a powerful structure for couples who wish to accelerate their growth and learn a great deal about themselves in a short time.

If you have seen the value of releasing your usual defenses by listening with an open heart, the next step is to extend this gift of love for a whole day. You will know if and when the time has come to try.

The structure takes place over a two-day period, and consists of a commitment by one person to keep their heart open to their partner for the entire day. The following day their partner does the same. The commitment holds no matter what your partner says or does. You will not attack your partner in any way, for any reason, and you may not be defensive. You will be constantly alert for creative new ways to express your love.

You do not have to do everything your partner wishes, or accept outrageous behavior. A parent can be loving toward a child even while setting firm boundaries. When a child is most wounded, love is most needed.

You are being asked to play the part of a person with a perfectly open heart. I once read of an Italian actor who played the role of Jesus in a major film about his life. After the filming, the actor's life was profoundly altered. Even playing the part of a person with a perfectly open heart can apparently have a remarkable healing effect! For an entire day, you put aside all fear-based behavior and act toward your partner as though you don't have an ego.

Your partner can revel for a day in something they have likely never experienced in their whole life: They can relax and be who they are, knowing they will not be judged or blamed.

If you fail to keep your heart open at a particular moment, don't defend it or apologize. Simply stop and do whatever is necessary to connect once again with your heart, restoring yourself again to a place of non-judgment. You are not asked to be perfect, but you are asked not to make excuses. Do whatever it takes to honor your commitment, though it may feel profoundly difficult.

If you feel that your partner's behavior is making it impossible for you to be loving, don't give energy to this feeling. If you have the intention, the Universe will lean in your direction and meet you with the help you need. Although keeping your commitment can sometimes be emotionally strenuous, it's also an opportunity for immense growth.

As the feeling of safety in your relationship increases through this process, deeper levels of pain may emerge for the first time in your life. Since nothing can be released until it is first made conscious, your wounds can now at last be healed. At times you might both temporarily wish you had chosen a path of less intensity. But there is a joy in doing this work, for you are not only healing yourselves, but the split between men and women as well. Ultimately, you are helping to heal all the conflict and pain that resides in the world. Another lovely variation of doing this is to give your partner a Day of Grace without telling them. A special pleasure arises from the purity of such a gift.

The Importance of Doing It Both Ways

Both roles in the Day of Grace are profoundly valuable. For me, just to be able to have full permission to be who I am and feel safe has significantly increased my level of trust. I have come to know that Martha will be there for me no matter how unsavory my moods. The fact that I have felt so unconditionally accepted has helped me toward making peace with my own imperfections.

Yet playing the other role is of equal, if not greater, benefit. Were

I to be the "safe" one all the time, there would be an imbalance. The value lies in playing the roles of both wounded and healer in succession, which shakes me loose from my conditioning more powerfully than either role possibly could by itself.

When we first started, I looked forward to the days when Martha would play the role of healer. But I soon found that, if anything, the days I was healer were even more rewarding. In helping to heal Martha, I was healing something similar in myself.

Often when I embarked on the day, I would encounter many occasions when I would be about to react negatively to things Martha had said or done. These became opportunities to allow in another dimension of awareness, and to make a different choice.

As time went on, I began to find new and more creative ways of expressing my love during these special days. For example, in communicating about some practical matter, such as the need to pay the bills, it's possible to speak without attacking, in a perfectly neutral fashion. But it's also possible to say the same thing with the heart engaged. I began to be interested in the tone of voice that I used for the most mundane communications. It was so much more possible than I had imagined to express my love in a variety of subtle ways. The opportunities were virtually unlimited! What had started as an exercise, developed a life of its own, taking us far beyond any structure.

The Day of Grace is a blessing of the highest order. It has shown me how to let go of my belief that I am a victim of my partner's moods. No matter what the content, I always have the option of choosing love, which is more powerful than fear.

Thoughts from Martha

I think that I, too, have become a better listener over the years. This is mainly because I've had the chance to appreciate the enormous benefits that come to me when I'm able to hear and deeply take in Don's reality. Even though most people would assume there's more satisfaction in being heard than in listening, I, like Don, have found the rewards of the latter to be even deeper and more fulfilling, in the long run.

This wasn't obvious at the beginning. When we first started doing Openhearted Listening, hearing and validating Don's point of view could be a real challenge for me. Even though I struggled to follow the process, there was often a voice within me railing in protest. Sometimes this voice would urge me to retaliate against Don for (as I saw it) unfairly accusing me. For example, he would sometimes tell me how it bothered him when I left piles of books and papers from unfinished projects all over the house. Immediately my mind would fasten on the fact that Don himself was often messy and unaware of his mess. Who is he to criticize me about that? I would think. My messes are nothing compared to his.

Sometimes my defensiveness took the form of indignation at being controlled, as it did when he spoke to me about my difficulty in saying no to others, and its effect on him. He was pointing out my tendency to agree to more social engagements, work commitments, personal favors, and so on, than I could possibly follow through on—at least without bringing chaos in its wake. It was something I really needed to hear, but at the time, all I was aware of was my own ego inwardly screaming, Look, you're not my social manager. I'm in charge of my life, not you! I won't have you telling me what to do, trying to control my life!

Such difficulties will be familiar to anyone who's tried Openhearted Listening. It is indeed a challenge. For untold thousands of years of evolution, we've been programmed with a fight-or-flight reflex, so deep and instinctive that it possesses us before we've even had a chance to see what's going on. Refusing to get defensive means going against this instinct. Fortunately, Don and I take very seriously our commitment to the discipline of listening to each other, so there's never any question of not doing it. And through our persistence over the years, the structure of listening, as well as the habit of non-defensiveness that must be at its core, have become second nature. The benefits of this have been immense, touching every aspect of our lives.

Now I can't imagine being without this tool. Even though I occasionally feel defensive around the issues Don brings me, my whole biochemical reaction has softened. When Don's feedback collides with my reality, a little red light goes on to warn me: Just step back a minute. See if you can appreciate his reality. See if there isn't something in it for you. (There always is, of course.)

When listening seems especially hard, I put my story aside for the moment, stay with my breathing, and watch my thoughts until they settle down—a kind of meditation. On rare occasions in the past when this seemed virtually impossible, I first had to realize how I had become so deeply ensconced in my own pain-making mechanisms that no matter what I did, the knot got tighter. No escape was apparent. Out of desperation I would call inwardly for the most available form of spiritual help I knew. Inevitably the response came through my surrender: my willingness to get out of my own way and let in a wisdom from a totally different plane. My fear would relax and my heart would soften. At last I was able to feel my way into Don's emotions, expanding my awareness to include his reality. The empathy I'd experience was totally relieving and refreshing. What a gift!

If I could whisper into the ear of every person entering into the adventure of Openhearted Listening, here is what I would say: "Relax and fill your mind and heart with the knowledge that this person before you, your partner and friend, has different perspectives from you, but this person is not your enemy. At heart they want the same thing in life as you. Even if you feel they didn't get the story 'right,' what you are validating is simply the existence of their human feelings. These may have been triggered by something you did, intentionally or unintentionally, but they are still no more than feelings. All of your partner's perceptions are subjectively true, just as yours are always true. Your partner deserves compassion, no less than you. Trust that there is the wisdom within you to remind you to soften and surrender to the simple, elegant, and sublime art of listening."

CHAPTER 3

Asking Your Partner for Change

The Usual Responses Don't Work

How many times have you had the following experience? You tell your partner there's something they do on a regular basis that really bothers you. They reply, "Oh, sure, I can see I've really been unconscious. I understand how that would bother you, and of course I'll be glad to change. If I forget, please remind me." Chances are, not very often.

Some of the most intense difficulties in being a couple stem from our frustration with our partner's behavior. No one, after the initial romantic stage, can avoid being annoyed or frustrated by some of their partner's habits. In a healthy relationship, we should be able to communicate about such disturbances, ask our partner respectfully to alter the offending behavior, and expect them to at least listen carefully and take our request seriously.

But the reality is generally otherwise. More likely, you respond to your partner's undesirable behavior like this:

You attack. "You're such a total slob! What's the matter with you, didn't you ever learn basic manners? Why the hell don't you clean up after yourself?" In response to such an attack, your partner is likely to resent you for not accepting their somewhat more casual relationship to order. Even if they do honor the request, they still resent you for the highly disrespectful way that you asked. If they don't honor it, there are bad feelings on both sides.

You resign yourself and resent. After fruitless attempts to get your partner to change, you resign yourself to the fact that they will never change. In so doing, you bury your negative feelings and end up resenting your partner. Resignation, while it may superficially resemble acceptance, is quite far removed from the feeling of peace that accompanies the latter.

You manipulate. Your style is more indirect, so you use subtle means to control your partner's behavior. People may accuse you of manipulation. What they usually mean is that you're not being forthright about trying to influence them. Nothing is wrong with trying to affect your partner's behavior, but it feels a lot better to both parties when you do so openly and with awareness. Instead of making manipulation into a sin, learn to be conscious about the ways you influence each other.

None of these responses addresses the real issue or elicits a lasting change. What *does* work is becoming allies with your partner, avoiding blame, and working together to be more conscious about what doesn't feel good. It's a challenge to deal wisely with annoying habits, but it's the best way to keep them from casting a shadow on your harmony.

Control and Surrender

If I am using my relationship to further my spiritual growth, how do I justify asking my partner to change their behavior? Doesn't this go against the common spiritual dictate that says I should accept my partner just as they are?

You both need to communicate effectively about what bothers you and to accept with grace your partner's imperfections. If communication is missing, you become a martyr with growing resentments. If you lack acceptance, you become a sophisticated nag, which can be very annoying to be around. The first represents control, the second surrender. For a harmonious intimacy, control and surrender must be purified of their fearful aspects.

Fearful control emerges as an authoritative and bossy style. Your manner conveys the feeling that your partner had better do as you wish, or you will make their life miserable. Those caught up in fearful control will try frequently to take charge of their partner's behavior in order to lessen their own feeling of fear or inadequacy.

Fearful surrender displays itself as weakness, placating and submissive. You put out the message that you are powerless, and that your partner may do whatever they wish with you. Anyone caught up in this state will invite being controlled unhealthily.

Destructive control and surrender often attract each other. Although they may seem like opposites, they are actually opposite sides of the same coin. Neither is a whole response or a genuine acknowledgment of your love. However, control and surrender can have an entirely different flavor when they arise from a place of respect for both yourself and your partner.

Healthy control is neither bullying nor manipulative. Rather, it represents the masculine force elevated to its highest potential. It arises from the realization that you are not a victim of the world you see; that you have the choice to alter your consciousness and master your circumstances. It is a recognition of the ways that you contribute, outwardly and inwardly, to whatever feels out of tune. It shows a willingness to say no to these harmful patterns. Healthy control may manifest as self-discipline, taking charge of your attitude, diet, exercise, or habits. It can also display itself as a firm and respectful "no" to your partner, when their behavior doesn't work for you.

Healthy surrender is not submission, nor is it self-abnegation. Rather, it is the feminine aspect elevated to its highest potential (either sex does well to bring masculine and feminine into balance within themselves). To surrender is to cease resisting, to be less brittle, more receptive and penetrable. If you don't like what is happening, take that as a cue to relax. Like water, continually shifting its shape, blend with what is happening. Healthy surrender manifests both as a loving acceptance of your own imperfections, and as a willingness to allow your partner to be who they are, allowing for those traits that you may not find too attractive.

Who Is Responsible for My Feelings?

When I ask my partner for change, am I implying that their behavior is the source of my bad feelings? After all, am I not responsible for the way I feel? Anyone with much exposure to New Age thinking will be tempted to agree instantly. In sophisticated spiritual circles it has become a virtual cliché.

But it doesn't seem at all obvious that I am responsible for my feelings. Almost all of us believe intuitively that if you criticize someone in an unkind manner, and they immediately feel bad, it's your fault for causing them to feel that way. It pays to assess with honesty if perhaps, underneath my spiritually correct belief structure, I still believe that my partner is the source of my unhappiness.

One way of telling is by watching the extent to which I blame my partner for the way I feel. Can I believe I am responsible for my feelings and simultaneously denounce my partner for making me feel that way? Obviously not. But if I am responsible for my feelings, is there appropriate justification for asking my partner to change behavior that is annoying me? We think there is. It's possible to take responsibility for my feelings and still reasonably ask my partner to change their behavior. But it is important to be aware of my motivation.

When Fear Asks for Change

When you ask for a change of behavior, your request can arise out of fear or love. For instance, if you're the sort of person whose insecurity requires you to plan your vacation out to the last detail, while your partner likes to make travel decisions impulsively, you may well become frustrated or annoyed with them. If you request that they plan more and be more organized, like you, they may feel you are rigid and constricted. Your fear is asking them to change.

Whenever you blame your partner for your uncomfortable emotional state, you are indulging in an ego-based request for change. Your request will likely come through with the message that there is something wrong with them. Your partner will feel judged, and in all likelihood not want to honor the request. They may well feel that you are trying unfairly to control them, or to deny some essential aspect of their being. Their reluctance to honor your request will have a truth to it.

For example, Frank tells Lynn it really worries him when she goes off climbing mountains. He asks her to renounce such dangerous activity and find a safer form of recreation. Since this request is fear-based, it will have a quality that doesn't feel right to Lynn. For her, climbing is an indispensable expression of who she is, and so she probably won't have much interest in accommodating him. She might, however, explore Frank's fear with him, and ask him if there is any way, short of giving up something that really nourishes her, that she can help him deal with his fear.

Or say you and your partner come from widely different backgrounds. She's from a family that emphasized privacy over intimacy, while your family shared everything at privacy's expense. In such a case, she might be uncomfortable with your style of intimacy, which she perceives as not respecting her boundaries. And you might equally be uncomfortable with her style, perceiving it as withholding.

If she asks you to change, she may be failing to see that your way of relating, although different from hers, is as valid as her own. Again, these are not healthy grounds for you to want to change. However, the knowledge of each other's past may certainly bring a new awareness and a greater respect for the other.

Or perhaps someone might ask their partner to be more rational, to stop allowing themselves to be so led by their feelings. The futility of such a request was expressed in a cartoon we saw recently, showing a dog and a cat lying in bed together, both looking sullen. The cat was saying, "Look, I'm not aloof, I'm a goddamned *cat*, okay?" Asking partners to alter something essential in their nature only arouses conflict.

Sometimes, the way a request is initially framed may stimulate in your partner a fear that if they said yes, they would have to give up something important. A woman is frightened by the intensity of her partner's anger, and asks him not to get angry with her. While he may have some learning to do about expressing his anger more wisely, he may also feel that there's something fundamentally unfair about his partner's request. And there is. To ask your partner not to have certain feelings is tantamount to asking them to abandon their humanity.

The woman, however, might acknowledge to her partner that he needed to be able to get angry, just as she needed to be able to feel safe. Then she might ask if he was willing to work together to find a way of dealing with anger that felt safe to her. With such a request, her partner is not being asked to give up anything essential.

When Love Asks for Change

Request for change can have a motive different from fear. In a spiritual relationship, one of our functions is to serve each other in the role of teacher, since there are many discordant areas of our being about which our partner has unique knowledge.

It's as if you were learning a martial art and you had a teacher who saw that you weren't putting your full effort into a move. The teacher coaxes you lovingly, "Come on, I know you can do better than that. Put your whole attention into the movement." Such a teacher serves you by not accepting anything less than your best. In fact, that is precisely why you have employed him or her, to help you be more conscious.

Similarly, you can look upon your partner as someone with whom you've contracted to help the both of you live more consciously. You are inviting each other to look more closely at the very things that you've come into this world to heal in yourself. Whether by direct request or through an innate understanding, you ask your partner to tell you when they sense that your behavior might not be in alignment with your deepest purpose. If your candle flickers, you ask them to please share their light with you. You pledge to do the same for them.

In our relationship, Martha's requests for change in my behavior have often revolved around my failure to pick up after myself. If our life together were a musical composition, such behavior would be a note or passage that was out of tune. The first signal of my out-of-tune behavior would show up in Martha's discomfort. It can be an act of love for her to ask that I play more in tune. I still sometimes cringe at being reminded of my shortcomings, but underneath, I sense that what Martha is asking of me would be a gift to me, were I to do it. If I don't feel the value for myself in her request, then even if I follow it, I'm going to do so resentfully, which isn't going to feel right.

Your partner will serve as your spiritual teacher if you have the ears to hear and are willing to abandon your defenses. Having lived with you and experienced the consequences of your habits and tendencies, your partner is likely to be acutely aware of those areas where you are most out of touch. Of course, it's preferable that they point out imperfections lovingly rather than conveying, "Oh God, there you go again!" When you feel more accepted, you're less likely to get defensive and push away the truth of what is being said. Your partner can serve as the voice of your deeper self, asking you to examine an aspect of your life that could be more in harmony.

Having Faith in Your Partner

I once performed with a small-town symphony orchestra. We were playing a piece with a big solo for the French horn section, which tended to play rather sloppily and frequently hit wrong notes. One day a famous conductor, an imposing and dignified man, came to conduct the dress rehearsal and concert. During their solo, the horns again hit a few bloopers. The regular conductor had come to expect this, and had gotten used to it. But the guest conductor stopped them short and asked them to repeat the passage. When again a few notes were missed, he brought everything to a dead halt and looked at them piercingly.

"*That simply won't do!*" he intoned, in a manner that I've never forgotten. That was all he said. On the next try, the horns got it right. They got it right at the concert. They succeeded not only because of their fear of the distinguished conductor, but because he believed they were capable.

You can contribute to the success of your partner in changing unwanted behaviors by believing in their capacity to change. Studies repeatedly show that students who have difficulties continue to do poorly when their teachers have little faith in them. When these same students work with teachers who believe in them, they perform surprisingly well.

Of course, there is the temptation to dismiss your partner as one who has proven repeatedly that they can't change. Many send their partners the message: You have never changed and never will. Your conscious and unconscious attitude about your partner's capacity to change sends them a message they take seriously. It often becomes a self-fulfilling prophecy. It is worth cultivating the perspective that your partner, despite past failures, is quite capable of moving together with you toward greater awareness.

Common Destructive Patterns

Certain forms of unconscious behavior are quite prevalent. If you recognize any of the following in your relationship, they might serve as useful starting places to practice asking for a change in behavior.

Discouragement—One partner will make a suggestion or share a dream for the future, and the other will instantly find flaws or objections. This will soon discourage the first partner from sharing ideas. Become allies in creating an atmosphere of emotional safety when one of you shares an idea or a vision.

Correction—How many times have we witnessed someone telling a story, only to be annoyingly corrected by their partner with some irrelevancy? A flow is interrupted for no good reason. Once Martha was expressing how impressed she was that our son had gotten to go up in both a balloon and a helicopter within a month's time. I promptly informed her that it wasn't a month, it was six weeks. Her enthusiasm was effectively punctured, and there was no place to go with it. My correction had served no useful purpose. Fortunately, she caught what had happened, and used it to frame a request to me that I be more conscious of my motives when feeling the need to correct her. Since then, I've noticed how often the urge to provide "greater accuracy" has no redeeming social value. It's allowed me to put into practice the truth that many things are better left unsaid.

Interruption—In some subcultures, such as the one I grew up in around New York City, it is considered all right to break in. In other cultures it is considered the height of rudeness. The one being interrupted may feel as if their partner has no interest in what is being said, and can't wait to speak their own more worthwhile piece. If you don't appreciate being interrupted, here's an opportunity to let the interrupter know that you are bothered, without blaming them. Should they forget and interrupt again, avoid responding in anger or putting up with it in hurt silence. Instead, try saying in a pleasant tone, "Just a second, wait till I'm finished."

A Difficult Request

Martha, by virtue of being so close to me, perceives many unaware aspects of my behavior. As a woman, she can see clearly in areas where I, as a man, tend to be less insightful. I've learned to have a great respect for her perceptions of my behavior. When she asks me for a behavior change, it usually has a power and a rightness to it. I've learned not to dismiss her observations too glibly. I may safely assume that in her requests, there's a good chance that there'll be something for me to look at.

In particular, I recall one request that was very hard for me to hear. Among my male friends, we have an easy and direct way of putting forth our personal needs, assuming that our friends will do likewise, working things out without conflict. As a result, I had a habit with Martha of communicating my wishes forcefully, assuming that if she had a contrary desire she would make it known, after which we could negotiate.

It tended not to work out that way. Martha felt I often prevailed with my more dominant manner, seeming to lack interest in her possibly different wishes. Many women have experienced this with men.

I once put out quite unequivocally, for example, that I wanted to go to the hot springs over vacation, as I felt the need for some deep relaxation. Martha didn't find it so easy to break in and let me know she had a real yen for the mountains, and that we needed to negotiate. Instead she built up resentment. I had put my needs out so strongly that they seemed to brook no contradiction.

After many failed attempts to understand, I finally got that she was not asking me to do whatever she wanted, or to sacrifice the strength of my feelings. I learned, after much struggle, to make a seemingly minor, but crucial change: After putting out my strong urge that we do a certain thing, I would ask her, "And what would you like to do?" Such a simple addition! Yet it made all the difference to Martha, who felt at last she didn't have to yell to be heard.

If you take an inner snapshot whenever one of you does something that bothers the other, you may perceive a pattern that connects the various incidents. For example, one major theme might occur when your partner is feeling hurt or angry. Perhaps you'd like for them to be conscious of their feelings, articulate them without blame, and communicate what they want from you, rather than just withdraw or criticize. Many couples struggle with this issue.

A Central Request

A few years ago, Martha and I seemed to be going through some rapids in the stream. We were quarreling more often than I felt comfortable with. Something was nagging at me for a long time, but I couldn't quite put my finger on it.

One day when we had just completed a run together on a back road, I realized there was something essential I had been wanting from Martha without having articulated it. I suspect that intimacies often contain a quintessential unstated request, something fundamental that we want from our partner and haven't asked for in a clear, direct way.

I had been noticing conflict between us whenever I would get into one of my deep, dark Russian-Jewish moods. I sensed Martha's fear and discomfort with me at such times, and her interest in getting me quickly out of my state so she could feel at ease once again. It felt as though she had doubts as to whether I would ever emerge from this darkness. I noticed she would either try to make things better, or get snippy with me. Sometimes her change was rather subtle. In either case, I hadn't been feeling the sense of safety that comes when my partner accepts me. I had never been clear enough about this, but on that sparkling fall day in Vermont, I asked Martha directly if she would hear a really fundamental request.

I began to speak. "I want you to honor and respect my rhythms and see the positive contribution my darkness brings into my life. I want you to stop treating my darkness as a disease to be cured. I want to know it is deeply okay with you that I go as fully as needed into my darkness. I want your support in getting to the very bottom. I want you to have faith in my process and in me. Please hear me, I want this with my whole being."

Martha was able to hear me and respond favorably. She promised to be there for me whenever I entered my depths. And she has. Not surprisingly, in feeling her support, I have found that I need to enter the darkness less often.

When Ego Contaminates a True Message

A common difficulty with many couples is the intrusion of blame into an otherwise legitimate message. Sometimes your partner's message originates from a clear perception of an imperfection, but your behavior has touched a raw place in them, so their communication doesn't come through in a totally loving fashion. You are receiving a confusing combination of a legitimate message that you need to hear, laced with a quality of blame, which is not valid, and which makes it harder for you to receive the truth in the message.

While the closing of the heart is certainly a mistake, not listening because blame is present is also a mistake. Even if your partner seems to be in their ego when they are asking for a change, there may be, lurking underneath the blame, some truth that you need to examine.

The Key to Asking

One of the best ways to improve the quality of your relationship is to learn the art of asking effectively for what you want. Those who become proficient tend to attain their desires frequently, while couples who have difficulty asking will end up not getting many of their needs met. As a result, resentment will accumulate through the years and poison the relationship.

Two mistakes are commonly made. First, you may avoid asking for what you want altogether. If past attempts to ask, dating back to childhood, have brought failure and unpleasantness, you may have formed a rigid notion that there's no use in asking. According to this belief, asking leads to pain and frustration, which you can best avoid by relinquishing any hope of getting your needs met.

There are other reasons why you may refuse to ask. Perhaps, suffering from a lack of kindness to yourself, you harbor a belief that you don't deserve to have your needs met. Or you may entertain the unrealistic notion that your partner should know you well enough to anticipate all of your wishes without you having to tell them. Whatever the reason, your refusal to ask guarantees frustration and leads to resentment in the long run.

Second, you may ask in the wrong way. The most important factor in asking is the effect it has on your partner's feeling about themselves. In general, complaint, blame, criticism, or any negativity in your voice, however subtle, tends to elicit in others a feeling of guilt, which shuts them down and renders them far less receptive to your request.

When you ask, it is tempting to imply that your partner hasn't been doing enough. If Martha says in a slightly complaining tone, "I've been working really hard all day long; would you mind folding the laundry?" I notice myself beginning to feel guilty: Uh, oh, she's the one who's been working hard and I haven't been pulling my weight. I tend to resist such requests. But if instead she says with a genuine smile, "I'd love it if you would fold the laundry," I find myself more often responding positively. If you eliminate complaint or blame from your asking, chances are far better you'll receive a favorable response.

The way you feel about yourself also comes through in your asking. If you feel unworthy, your request may have an apologetic flavor, which can transmit the message that you don't deserve compliance. Low self-esteem breeds discomfort with asking directly. But an indirect and indecisive manner of asking often feels annoying and manipulative.

It is important that you feel good about yourself, so that you convey a comfortable quality when asking, one that suggests you deserve to get your needs met and invites cooperation. In short, your attitude toward yourself tends to elicit what you believe you deserve.

Be aware of the difference between a request and a demand. A request spoken with a harsh tone can sound suspiciously like a demand, even though most of us respond far less favorably to the latter. Some people in particular, often men, have a forceful negative reaction when they believe they are being told what to do. One way of avoiding this is to make it plain that it is all right for your partner to say no. In a healthy relationship, it's okay to ask for what you want at any time, and it's equally okay for the other to say no.

We make a distinction between what we call the overhand and the underhand approach to asking. The former points a finger, like an angry parent scolding a misbehaving child. It leads to resistance with your partner, just as it would for a parent with a child. The latter approach is like a gesture with the palm up, using the index finger the way you would lovingly coax a hesitant one-year-old to take a few steps. This style of asking makes your request more enticing.

The ultimate test of skill in asking comes with emotionally charged issues. Once you became comfortable with asking, it will be possible to convey a more persuasive message: "I want something, and I know it's hard for you to give it to me. You are not bad because you haven't given it, and I'm not bad for wanting it. Can we find some meeting ground where we could lovingly explore this together?"

Saying No

If you need to say no to a request, it's still important to stay conscious of your heart. For years, a predictable pattern developed when, on certain occasions, Martha would ask me to do an errand, and it went something like this:

Martha: You're going to town today?

Me: Mm hmm.

Martha: Would you mind stopping by the bank and depositing these checks?

Me: [in a weary, complaining tone] Look, I've got so much to do, and I'm rushed as it is. I don't even have time to do all my own chores. If I try to squeeze in the bank as well, I'll be totally stressed out.

Martha: Okay, okay, forget it, I was just asking.

Needless to say, we both came away from such exchanges feeling worse. As we learned to keep our hearts open when we said no, such dialogues began to sound more like this:

Martha: You're going to town today?

Me: Mm hmm.

Martha: Would you mind stopping by the bank and depositing these checks?

Me: [in an amiable tone] I'm really sorry, I'd love to help you, but there just isn't enough time today. I'd be happy to do it next chance I get.

We are both left with a different feeling. With no need to explain, justify, or defend, the heart remains open. As a result, Martha, knowing that she will feel respected whether the answer is yes or no, feels more relaxed in asking for what she wants.

However trivial this example might seem, life consists of thousands of such moments. If both of you know that you deserve to have your needs met, that you can ask for what you want in a graceful way, and that your partner will take your request seriously and respond with an open heart, the emotional climate in your home will improve noticeably.

The Loving Request

A loving request has the following characteristics:

Good timing—If your partner is upset, they're unlikely to be open to hearing you. It is a service to you both to take into account their emotional state when communicating something difficult.

Directness—Learn to ask directly and without apology for what you want. Instead of saying, "I wish you would hold me more often," try, "Will you hold me now?" If you play it safe out of fear that you'll be rejected, you actually make it more difficult for your partner to see what you want. Naturally, they tend to retreat when they're getting mixed messages.

Explicitness—It helps your partner if you can make your requests as specific as possible. When your request is broad and general, it often comes across as too vague to be of much use. Instead of "I'd like you to help me out more in the kitchen," try, "How about you do the dishes and clean up two nights a week?"

Positive form—It's also easier to respond favorably when a request is put in a positive light. For example, rather than saying, "I want you to stop spending so much time with your friends and ignoring me," say "I'd like to request that we spend a good stretch of uninterrupted time together each week." Ask yourself if you might find it easier to say yes to the latter request.

Sensitivity—If your request includes a critique of your partner's imperfections, be especially sensitive in the way you ask. In pointing out areas of their unconscious behavior or misperception of you, make sure you don't come across as blaming or patronizing. This tends to erode your partner's sense of their own value, which may already be fragile. If you feel your partner could be doing better, be aware of how you would like to be told about one of your own shortcomings. At some level, there needs to be the awareness that you are both doing the best you can.

Here is a request as it gets delivered by the ego: "God, you were really awful at the party last night! You behaved like a mentally deranged two-year-old after you had a few drinks. I can't begin to tell you how embarrassing it was for me! I really want you to stop drinking at parties, since you obviously can't handle the stuff."

Here is the same request made from a more open heart: "I'd be a lot more comfortable if you could be more conscious of the way you are at parties. I was uneasy with the way you behaved last night. You seemed different after a couple of drinks. You certainly said and did things that are not reflective of who you really are. This isn't the first time it's happened. I respect that you need to relax and unwind, but I would like you to take a close look at what you are doing when you drink at parties."

There is nothing "bad" about people when they are unconscious or unskillful. But they might have richer, deeper relationships if they were more tuned in. Pointing out their blindness need not be a judgment; it can be an invitation to greater awareness.

Here's another example of a loving request: "Last night when you told the kids to clean up the mess they'd made in the living room, I felt sad. You had a harsh tone in your voice that I think you weren't aware of. It felt as though you were telling the kids they were bad, rather than that their actions weren't acceptable. I feel pain whenever you use that tone with the children. You've been doing it more often lately. I know we both want our children to grow up feeling good about themselves. In many ways you're a wonderful parent, and I know you were feeling stressed out and frustrated last night. I'd just like you to listen more closely to your tone of voice when you set boundaries with the kids."

Responding to the Request

When your partner makes a request, don't get immediately defensive. We recommend treating requests as a variation of Openhearted Listening. When your partner says that they have a request, make a commitment to keep your ego out of the way, to mirror, and to validate. It helps to stay aware of your body and your breath, and to say no to the urge to shut down. It also helps to remember that it's perfectly acceptable to make mistakes. They are perhaps discussing one of your imperfections, but you are still okay.

Once they make the request, mirror it back to them to make sure it's properly understood. Then show your partner that you understand the emotional reality behind the request. If you feel defensive, your partner's request may seem unreasonable. If that's the case, make a special effort to talk about the feelings that gave rise to the request, in order to understand with some empathy the nature of their frustration. See what needs aren't being met. It can be helpful to ask yourself what reason they might have for making such a request. When Martha and I ask ourselves this question, we can always see some way in which the other's request makes sense. When you show that you understand what led your partner to ask, you are validating their request. Of course, this doesn't imply that you necessarily will do what they ask.

If you do say no, be aware of your style. At one time or another, we've all given responses similar to: "What? Are you kidding? No way I could do that!" Of course your partner will feel unheard, and resentment (which you will inevitably receive back) will likely start to build.

Consider how your partner might feel if instead you responded in this spirit: "I can see you've been frustrated about this, and I understand your frustration. Of course you'd want a change. I think your desire is reasonable. For me your request in the form that you gave it doesn't work, because then my needs aren't being met. But I am interested in finding a way for us both to get our needs met, even though we don't yet know what that way is." The chances are far greater for an eventual resolution.

Clayton and Heather found this approach useful. They were an active professional couple, without children, in their mid-thirties. Clayton loved golf but felt guilty about spending so much of his spare time on the course, away from Heather. His solution was to ask her to play golf once a week with him. But Heather, although she played on occasion, didn't particularly enjoy the game. At first she considered the request unreasonable, since she had made her distaste plain to him. She was tempted to blurt out that she hated golf.

Rather than succumb to the temptation, she asked Clayton why he had asked her to play golf. When Clayton shared his feelings, Heather saw that he really wanted to connect regularly by doing something physically enjoyable together. She told him that she saw what he really wanted, and although golf wasn't a suitable answer for her, she would try to find other outdoor activities they could enjoy together (hiking and cross-country skiing eventually proved to be the answer).

Differences in Style

Stylistic differences frequently give rise to the wish that one's partner were more like oneself. Actually, it isn't uncommon to find very different people attracted to each other—an orderly partner with a more casual one, for example. This need not present a problem, unless resentment has begun building in other areas, in which case the orderly person may accuse their partner of being a slob, while the more casual one might denounce the other as being rigid and uptight. When differences are not respected, conflict results.

Winston and Helen were an older couple with deep New England roots. He was about sixty-five, with a full and distinguished head of white hair, and the natural politeness that comes from tradition and an ease with oneself. Helen, about five years younger, had obviously put a great deal of care into her body and dress. They were a handsome couple, who had learned to step gracefully around each other's foibles. Except for one issue.

"You never like to tell me what's bothering you," Helen began, "and it sometimes drives me crazy. So why don't you go first."

Winston smiled. "You're right. It *is* hard for me to let you know when I'm displeased. I was brought up to keep my uncomfortable feelings to myself. But this has bothered me for many years, so I guess I'm willing to let you know about it.

"You frequently get excited about all these 'New Age' things. First there was macrobiotic cooking. Then it was the I Ching. The latest is rebirthing. Whenever you get involved in something new, it's as if nothing else exists; it takes you over completely. You want to talk about it everywhere. Now I have nothing against this. I'm glad to see you doing things you're passionate about. But you want me to go along. You make me feel I'm kind of an old fuddy-duddy 'cause I don't share your enthusiasm. If you want to know the truth . . ." he hesitated, then went on, "a lot of these things just don't interest me that much."

Helen interrupted with an edge to her voice. "I'm quite aware of that. If you would only show a little more interest and not dismiss it all so readily. I feel your mind is closed to new things. You make these subtly patronizing remarks to our kids about my 'interests.' It makes me uncomfortable. I feel put down."

"That's interesting," Winston replied. "I experience exactly the same thing. When we're with our children, I hear you making remarks to them that imply there's something wrong with me because I'm not doing iridology or rebirthing or whatnot. Frankly, I resent it."

This was a new development for a couple that had managed for forty years to avoid fighting. We suggested that each make a request of the other, one at a time, so they could be heard. They agreed that Winston would go first.

"I would like for you to be more respectful of my ways. I'm a little more conservative than you are, and I'm simply not comfortable with some of the things you get involved with."

At this point Helen started fidgeting. She wasn't used to being asked to change her behavior. Her body language was expressing nervousness and discomfort, even though she was trying to control herself. We asked her to breathe and to sit quietly with a receptive posture. She acknowledged this was difficult for her, but she made an effort to calm herself and remain present.

Winston continued. "I want it to be all right that I have a different set of beliefs and values from you. And when we visit the children, I'd like you to respect our differences. I don't want to feel there's something wrong with me for differing with you."

Helen's ambiguity was clearly visible. On the one hand, she was grateful to have her husband say what had been bothering him for so many decades. On the other hand, she had her own view of the situation. She felt Winston was being unfair by leaving certain things out.

"Well, I guess I understand what you mean. You want me to make it okay that you are an old stick-in-the-mud . . ."

"Come on, Helen, that's not allowed in this process," I interrupted. "Not even in jest." It's true that joking remarks are often employed as unconscious forms of attack, which is why we encourage couples not to poke fun at their partners during the process.

She smiled. " Okay, you're right, I was poking a bit, and I'm sorry. I understand that you want me to show you respect even when you don't share my interests. You want me to be more careful how I talk about you. That's reasonable. You shouldn't have to share all my beliefs and enthusiasms. I'm willing to allow you your own ways, and to watch my tongue around the children. If I forget, I give you permission to let me know."

Winston beamed with relief, and in a courtly manner thanked his partner.

The next time we met, Winston agreed to listen to Helen's request. She began:

"I feel an equal desire to ask of you that you show more respect for my interests. I'm aware that you don't share most of them, and probably think many of them are rather strange. That's fine with me. What I don't like are the little innuendoes you make around our kids, or our friends, that imply, "Oh, there goes Helen again, off on one of her bizarre New Age kicks. I guess I'll have to put up with yet another piece of weirdness until she outgrows this one . . ."

"Come on, I think you might be exaggerating just a hair," Winston interrupted.

"Winston!" I had to say. "That's not allowed."

"Why not?" he asked. "She *was* exaggerating! Am I supposed to just let her get away with it?"

"Frankly, yes. In the first place, you were interrupting. In the second place, if it were you, would you want Helen to be the one to decide when you were exaggerating?"

Winston heaved a sigh. " Okay, I do know what that feels like. I'm sorry, go ahead, I won't interrupt."

"Basically, I want the same thing you do," Helen continued. "I want to feel that who I am and what I like is okay with you, even though you don't personally relate to it. I want you to respect the path I've chosen, and to watch how you speak of my interests in front of others, especially the children."

Perhaps as a result of Helen listening to his request, Winston was able to respond rather easily. "I think I understand what you want of me. It's pretty much what I want from you. You want me to respect the way you feel, no matter how differently I see it. And you want me to refrain from subtle put-downs in front of the children."

"Not just the children," Helen replied. "Everyone."

"Yes . . . everyone. You want me to be careful all the time how I speak about your interests. And actually, it's easy for me to see what a reasonable request that is, especially after our last session. I would be happy to do that, my dear."

When Your Partner Forgets

Many requests for change take the form of asking your partner to break a deeply entrenched habit. It's unreasonable to expect a sudden and complete change. Undoing a lifetime of mechanical conditioning takes time., and your partner will sometimes forget.

One couple we met used a signal to help them remember. Marcy, a rather shy computer programmer in her mid-twenties, had been with Jed only a year. They got along well, except that Jed, a popular professor of literature at a small college, tended to take over at social gatherings with his witty and insightful conversation. Marcy felt squeezed out, unimportant, invisible. She requested that he listen more and leave space for her to speak.

Jed acknowledged that he tended to monopolize things, and

agreed he wanted to break the habit. Marcy said to him, "I don't expect you to be perfect about this, I know you will sometimes forget. When you do, would it be all right if I reminded you? And if so, what would work best?"

Jed told Marcy that placing her hand on his arm could be the signal for him to pay attention. The agreement worked very well. Over time, Jed needed to feel the touch of Marcy's hand less often.

If you are the one being asked for a change, you may sense the value of your partner's request, but doubt whether you have the capacity to change. If so, ask for their assistance to help you remember. In this process, you have become real allies, joining forces to help each other live a more conscious life.

At our couples weekends, we sometimes have people exclaiming with some passion that they want a partner who accepts them the way they are. But if they insist on maintaining all of their unconscious habits, they will probably end up with a partner who harbors an increasing reservoir of resentment. The person unwilling to change may become the recipient of nagging, withdrawal, direct or indirect anger, sabotage, or sexual shutdown.

You may have neither the desire nor the capacity to alter your essential core, but you can certainly transform the way you express it. In so doing, you may reveal more interesting aspects of yourself, and become a lot easier to live with. There is no person better equipped to help you in this noble task than your ever-loving partner.

Thoughts from Martha

Many benefits come from asking for change skillfully. The way in which I come to Don with my request has an impact on his willingness to consider my request. But I've also learned much about the benefits of being asked for change. I used to think of such a request as a demand for a sacrifice. However, I now realize from experience that I'm usually being offered a gift.

An encounter I once had with a friend helped me see the truth of this. She was doing something that bothered me, a small thing, but because it kept happening, it was getting under my skin. I knew that if I just held on to my negative feelings, they would fester inside me. So with some trepidation, anticipating what I was sure would be her reaction, I brought my issue to her. Her response startled me. She not only acknowledged without defensiveness her part in the dynamic, she thanked me for telling her about it. "I'm grateful to you for having the courage to bring this to me," she said. "I would never have known this about myself. Thank you."

The beauty of her attitude struck me. It was a gift to be given honest feedback. It made me think about my own reaction when Don brought requests for change to me. At the time, he had been trying to tell me about a harsh tone of voice I often used when telling him about the messes he sometimes left around the house. It was hard for me to hear this, because I was so taken up by my own righteous indignation. In my mind, it was Don who was creating the problem. He was the one making a mess (didn't I have a right to scold him for that?), and then dodging the issue by criticizing my tone of voice. We had gone around a number of times on this issue, but it never seemed to resolve.

I considered the matter in light of my friend's response. Could it be that Don's willingness to keep bringing this issue to me, over and over, was actually a gift? I saw that my tone of voice was having an impact on his ability to hear me, on his desire to change. Whenever he heard my scolding tone, he would dig in his heels. As a result, I was seldom satisfied with the outcome. Once I saw this, my defensiveness began to melt away. For the first time I truly heard the sound of my voice when I spoke to Don. I had learned something invaluable about myself, one more piece of my unconsciousness come to light.

I was now able to validate Don's frustration, and a great tension between us was released. With a willing heart, I was able to offer him what he had been asking, which was for me to accept responsibility for my own piece of the dynamic, and to ask for change respectfully. It was an important breakthrough for us. What I had been seeing as a great annoyance—Don's request for change—I could now regard as a blessing.

It's never really a sacrifice to be asked for change. The ego always thinks, Oh boy, if I have to do this, I'm going to lose out. If we could just look down on ourselves from a higher perspective, we would see the beauty and benefit of being asked for change. I want to know where I am unconscious. Every time Don tells me how something I do rubs him the wrong way, it shines a light on my dark, murky areas. Over time, I began to see patterns I was unaware of, filling in the pieces of my mosaic. Welcoming Don's feedback, rather than resisting it, makes it easier for him to bring up issues in a gracious and supportive way, so I am doubly rewarded. I am learning about my own blind spots, and at the same time, I'm opening the door to a more harmonious interaction between us.

This is so much what I really want. I am committed in this life to becoming a more conscious being. With the invaluable aid of Don's honesty, which adds so much clarity to my own introspection, I continue to push back the darkness and to allow my essence a fuller expression. This is a gift beyond measure.

CHAPTER 4

Giving and Receiving

What Spirit Do You Emit?

We have emphasized transforming what doesn't feel good in the relationship, This is often hard work. A more pleasant part of intimacy is learning together what makes both parties feel loved and cared for.

I recently heard about a teacher who spent years trying to discern which parenting style led to happy, well-adjusted children. She was acquainted with the parents of hundreds of children that she taught, and had carefully observed parent-child interactions for decades. In all her years of teaching, she found one reliable factor that made a difference. Of all the parents who came to school to pick up their children, there were some who really showed by their manner how glad they were to see their children. Not surprisingly, these tended to be the parents of the happiest, most secure children. Their children knew they were loved.

Another example of this kind of manifested love occurs when you phone somebody who hasn't heard from you in a while. Watch the positive effect it has on your mood if their immediate response is obvious delight at hearing from you. I have a friend whose special gift is to convey such pleasure on hearing from me, whenever I phone. I am always affected by his offering.

It's instructive to observe the quality of energy you put out when you first see someone, whether it's been a gap of five years with an old friend, or just a day at work. When you first greet your partner at the end of a day, does your manner convey that you're truly glad to see them? Imagine the difference if your partner imparted that feeling regularly to you. Often the first thing partners do when they get together is complain about their life or go instantly off to their own individual worlds. It's good to share the things that bother you, or to take care of your need for privacy. But when you spend time with someone, try putting aside your needs and complaints, and focus on communicating a basic feeling of goodwill.

Parting for the day is another especially good time to be watchful. When you say good-bye to your partner in the morning, what is the quality of the last lingering moment between you? Whatever the feeling, it tends to remain with both of you for the rest of the day, coloring your moods and activities. Whether you part with a complaint, a casual peck on the cheek, or a deep, loving connection, you tend to carry it with you into your day.

A dear friend of ours who had recently lost her husband to cancer was visiting. She told us they had grown extremely close the final year. His dying had brought a great richness and poignancy to her life. I was leaving the house for the day, and Martha was preoccupied in the kitchen. She gave me a pleasant, but rather perfunctory good-bye. After I left, our friend asked Martha, "If that were the very last time you were ever going to see Don, would you be satisfied with the way that you said good-bye?" There was no need to answer.

Approach with Care

Do you remember as a child when your parents would yell across the house or down the stairs, commanding you to clean up some mess immediately? We usually have quite a few memories of someone entering our mental space and shattering our peace in an abrupt and harsh manner. When someone enters our world intrusively, we tend immediately to assume a defensive posture. Often we forget to approach our partner with awareness. Sometimes we burst in with a complaint, which is likely to feel mean or abrasive. The first few seconds of an interaction can set the tone for much of what lies ahead. Be mindful when approaching your partner.

What Do I Convey to My Partner?

A skillful parent dealing with a child's unacceptable behavior conveys a message that the behavior is not okay, although the child herself is accepted. The child, feeling safe and loved, is more likely to receive the message. A less skillful parent, however, sets limits with a scowl. Their body language, tone of voice, and manner convey that something is wrong with the child; that the child doesn't deserve love.

If you're not satisfied with the feeling coming from your partner, you might ask yourself, How often do you smile lovingly? How often do you acknowledge them? How often do you appreciate

them for fixing things around the house, for making tasty, healthy [meals? ...] ut into an often stressful world to bring home [...]g your clothes clean over the years? How often do [...] irectly that you're glad they're in your life?

[...] eenly aware of the quality of energy coming from [...] t we're oblivious to what we put out ourselves. If I [...] r to sense the slightest nuance in my tone of voice, [...] hat I am equally sensitive to theirs? It would feel so good to me if my partner were respectful to me, forgave my mistakes, overlooked my shortcomings, appreciated and acknowledged my virtues. Do I do the same for them?

The essence of an intimate relationship, happy or otherwise, lies in the hundreds of little interactions that make up daily life. There is much learning when you bring more consciousness to these transactions.

It's Not the Content

When conflict arises in intimacy, it is seldom for the reasons we think. Partners who are upset with each other tend to attribute their negative feelings to the content of what happened: what was said, what was done or not done. In reality, the major exchange of energy takes place at a deeper, nonverbal level.

Underneath the verbal exchange there exists a whole world of communication, usually lost to the conscious mind. It can be found in the look in your eyes, the muscles in your face, your tone of voice, your body language, and perhaps even at a more subtle vibrational level. Your negative reactions to each other come not from your words, but almost entirely from a perception at this deeper level that your partner is not wishing you well. In such cases, disagreement easily becomes laced with bitterness and resentment. However, if you can feel a loving quality coming from your partner, even disagreement can lead to a valuable mutual exploration in which your differences are complementary, rather than antagonistic. Despite your differences, the two of you can feel like allies.

To get to this core of feeling in your relationship, you need to delve beneath the content to the level of nonverbal exchange. In particular, you have to be aware if you are supporting your partner's being, or negating it.

The Essential Message: Support or Denial

An elegant simplicity lies at the heart of your nonverbal message: either you are wishing your partner happiness, glad they are alive, loving them; or you're not wishing them well, withholding love, passing judgment because they are unforgivably flawed. Each moment you are with your partner, you can't help but transmit one of those messages at the most primordial level—through your smile or lack thereof, the softness of your expression, the nuances in your voice. Underneath the content, the feeling of wishing your partner well is either present or absent, and herein lies the essence of your communication.

You can become sensitive to this phenomenon, if you start observing your inner responses in a variety of situations. How do you feel when one of your coworkers scowls, or when a cashier snaps at you? How do you feel when your partner's tone of voice has an edge? Notice how you often come away from such an interaction feeling a little less alive, more contracted, vaguely uncomfortable—the by-product of assimilating the energy exuded by somebody not wishing you well. On the contrary, when you are with somebody who smiles at you or conveys good will, you leave their presence feeling a little more alive, happy, or whole. If you observe many such moments, you may be surprised to find just how impressionable you are in the presence of others.

This is something I've learned about myself later in life. Through the years, I've noticed how very sensitive our son has been to the slightest affirmation or denial. But then with a little scrutiny, I observe myself in Martha's presence, and discover that I, too, am affected to a similar degree by whether she says something to me with a hint of disapproval in her voice, or whether she gives me a smile.

Observing the Nuances in Daily Life

We all want our partner to treat us with love and respect. But are we putting out that quality to them? Are we sending forth a great deal of love and not getting it back, or are we in fact receiving from our partner pretty much what we are putting out? Those who are not satisfied with their relationship might look closely at what they are conveying, especially nonverbally. Chances are they will find they are not giving forth what they would like back. To see this connection can be a moment of truth.

Many of us wait for our partner to show us love so that we can then respond in kind. This is not unlike the Arabs and the Israelis, or other traditional enemies: each waiting for the other to cease aggressive actions so that peace may finally blossom. Although many opportunities may exist to make the first move, observe how the ego is always reluctant to do so.

In any relationship, but especially an intimate one, it is quite revealing to become aware of the nuances of your communication. If you have children, listen to your tone of voice when you talk to them. Many parents address their children with little respect. Some almost always have a negative quality in their voice. You may have had parents who forgot to engage their hearts when they talked to you, and as a natural consequence, you have developed a similar habit of communication with your own children, and perhaps with your partner as well.

Tune in to the quality of your heart when you communicate to your partner about practical matters. Your message may sound cold, annoyed, or slightly blaming, or it can be conveyed warmly, with the heart engaged. Everyone has a specific mode of expressing discomfort and fear. Some have obvious anger in their voice; others nag, lecture, or whine. Some may become sarcastic, cold, or numb, while others plaster on an artificial coating of niceness. Hearing a tape or seeing a video of ourselves, we might sometimes be shocked to realize how little the quality of heart shines through. The heart gets shut down along the way, and the process becomes painful. Those around us may get used to our style, but in all cases, the lack of love is deeply felt.

It is very useful to pay attention to the quality of the energy in your home when you are not engaged in communication. Two people can be in different rooms in the house, each involved in their own activity, and yet there can be a palpable feeling of harmony and connection between them. Or, the energy can be that of two isolated people, walled in and lonely in their individual pursuits. In some homes, you can feel the heaviness of resentment even without a word being spoken. That disagreeable quality results from thousands of little negative interactions, stemming from feelings that have remained undealt with over the years. Fortunately, there is no need to put up with such an undesirable circumstance. It is possible to learn how to clean things up as they occur. As your intimacy deepens, your mutual sensitivity will increase, and you will both know when harmony is lost. Rather than resigning yourself to it, using it as an excuse to blame your partner, or allowing it to spiral downward into serious negativity, you can say to your partner, without blame, "I don't know what's happening, but I'm feeling that things are a little off between us. Are you feeling that way, too? Do you want to reestablish connection?"

There is no need to make the failure to engage the heart into another sin. A negative or uncomfortable quality between two people is merely feedback, inviting investigation. In exploring together all the unconscious ways we nonverbally convey a lack of love, we are helping each other wake up and live with more awareness. Becoming more conscious of the subtle messages we continually transmit in our daily life may help heal the emotional climate in our homes.

The Instant Replay

One of the most useful tools for us has been what we call "the instant replay." If one of us says something to the other that comes across with a lack of love or respect, the other responds, "Would you do a replay?" This is not asked combatively or sarcastically. It is an invitation to become more thoroughly aware of what we have just communicated.

When Martha asks that of me, I pause, breathe, and do a slow, careful run-through in my mind, not only of the words I just spoke, but of the tone of my voice, the posture of my body, and, especially, what I was feeling in my heart at that moment. Invariably on such occasions I realize that Martha was motivated to request the replay because I was unconsciously conveying a message that was less than loving. As a result, I get a chance to ask myself what I really wished to communicate.

Usually it is not my intention to transmit an unloving message, although on some occasions I may discover an unconscious negative feeling toward Martha that lies behind my unloving communication. Perhaps I'm feeling irritable for reasons having to do with body chemistry, sleep deprivation, caffeine or sugar overdose. Perhaps I'm worrying about our finances. Whatever the reason, I now have the choice to communicate with a different spirit, and to communicate my feeling directly. This time I attempt to convey the same content, but with my heart open. What would have normally festered as resentment now has a chance to be made conscious and dealt with. It feels a lot better to me, as well as to Martha.

The Mutual Replay

When I was a teenager, I became totally enamored of the bassoon. I loved the way it expressed both the profound and the comic, and was fascinated by its capacity to move from an almost human plaint in a tenor register to a solemn and sepulchral quality in the bottom notes. I found an old bassoon, learned it quickly, and eventually became a professional bassoonist.

In the act of learning it became clear that practicing is an art. To master an instrument, you have to spend considerable time going over passages that challenge the fingers. Whenever you make a mistake, it is necessary to focus on what was happening at the moment of error. It doesn't work merely to substitute the correct note and continue. You have to go back several notes before the mistake and play the passage through correctly and with awareness. If you don't, you're likely to make the same mistake the next time.

Learning to be intimate is quite similar. In music you can spot a mistake if you know how to listen, because it simply doesn't sound right. In an intimacy, if you are able to listen, you can tell a mistake because it doesn't feel right—to either party. Mistakes are those moments when you have lost or forgotten the way: when you respond without love to your partner. A mistake by one often leads to a mistake by the other, resulting either in a fight or an emotional shutdown. Unlike good musicians, who know that wrong notes must be corrected, intimate partners are prone to spend a lifetime endlessly repeating the same mistakes. Many of us are painfully aware how the mere mention of a certain topic leads to instant defensiveness so acute that no discussion is possible.

The stubbornly conditioned mind sorely needs retraining in how to relate to its mistakes. The mutual replay is a tool that has taught us much about our own roles in creating and perpetuating negative feelings. A hostile interaction requires two participants. If just one keeps their heart open, a fight is impossible. If you have a child, check it out with them. When the child comes to you angry or upset and you respond with love, there is no real conflict. But when a negative exchange has occurred, there was always some point when each person forgot to keep their heart open, and has thus contributed to the same weary, unfulfilling pattern.

Martha and I were driving from our home in Vermont to the coast of Maine, where we were to catch a ferry to an island in order to give a workshop there. It was a long drive. I knew that she had wanted to stop off in Augusta, where she knew of a restaurant offering healthy food. I had assumed that she knew where the restaurant was. In an overstressed state and feeling grumpy, I responded, as you will see, quite poorly. Here's what occurred:

Me: Okay, we're in Augusta, where's the restaurant?
Martha: I don't know. We're going to have to stop and look it up.
Me: What?? You don't know where it *is*??
Martha: No. Let's just stop at a gas station and find a phone book.
Me: I thought you knew where it was! You expect me to drive all over a town I don't even know, looking for some restaurant? Don't you understand, we're on a schedule. I don't want to even think about missing the ferry. We can't take the time.
Martha: Well! So my needs don't count, once again. You just get to decide what we do. I suppose we can have some delicious french fries and coleslaw at some greasy spoon. Okay, drive on, get your own way!

And so on. Does it sound familiar?

Most of us beyond the early romantic stages of intimacy have experienced such exchanges countless times. An intimacy devoted to becoming conscious can make good use of such encounters. Instead of justifying why we closed our heart to our partner, we can instead go back over the dialogue and try to find where each of us lost our way. Each gets a chance for a separate replay. Our partner repeats whatever triggered our negative response, and we get to give a new response, this time with the heart open.

To do the mutual replay effectively, it is essential to wait until after you have ceased harboring negative feelings. After Martha and I had calmed down a bit, I did my replay first:

Me: Okay, we're in Augusta, where's the restaurant?
Martha: I don't know. We're going to have to stop and look it up.
Me: (taking a deep breath) Oh boy, I can feel myself beginning to get uptight. I'm concerned that if we have to drive around a strange town for a long time, it might cut our margin for the ferry kind of close. I don't want to have a stressful drive and be worrying about time. What do you think?

Notice that I didn't have to suppress my feeling of concern, to pretend I was feeling something other than what I was. Instead, I located a different place in my being where I could look at my fear rather than drown in it.

For her replay, Martha was able to greet my scared little boy fear with more compassion, while staying in touch with the integrity of her totally legitimate desire. Again, we went back to what triggered her to lose her way.

Me: I thought you knew where it was! You expect me to drive all over a town I don't even know looking for some restaurant? Don't you understand, we're on a schedule. I don't want to even think about missing the ferry. We can't take the time.
Martha: I understand, you're really concerned about not feeling rushed for the ferry. I don't want us to feel rushed, either. But I would enjoy a healthy meal, if it were possible without feeling the time pressure. How about stopping at that gas station and just asking? If it seems like it will be a hassle, or take a lot of time, I'm willing to forgo it.

Not only did our new responses feel better to receive, they felt a lot better to give. Paradoxically, much of our annoyance at our partner stems not so much from the way they are with us, but from our own disrespect toward them. Why is this? Why would we be annoyed at them for the same thing we do?

The answer is that when we act unlovingly to our partner, we feel guilty at some level. Now their very presence reminds us of what we dislike about ourselves, and we end up disliking them for being such a reminder. The worse we act toward them, the more we resent them. We then act even more unlovingly, which further increases our guilt. A vicious circle results, which can lead to a complete emotional shutdown.

When we start responding to our partner with more kindness, it has the unexpected consequence of *our* liking *them* more. As we respond to their fear and hurt with an open heart, we feel better about ourselves, which in turn causes us to act more lovingly. Our partner's presence now triggers in us a good feeling about ourselves, and our attitude softens toward them. In this way, the vicious circle is transformed.

The Importance of Acknowledgment

One of the most effective ways of demonstrating this kindness is through frequent acknowledgment of what we appreciate about each other. Most of us spend considerable time in the world of criticism and negativity. Much of our conversation is taken up with observations of what our partner or others do that we don't like. A generally negative atmosphere is common in many homes. It is impressive how quickly acknowledgment can change this.

Many of us didn't have parents who acknowledged us frequently and sincerely. A truly felt acknowledgment can feel good because we have long been hungering to hear an appreciation of our unique worth.

Some of us use false acknowledgment, or flattery, in an attempt to feel better about ourselves. Feeling unworthy, we are concerned that our partner will finally discover the awful truth about us, and end up leaving or ceasing to love us. One unconscious strategy for avoiding this catastrophe is to flatter our partner in order to win their approval. Such flattery feels uncomfortable to both. But not expressing honest appreciation is also damaging.

For years, I had trouble expressing appreciation, because I confused flattery with real acknowledgment. I almost never told a friend that I really loved them. I was too embarrassed. My difficulty originated when I was a child. I would occasionally observe people who employed flattery in an attempt to manipulate others, to sell them something, or to purchase affection.

With a child's sensitivity, I felt an aversion to the lack of honesty involved in such behavior. But I also had evidently developed an unconscious belief that all people who say nice things to others are manipulators and phonies. To this day, it's not easy for me to express appreciation to a friend. It has taken me a long time to learn that when acknowledgment comes forth out of love, it feels good to give, and the receiver experiences it as the real thing.

I love to be acknowledged by my partner. I delight when Martha notices my parenting skills and acknowledges me for being a good father. By reminding me of my inherent goodness, it softens my dislike of myself. Through genuine appreciation, freely offered, we can help each other heal our feeling of unworthiness.

Acknowledgments are more effective when they are specific. It is one thing to offer a child vague praise, such as "That's a nice picture." It's more effective to say, "I really like the way you drew those clouds so fluffy." In the latter case, your child will more likely feel truly seen. Obscure pronouncements to your partner about everlasting love aren't effective, compared to focusing on something you find special in the moment.

Look upon your partner without the burden of the past. See their beauty, their suffering, their earnestness, their humanness, their basic goodness, and above all, the things that make them special. Allow yourself frequent moments of appreciation, and then tell them what you are appreciating. Just as children need, every day, to receive the nourishment of acknowledgment, your partner, who, like you, is carrying the wound of unworthiness, can use the same nourishment.

Making Your Partner Feel Loved

Imagine if you made a list of the ways your partner could make you feel loved, and imagine them studying it seriously with the intention of making sure you felt their love every day. How much difference would that make in your relationship? How much easier would it be to forgive your partner's imperfections? Imagine the value of doing the same for your partner.

Usually, it is the simple gestures that have the greatest effect. I love it when Martha smiles at me, offers to massage my head, makes something for dinner that she knows I love, acknowledges my efforts to change unwanted behavior patterns, encourages me to take time for myself, buys me a special little gift, suggests an overnight together at an inn, overlooks a mistake, or responds to my ego with love. Little demonstrations of care set the tone for a relationship, and have immense power to dissolve negativity. Become familiar with the specific gestures that work for your partner, and make a priority of doing them regularly. In addition, communicate in detail to your partner what makes you feel loved. When you both take the initiative to make sure the other feels well loved, the relationship will handle the difficulties with far more grace.

The Importance of Receiving

Receiving the gift of acknowledgment is as important as giving it, for it completes the circuit. Many are made uncomfortable by it. When they get acknowledged, they dismiss it, or they say something disparaging about themselves. They may also deflect the compliment by instantly praising the other in response. It probably feels better to the giver of the compliment if the other person simply receives it graciously.

The great hindrance to receiving is the feeling of unworthiness. If you or your partner has difficulty receiving, you can be sure that feelings such as guilt, shame, or inadequacy are lurking in the shadows. In helping each other to receive gracefully, you will be uncovering and dealing with fundamental issues of self-worth.

If you have the tendency to avoid receiving, the next time someone gives you an acknowledgment, try simply to look the giver in the eye, breathe, connect with your worthiness to receive, admit the gift fully into your being, and then say, "Thank you." Remain for a moment with the feeling, and be aware that the giving and receiving circuit has been completed.

Sometimes Martha or I will notice that our gift to the other isn't being received. At such times, our custom is to remind our partner that it's time for receiving practice. The gift is given again, and this time consciously received. We have caught ourselves so many times in the act of deflecting gifts, that we have become more aware of keeping that all-important circuitry open.

We highly recommend that you and your partner learn to receive as a basic act of self-love. You can't fully give love without loving yourself. Developing the capacity to receive will make your giving more complete.

Thoughts from Martha

One of the most important lessons Don and I have learned over time is that giving and receiving don't have to cease when there's conflict. Even in the midst of tension or bad feeling, we can still make gestures of kindness. When we are weary of the pain, and our tolerance for negativity is low, we have learned how to access, from underneath our differences, our soul connection. Souls speak to each other all the time. Our soul wishes our partner well at the deepest level. Even when obscured by resentment or conflict, the sun continues to shine behind the passing clouds.

We devote a good deal of space in this book to processing conflict, but sometimes there's a quicker route home. When Don and I get into our most difficult feelings, the darkness can seem all-encompassing. We're caught up in the "movie" of our lives, and any positive outcome feels like it's beyond us. This is often the time when it helps to try something entirely different—to offer a gesture of love unconnected with what we've been fighting about. When I do this, I don't necessarily have to admit I was wrong, or even say that I want to make up. I only have to open my heart the tiniest little bit, enough to do some small thing that makes Don's life easier, or makes him feel a bit of love. I may offer him a head massage, or invite him for a walk. It may be as simple as a smile, or a kind touch. I once read about a couple who in times of bitter conflict would simply wink at each other—just enough of a gesture to show they weren't taking it all so seriously. These are all ways of saying, nonverbally, I realize I'm in a difficult place with you, but it isn't my bottom line.

It's hard to overstate the rewards of such gestures. When, under difficult circumstances, you give to your partner even in these small ways, the gift is returned multitudinously and the benefits are tangible. You can feel the tightness and constriction in your heart freeing up. One of the things I've learned from years of offering energetic body work is that giving and receiving are one and the same. When you offer love to your partner, you are also receiving. Your heart is awakened and enlarged by extending your gift—never more so than when your heart has been closed for a while.

Giving in hard moments will be easier if you practice giving at other times. One of the ways Don and I give and receive regularly is by offering daily acknowledgments. I love acknowledging Don each day because it enhances my awareness of his wonderful qualities; it makes me feel blessed. I also look for spontaneous moments when I can let him know how much I appreciate those qualities: his kindness, his patience with me, his strength and dignity. One thing I've always loved about Don is his wonderful deep bass singing voice. When I listen to the beauty and richness of his voice, both speaking and singing, my need to focus on his petty flaws is obliterated. I am filled with loving appreciation for who he is.

Regular practice of acknowledgment and spontaneous gestures of kindness nourish the relationship at a root level, like watering and fertilizing a garden. Most of the time it's easy to do, not a big deal or a great effort. But whether easy or hard, whether in moments of conflict or of peace, my experience has been that the simplest gestures of kindness can be the most powerful in changing the course of a relationship.

CHAPTER 5

Avoiding Intimacy

Why Are We Afraid of Intimacy?

Many people who wonder why their relationship isn't flourishing blame their partner or themselves. What they often fail to realize is that though they may crave intimacy, at another level they are likely to be terrified of it.

One side of us truly hungers for intimacy. We sense there is a great beauty in opening up our boundaries and letting another person in. But our craving for closeness is matched by an aversion of equal strength. What lies behind the part of us that fears intimacy?

Opening up our boundaries entails letting go of control and dropping our defenses. Most people are uncomfortable being so vulnerable. The origin of this discomfort can usually be found in the earliest part of our lives. As infants, we were wide open emotionally. But many of us were brought up by parents who, although they loved us, did not necessarily love us wisely. Their love was likely withheld from us when our behavior triggered their discomfort. As a result, we received a painful message at a deep level that we were flawed beings not always worthy of love.

From this unfortunate teaching, our minds concluded that to be emotionally open leads inevitably to pain. To protect ourselves from this pain, we sent ourselves the message not to be vulnerable, because it's not safe. We became skillful at erecting a variety of defenses against openness, and as adults, the part of us that remembers that painful early experience has some very good reasons to be afraid of opening up to intimacy. This fear of intimacy is usually not conscious. Many of us identify with the part of ourselves that wants intimacy, but we're less in touch with the other part. Because of the conflict between the two, we may well encourage and oppose intimacy at the same time. Our unconscious fear of intimacy emerges indirectly in our adulthood through a variety of behaviors that we call "escapes."

What Are Escapes?

Escapes are patterns of behavior that allow you to avoid the relationship. They are motivated by the often unconscious fear of intimacy. Escapes aren't "bad"; arising out of fear, they deserve understanding rather than condemnation. Moreover, fighting against escapes only gives them strength. What works better is to become familiar with them. By observing how the fear of intimacy displays itself in your daily life, you will detoxify the fear, which will then cease to have such a limiting effect on your relationship.

Like a garden, a relationship cannot flourish unless you put time into it. If you eliminate the escapes, you will find that you have a lot more time and energy to tend your garden.

When Is It an Escape?

What is the difference between an escape and merely taking some necessary and well-earned space for oneself? The person who goes out to work eight hours a day may not be indulging in an escape. But if, assuming no financial pressure, they find themselves working excessively and spending little time at home, then they are quite likely using work as an escape. Whether or not a certain behavior is an escape depends on whether the motivation for it is to avoid the relationship.

Is walking out on your partner in the middle of a difficult situation an escape? Not necessarily. If you are very upset, afraid you might say or do something you would later regret, it might be skillful for you to depart for a while, take a walk or do something physical, and calm down until you get some perspective. If you then come back to your partner and indicate that you are now ready to deal with the situation, then you have handled it wisely. However, if you're in the habit of walking away in order to avoid difficult situations altogether, you are indeed escaping.

Two people in a healthy intimacy will regularly spend time together. In addition, they will feel a natural desire to nourish themselves outside the relationship, through time alone, friendships, hobbies, recreation, volunteer work, and so on. Intimacy is enriched when both parties take what they find outside and bring it back to fertilize the relationship. This is not escape. Escapes are overcome by spending your time either being in the relationship or consciously nourishing yourself outside the relationship.

If you are in doubt as to whether your outside activities are escapes, review the following to find out:

- Take an honest look at your motives.

- Examine the amount of time spent outside the relationship against how much time you spend with your partner (time, that is, when you both have energy for each other). Most couples with unsatisfying relationships lack a healthy balance.

- Imagine that you suddenly were going to spend significantly more time together with your partner. What is your very first feeling? Is there resistance? Fear? Why *don't* you spend more time together? Many who escape convince themselves that they don't have enough time for intimacy.

Common Escapes

We put escapes into two categories. In the first are all the things we do in order to avoid spending time together. In the second are ways we avoid intimacy while being physically together.

Escapes to Avoid Time Together

- Television is one of the prime escapes in our culture. Millions of hours of potential intimacy are lost to the tube! Many foundering relationships would be well served if just this one escape could be eliminated.

- Reading is a wonderful activity for gaining knowledge, deepening perspectives, and relaxing. It can also be an escape. Many hide behind the newspaper each morning with a cup of coffee, rather than start the day with some kind of personal connection. Others spend many hours with a novel instead of having a conversation with their partner. In seeking to be informed about the world, we may well lose track of how little we are informed about those closest to us.

- Lists of things to do: We all have things to take care of, big and small, and there's never enough time to finish everything on the list. But if we are in the habit of using escapes to avoid relationship, it's easy to use the list as a reason not to relate. If we spend a lot of time with the list and little with our partner, perhaps that means it's easier to find something to do at the desk or in the kitchen than it is to confront our fear of intimacy. Since lists are a real part of life, we suggest setting aside regular time for your partner and putting it where it belongs—right at the top of the list!

- Alcohol and other drugs can be a major escape. This is a vast issue that goes beyond the scope of this book. If you or your partner are using chemicals to avoid intimacy, or for anything else, it may be wise to seek counseling.

- Eating is another major escape for some, and it isn't just the frequent forays into the kitchen, or the dullness that comes from eating too much, but all the extra time and energy spent on planning, shopping, and cooking. Satisfying the palate may become a substitute for love, and food a surrogate for intimacy.

- Children can be a common escape, especially for women. Children do require much quality time from their parents, and many parents don't spend enough. Nevertheless, check the time spent with your children and the time spent with your partner, and make sure they're balanced. Some women turn to their children when things get uncomfortable with their spouse. When parents escape from intimacy, it is actually a disservice to the whole family, since children feel more secure when they sense a strong bond between their parents.

- Work is a favored escape for many. We'll commonly encounter professional men whose wives resent them for not wanting to spend more time at home with the family. When they do come home, they experience their wives' complaining, which doesn't feel good. Not surprisingly, they find excuses to stay at work or go to as many professional meetings as they can, which in turn breeds more resentment.

- Sports, especially for men, are an easy avoidance. Those who use this escape may send a message that the private lives of their favorite sports heroes interest them more than the world of their partner.

- Illness or fatigue may be the only way we can find to avoid painful situations, when all else fails.

Escapes While Physically Present

- Anger is not always an escape; it can be a legitimate form of intimate expression. However, if you find yourself frequently getting angry at your partner, it may represent something else. The same is true if you find yourself habitually blaming your partner, instead of seeing things through their eyes.

- Arguing, or chronically taking issue, are common responses when one is more interested in being right than in understanding another's reality.

- Denial of feelings, while more common in men, is widespread among both sexes. The habit of emotional withdrawal, usually originating in early childhood, is often an attempt to escape from oneself; to protect oneself from guilt or other painful disturbance.

- Relating through the mind alone is subtle, and often not easy to recognize as an escape. Your attention is focused entirely on the content of what you are saying, during which time you are missing out on your own and your partner's emotional reality. The brain is engaged, the heart is not. (Men seem to do this more often than women.) But there is another way of relating in which, no matter what you are talking about, you are aware of the flow of energy between you and the other person. In addition to talking about something, you are also relating *with* someone. Many women long for their men to discover this way of relating.

- Gossiping and other forms of distracting small talk may not be seen as escapes from intimacy. To some extent, it is natural to talk about the people we know. Yet it is revealing to observe the state of our minds when we do so. It may be that our attention is directed at others because of the discomfort we feel in each other's presence. Occasionally, Martha and I make an agreement to spend a period of time, perhaps a week, without talking about other people. The results are interesting. There is usually quite a bit more silence.

- Niceness is one of the more common escapes, yet it too is often difficult to detect, since it has an ease and comfort to it. Through an unconscious mutual pact, partners who seek to avoid conflict, agree to get along well on the surface, burying whatever might upset the harmony. To the world, it looks as if they "have it all together," an impression that the couple finds comforting. The price for this surface harmony is the sacrificing of real depth.

The Ultimate Escape

One escape from intimacy is like the ocean in which we swim: It is so pervasive that it goes unnoticed. If I examine my daily consciousness, I find that my thoughts are constantly bouncing back and forth between the future and the past. This inner monologue keeps me from being present in my actual life as it is unrolling. The ultimate escape is my thought process. I observe myself to see if I am truly aware when I watch a sunset, listen to music, take a walk in the woods, or look into my partner's eyes. It becomes quickly apparent that if during these activities I am thinking about something, my attention is somewhere else. I am not really there. Because thought goes on continually, most of us spend the majority of our lives not present. This can be quite a revelation.

One of the most common forms of thinking is planning for the future. Although some planning is obviously necessary, check to see how often planning is the mechanical escape of a mind uncomfortable with the present moment. An insecure mind attempts to achieve security by controlling the future. There is value in consciously choosing to live with uncertainty. Staying with this feeling develops one's faith that they will be shown from within what to do when the appropriate time comes.

When Martha and I take a walk and find ourselves escaping into the future, one of us may suggest that we confine ourselves to being present. By returning to the present, where our life is actually taking place, we find the sights, sounds, smells, and companionship of our strolls far more vivid.

Communicating About Escapes

It is common to feel resentment when you perceive your partner avoiding intimacy. The two most familiar, but least effective, ways of handling this feeling are polar opposites. The first way is to bury the resentment and say nothing, for fear of creating disturbance. This breeds further resentment. The second way is to communicate *from* the resentment in a manner that destroys perspective. It is better to communicate *about* the feelings without being caught up in them.

We knew an artist named David whose wife, Rita, an editor, was spending a great deal of time with her friends but little time with him. David first expressed his resentful feelings in this fashion: "You're always going out with your friends and having a marvelous time, but you never want to spend any time with me. It seems kind of self-centered. You have no regard for *my* feelings. Sometimes I think I'd be better off living alone." Obviously, communications of this kind made Rita want to spend even less time with David.

David was allowing his resentment to fill his being so that there was no space around it. This resulted in a communication from David that was so judgmental, it was difficult for Rita to hear the pain underneath. David needed to locate a part of himself that could create some space around his feelings, witness them, and then talk about them. He also needed to view the situation as a dynamic between the two of them, rather than something bad that Rita was doing to him.

When he gained some perspective, David was able to express a message with a very different flavor, while denying none of his feelings: "Rita, I notice there's a common pattern we get into, which makes me uncomfortable. You go off with your friends, then I feel out of touch with you and get resentful. Then you resent me for trying to inhibit your freedom, and we're off and running. I want you to have enjoyable times with your friends, and I also want to feel nourished by our relationship. I don't think it has to be either/or. I'd like for us to work together to find a different way of dealing with this, even though I'm not sure how."

This mode of expression made an important difference in the outcome. Without denying any of his feelings, David was now offering an invitation to work together toward a mutually acceptable solution. By abandoning the belief that his partner was the cause of his unhappiness, he stopped coming across as blaming. When David talked about his feelings, rather than using them to attack his partner, Rita was able to hear him without getting defensive, and the resolution was under way.

The Road Less Traveled

Eliminating escapes can be challenging work. We are constantly given choices in a relationship, one of which is usually more comfortable and familiar. Our attachment to the familiar keeps us confined in a narrow world. When M. Scott Peck wrote *The Road Less Traveled,* he touched on an important truth. To take the road less traveled means to have the courage to make the less secure choice. In the interest of greater aliveness, newness, or truth, one has to enter consciously into discomfort.

Though eliminating an escape is often uncomfortable, a far more insidious kind of discomfort results when we fail to do so. The road more traveled often brings dullness and mediocrity, a range of experience restricted by habit, and a life lived in constant fear of change.

Watch for escapes especially when one of you is in pain. Many have a tendency to pull away when they are hurting, physically or emotionally. It's also tempting to run away when your partner is upset or in pain. But times of pain can actually deepen your intimacy, if you have the skill and the courage to create a spaciousness that makes the pain acceptable.

If you sense the value of eliminating escapes, you might suggest that your partner point out when they suspect you are escaping. Promise not to get defensive, and to check it out. A mutual investigation of escapes can lead to major personal insights, as well as greater depths of intimacy.

What Are Your Priorities?

We often ask couples if they ever spend sizeable blocks of time together, doing things they enjoy. For couples who are having problems, the answer is usually "seldom." They say they are too busy.

Your behavior is a direct result of your priorities. If you want to know what the priorities are in your life, watch how you spend your time. It can be very revealing. Is keeping your body healthy a high priority? If yes, then you will make time to exercise. If you say that you don't have time to exercise, what you mean is that exercise is not as important or interesting as reading the newspaper, watching TV, or whatever it is that you do instead. Is being in an intimate relationship high on your priority list? If you don't spend much quality time with your partner, then it's not.

What are your deepest wishes? If you were on your deathbed, would you wish that you had done more business, become more accomplished, or had more experiences? Or maybe you would wish that you had loved more. If your escapes are keeping you from fulfilling your deepest wishes, then you have found out something of real value. Perhaps if you determined your true priorities, your escapes would naturally diminish.

Taking Regular Time Together

Taking regular time together is essential for the health of the relationship. Find time when you are alert and unhurried, and keep in mind that the time has to be sufficiently long. Sometimes after coming from highly separate worlds, it takes a while to blend into each other's energy field. An hour or two is better than nothing, but we find that it usually isn't enough to reach certain intimate depths.

We find it valuable to have at least four consecutive hours of absolutely uninterrupted time each week (if you have an infant, shorter, more frequent stretches will be necessary for a while). This means you're not dealing with the phone, the children, or the things that need to be done. Watching movies or TV together, while perfectly fine, doesn't count here, because you are not really relating to each other. You might take a walk, go out to dinner, make love, engage in a massage, sit by a stream, or do anything together where you feel connected. A flourishing intimacy requires tending.

If you find yourself resisting the idea of regular weekly time together, explore the origin of that resistance. Perhaps you are afraid that painful issues would arise and lead to conflict. Maybe you are afraid of finding out that you don't really love your partner, or they you. Or perhaps there are sexual fears. Certainly, one way to avoid confronting these painful possibilities is to ensure that you don't spend much time together.

You are kept apart by the fear of what would happen if you were to come together. The longer you are apart, the more the fear insists that there's nothing there worth coming together for. Over time, the barrier between you becomes thicker and more impenetrable. This is the same kind of difficulty that confronts out-of-shape people who avoid exercise; when they commence, it may feel uncomfortable for a while. It may be scary to begin joining after a long separation. There is a need here for courage.

Perhaps conflict or deadness in a relationship is an invitation to awaken. Can you use this marvelous opportunity to help each other become more conscious? Eliminating your escapes is a major step in this direction.

Thoughts from Martha

Sometimes it's assumed that the woman in a relationship is always the one who desires more intimacy, and that the man is the one who resists it. I used to believe this, too, but I now see that the reverse is often true. Intimacy can hold terrors for all of us. My own encounter with avoidance—and my subsequent journey back to still deeper intimacy and friendship—has made this clear to me.

When Don and I first met in Alaska, I had a powerful, seemingly cosmic opening. For a few relatively undisturbed years, we reveled in the intimacy of our simple life together. However, after an extended honeymoon period, the romantic glow began to fade. The reality of living with another human being—a being with noticeable imperfections—was setting in. Soon the two of us started experiencing our different ways of shutting down, and the dance of conflict began.

Later, when we moved to California, had a child, and seriously had to earn a living, the stress increased. We had no models to help us deal with it, no understanding of how to keep our flame alive in the midst of our differences. We allowed a barrier to develop between us, and intimacy receded. The more this happened, the more tempting it was to escape our challenges altogether.

Meanwhile I was connecting with a circle of women friends in whose company I discovered deep fulfillment. At first this seemed like an enjoyable, nourishing expansion, and of course in many ways it was. But it was far easier to be around other women who "understood" than to struggle with Don to bridge our differences. I began putting more energy into these other relationships, and less into my marriage. I never fully let in Don's grumbled protest: "I wish you had the same juice for us that you do for your women friends." I would get defensive, claiming that he wanted too much from me. We had many a fruitless argument.

For a long time, we felt stuck in this impasse. However, Don and I remained committed to looking honestly at what was going on between us, and over time I began to see the limitations of my avoidance. At first, I hadn't been clear about the difference between having healthy friendships with other women, and using these relationships to escape from intimacy. What was unhealthy about this was that I was putting all my emotional intensity into my friendships at the expense of my marriage. I found that the intensity of these relationships could be uncomfortably similar to having an affair. By escaping the discomfort I was feeling with Don, I was shirking the challenges that would allow us to have a strong and nourishing intimacy at another level.

Another revelation was seeing that I had been carrying an irrational fear of losing my own identity in intimacy. When I let go of that fear, I could see that being intimate with Don was not a threat to the person I was, or wanted to be. Indeed, Don had always fully supported my having close women friends; he simply wanted to give our relationship its due priority.

To shed these burdens was a great relief. I had been troubled all along by the pain I was triggering in Don through my withholding of love. My conscience prodded me to look more closely at the choices I was making, and to alter them. But what I hadn't seen clearly was how much pain I had been causing myself. Deep down, I realized I was depriving myself of a great source of fulfillment. Even my relationships *with women friends had suffered. As long as I was using them to avoid intimacy with Don, I sensed it in my inner being and was dissatisfied.*

True intimacy does not detract from a woman's individuality, if she has good boundaries; in fact, the stronger she feels in her own being, the more easily she can share herself with her partner. Having good boundaries means that you are in charge of defining how much you give to others and how much you give to yourself. So when you do give, you give wholeheartedly, without the fear of being overwhelmed.

Eventually I was able to offer Don the commitment he was seeking from me, not by renouncing my identity as a woman, but by actually giving it fuller expression. I came to see that women have a special gift to share with men, a perhaps ancient responsibility to their role as hearthkeepers of the relationship. For a long time, I couldn't be in this role fully because I wasn't connected to my deepest core, my essence. When I came to feel this connection—through my path of meditation—it allowed my relationship with Don to assume its rightful proportion. Since then, my heart has opened more and more to this amazing being, my traveling companion of this lifetime.

CHAPTER 6

Anger

Anger Is a Teaching

Throughout history, we humans have used our anger in an attempt to get rid of fear and pain. Some of us have turned our anger in on ourselves, creating massive guilt. Or we have repressed our anger, leading to depression or illness. Whatever the pattern, anger is one of the most difficult realities to face in a relationship. When we look at relationships that end in separation, get painfully stuck in perpetual conflict, or go dead, we inevitably find anger, either in direct outbursts or simmering under the surface.

Though anger is sometimes viewed as an obstacle to the spiritual life, it's not just a regrettable aberration to be stamped out. When you push away anger, you are also stifling your inner fire. In a true intimacy, it is important for both parties to allow anger a proper place in the relationship. Like all uncomfortable traits, anger is not meant to be eliminated, but purified and transformed. In it lie the seeds for something of great value. In working together with our anger, we act as alchemists, burning away the impurities and transmuting the anger into the purity of passion.

If you honor your precious fire, if you seek to know it and live it in a way that is aligned with your higher purpose, you will not want to waste it by imposing it thoughtlessly on your partner. You will cherish your fire and use it for the good of the whole, knowing it arises from the depths of your being.

Learning to Get Angry ... or to Stop

We are all climbing the same mountain, but we approach it from different directions. If your anger erupts with ease, redirecting it is your task. If you bury your anger, your initial work is to feel it and have the courage to express it.

Some erupt easily, frequently attacking their partner and trying to make them feel guilty. Those who are quick with their anger often justify it by pointing to how badly their partner has been behaving. Additionally, they may point out that repressing anger is dishonest and harmful, and that it's okay for them to have all their feelings. Therefore, they believe that all expressions of anger are both justified and helpful.

We designated this attitude earlier on as the Psychological Mistake. It is true that anger is a perfectly valid feeling whose repression can be harmful. However, you cannot justify indulging in it frequently and yet remain at peace. Those who tend to give in to it too often need to create a place within themselves where they can view their anger with some detachment. In the act of developing an inner witness to their anger, they will learn how to stop indulging in it mechanically. Their anger will become redirected as they become familiar with its roots in the past. It will wither away, as they challenge their beliefs and assumptions that underlie the blaming of others for one's own discomfort and pain.

Other people have difficulty expressing their anger, or, indeed, even feeling it. For many years, they have been sitting on their rage, perhaps partly from genetic makeup or cultural conditioning, partly because they were given a message as a child that it's not safe to be angry. Such people seldom, if ever, allow themselves to display anger. If they are aware of it, they may suppress it in the belief that it is wrong, a vice to be condemned, something unreasonable or unspiritual. We may recognize this as a form of the Spiritual Mistake, the undoing of which requires a different kind of work.

If this is your tendency, your first task is to realize that in your humanness you sometimes will get angry. This may not come easily if you don't feel safe with such feelings. When anger arises, all you may feel is a vague sense of discomfort, annoyance, irritability, withdrawal, or even numbness. You may need to ask yourself on such occasions: Could it be possible that I am angry?

It can be valuable to enlist the aid of your partner, who may be quite willing to educate you about the ways you hide your anger. You might want to ask them if they ever sense that you might be angry without being conscious of the fact. If the answer is yes, encourage them to ask you what you are feeling when such moments occur.

Once you start becoming aware of your anger, the next step is to create a safe environment for it, and to risk expressing it. If this work is not done, your anger will seep out indirectly, causing far more damage.

It's important always to remember that neither way of dealing with anger is bad, but the fact that neither feels satisfying can be considered an invitation to explore the reasons behind your anger, and can possibly lead to change. Whatever form your work takes, it helps to agree on some basics:

- It's okay for both you and your partner to be angry, acknowledging that it's sometimes very uncomfortable.
- You can work together to eliminate certain ways of expressing anger that bring unnecessary pain.
- You can explore your anger together, rather than assuming that if one of you is angry, it's because the other is bad. It takes a great deal of awareness to prevent anger from turning into a mechanism of attack, a means of making another feel guilty.

Anger from the Past

Anger will often erupt unexpectedly with a force that seems far out of proportion to the event that triggered it. In such cases, the anger may have little to do with the immediate situation, but represents something from your history.

We all bring a reservoir of stored anger into our relationships.

Once when Martha scolded me for being careless in the kitchen, I found myself in a rage, the strength of which truly astonished me. Martha's chiding had set off a memory, deeply buried in my brain, of the anger I had experienced as a child when I was unfairly (it felt to me) scolded for breaking a dish. My feelings erupted with the force of a long-bound energy, and Martha was the recipient of what felt like a totally unwarranted outburst. Our partner's behavior will frequently remind us of emotionally charged issues from our past, often involving our parents or siblings. This is called "transference," and in it lies the remarkable strength of much current anger.

It is not only childhood that contains our reservoir of past anger. Old anger may also arise out of our adult relationships, or from earlier times in our current relationship. If our partner has done something we have not forgiven, or acts repeatedly in a way that has bothered us through the years, these experiences are stored as resentment. A look, a tone of voice, or a subtle gesture from our partner can unleash this dormant negative energy, which may overwhelm our partner with its unexpected force.

A lot of the anger in intimacy is old rather than current. One task of a conscious intimacy is for both parties to become familiar with their own and each other's past anger. This recognition is valuable for two reasons. First, it is a great deal easier to accept your partner's anger being directed at you if you know that old emotions are actually being discharged. You will be less tempted to accuse your partner of overreacting, never a skillful response when someone is expressing a feeling.

Second, you can help your partner redirect their attention to the true source of their anger.

How is this accomplished? One couple told us about an event that had happened the day before. Nancy was trying to tell Dan something that had upset her about the children, and he seemed not to be paying much attention. Nancy suddenly got furious and accused him of never listening and not caring about her feelings. Dan, experienced in listening, was able to hear her feelings without defensiveness. After Nancy had fully discharged her anger and felt heard, Dan asked gently if she sensed that the anger was old, and had a familiar flavor to it.

Despite an urge to continue attacking, Nancy was willing to put aside the blaming portion of her emotion and sink into the raw feeling of rage. When she did so, she became aware that the feeling was actually that of a little girl, enraged because her parents continually dismissed her feelings. Dan's seeming indifference had set off these deeper emotions.

Because she now felt heard, Nancy was able to feel and express some of this rage, while no longer directing it at her partner. Afterwards she experienced a feeling of release, like the clean air after a thunderstorm. Dan had assisted her in the worthwhile task of clearing stored negativity from the deeper layers of consciousness. Both parties benefited from seeing the anger for what it really was.

The more you explore your anger, the more you're likely to discover a startling but significant truth: You are seldom upset for the reasons you think. Fearful emotions from the past, frozen beneath the surface of awareness, cast a powerful shadow that darkens our present reality. Perhaps our anger is really the voice of the frightened child, believing they have no power.

At a more metaphysical level, our anger may be connected with the belief that we are cut off from the Source, imprisoned in this separate body, soon to cease being. Fear is the continual presence of such a belief. Anyone would be angry at being dealt such a painful fate, given that our deepest truth tells us we deserve better. Our metaphysical anger is a loud No! to the God who seems to decree that we are finite—an unacceptable limitation for the infinite spirit.

Indirect Anger

When angry feelings don't get acknowledged and expressed, unfortunately they refuse to disappear. Instead, they remain in the system, where they are capable of doing damage within and without. By turning in on itself, the energy of anger can turn into chronic disease, depression, guilt, fatigue, insomnia, unaccountable failures, "accidents," and other forms of self-sabotage.

Outwardly, the energy of unexpressed anger declares itself to others in all kinds of indirect and harmful ways. When anger is direct, it can be a clear teaching for both parties, if they're willing to learn. But anger that seethes beneath the surface, emerging indirectly in its various disguises, is a more difficult teaching to assimilate.

You express anger indirectly toward your partner in a variety of ways. You may close down emotionally or sexually. Indirect anger frequently emerges as passive-aggressive behavior, which is the unconsciously motivated punishing of your partner by generating difficulty or pain. Examples of typical passive-aggressive actions are regularly being late, forgetting to do things, or creating seeming accidents. Indirect anger often comes out in a tone of voice that conveys a lack of love. It may emerge as a tendency to dwell on your partner's imperfections far more than on their beauty. Frequently it manifests as a tendency to get annoyed at trivial things. In short, when negative feelings are not expressed directly, they come out indirectly in a thousand ways.

Indirect anger can be more difficult to live with than direct anger (we're not speaking of physical violence). I prefer a burst of direct, no-nonsense anger from Martha, rather than having her simmer at me for a long period. Direct anger is like a visible wound whose symptoms call for instant action. Indirect anger is more like an internal hemorrhage, creating much damage before its harmful effects are noticed and dealt with. Whereas direct anger can be released, indirect anger festers. Learn to recognize anger in all its manifestations, so that it may be expressed directly. Then there is a chance for real communication, and the released anger, which may expand to include past anger, will allow the present to feel cleansed.

Escalation

A common pattern with anger occurs when each partner becomes angry at the other's anger. What starts as a mild annoyance bounces back and forth between the partners, gaining severity along the way, until it intensifies into rage.

For example, Martha and I had an appointment to go to our son's piano recital. She was late in getting home from a previous engagement. She had recently been late for a couple of appointments, and I didn't think she was going to be able to get herself ready to leave on time. I was mildly annoyed, and expressed it directly by being a bit withdrawn.

Martha didn't like my mood. We had been in a very loving state before she left, and my sudden withdrawal for no apparent reason was hard for her. She began to get angry with me, expressing her feelings indirectly by criticizing the way I had cooked the food we were bringing. I was upset by her tone of voice, and by her emphasis on what I had done wrong, rather than appreciating that I had taken time from several important tasks to do the cooking. In response, my annoyance intensified. I became louder and reproached her for not seeming ready to make our appointment on time.

Martha, who had been keeping close watch over the time and had planned it all out to the minute, became furious at me for being unfairly angry with her and assuming she would be late. At this point, she began loudly to inform me of the many ways I was severely wanting as a partner. What had started as the mildest of disturbances had expanded swiftly into a volcanic fight.

Afterwards we could look back and smile at the way our rage had blazed up from such a tiny spark. It so often begins with a look, a casual remark, or a subtly negative tone of voice. But when you are in a delicate or stressful emotional state, the ego loves to seize on what seems like virtually nothing and run with it. Your partner's fragile ego responds in kind by taking it further. Each gets angry at the other for their anger.

This is a good occasion for more consciousness. Whoever has the awareness can interrupt the escalation at any point, either by letting go into a more loving stance, or requesting Openhearted Listening. This is also a good time to go back and do a mutual replay.

What Do You Do with Anger?

It is not always wise to express anger the minute it appears. A sense of timing is important. There will be occasions to back off from the intensity for a period. Your anger may be so knotted, so full of tension and blaming, so completely inappropriate, that it may be better to take a respectful distance from your partner, rather than say or do something you will later regret. As you walk away, you should resist the temptation to judge yourself for being angry. Your anger, although it may be highly uncomfortable, is a valid part of the human experience, a piece of feedback with an important teaching for you. Don't try to rid yourself of the feeling immediately. It may help to find a quiet place just to be with yourself, making sure to breathe slowly, allowing the feeling to grace you with its teaching. On other occasions, when the confusion and turbulence are more manageable, you may want to share your anger. At these times you will want to learn to make its expression clean.

The distaste we feel for anger is truly understandable, given our human history of profoundly misusing it. But emotions themselves do not isolate. It is what people do with them that creates separation. There are very few role models for handling anger skillfully. We observe countless instances of anger with the heart closed, when righteous judgment prevails and the object of the anger is attacked and asked to feel guilty. But there can be another kind of anger.

There may be times when someone you love persists in acting in a way that you do not wish to tolerate. You don't have to pretend that certain actions don't bother you. You don't have to mask your discomfort with a feigned placidity. It is indeed a challenge to feel your anger without closing your heart. But remember, you have an interest, even when you're angry, in honoring your partner's being.

Have you ever watched a good mother, skillful and competent? She can get annoyed or angry with her children, but she sets firm boundaries in a way that conveys, I really don't like what you are doing . . . but I love you. Even in the midst of their mother's anger, the children feel safe.

There is another, less skillful way of setting limits with children. Those parents, in addition to conveying, I don't like what you are doing, also send the message, You are a bad child and don't deserve love. Children who receive this kind of anger over time are bound to feel bad about themselves.

Clean Anger

It is not difficult to perceive the difference between these two ways of expressing anger. One useful way of defining the contrast is to distinguish whether the quality of expression is clean or unclean. When you express anger to your partner, it is important to learn this vital distinction.

"Clean" and "unclean" are not used here as value judgments. With clean anger, you are as respectful as possible, without denying your feelings. Clean anger may be expressed with force and vigor, yet it always restricts its expression to the feeling itself. "I hate it when you do that!" or "I feel really angry when you don't keep your agreements!" are statements about me. I'm not pointing a judging finger at you, trying to make you feel guilty

"You're so selfish, you never give a damn about anyone but yourself!" is unclean anger. This is a judgment about the kind of person your partner is. Unclean anger is often marked by name-calling, or by absolute terms like "always" or "never." Unclean anger is verbal attack, designed to hurt. Intimate partners who use it have a knack for attacking their partner's most vulnerable area, evoking extraordinary guilt and pain.

Anger may be natural when it emerges, only to lose its truth when it gets worked over by the mind. When anger first appears, it has its own vital intensity, arising without a great deal of mental activity. But if you pay attention, you will notice that after a few moments, the raw anger begins to dissipate rapidly, at which point it undergoes a change in quality. Now the mind can keep it going only by justifying itself and blaming the other. At this point, when the anger moves to the head, it begins to have an artificial, more toxic quality. Anger stimulated by thought feels less satisfying, more like an indulgence. It will likely express itself as attack. Learn how to distinguish between the genuine anger of the moment and the mind's subsequent attempt to keep it going

If the two of you see the value of transforming unclean anger into clean anger, then you can join forces to work on cleaning up your anger. Along the way, you will have many opportunities to sharpen your skills. After a fight, the time is particularly suitable to learn from what transpired: "You were pretty good with your anger until you said I never give a damn about how you feel. That felt like hitting below the belt." Confront the way you express anger, rather than the simple fact that you get angry. You'll do better winnowing judgment from your anger rather than trying never to be angry.

Clean anger can actually be a practical and effective means of communication. When you are attacking, what will be received most directly is your own blame and judgment; the threatening aspect of your message will drown out the content. The recipient will become defensive, creating an impermeable communication barrier. But in the act of learning clean anger, you will find that it is possible, even while angry, to be aware at some level of your love for your partner. This quality will make it easier for them to feel accepted, and they'll be more likely to receive what you wish to convey.

Using the Body

Anger, like all other emotions, has a physical as well as a mental component. The physical component is especially significant for those interested in releasing their accumulated anger. Stored anger is no less dangerous than anything you take in from your environment or your diet. To clean up your inner environment, it's essential to express anger, releasing its toxicity from your body.

You can free yourself from this toxicity in creative ways. You may already have discovered that when you feel stuck, aerobic exercise or vigorous work can blast through stale or frozen feelings. At the end of a good run, I sometimes become aware of previously hidden anger.

Yoga is another helpful tool. By opening up the body, it keeps the channels unimpeded for all your energy to flow more freely, including your emotions. Furthermore, if you do yoga for any length of time, you may find that you have become more sensitive to subtle levels of feedback from the mind and body. By helping you tune into nuances, yoga turns the body into a more sensitive barometer of your feelings. Some of the ways my own body informs me of changed feelings are:

- shallow breathing
- less erect posture
- tight facial muscles
- contracted stomach
- hunched shoulders
- brittle voice

To release pent-up anger, you can also scream into a pillow, have a private tantrum, hit a couch repeatedly with a two-foot length of rubber hose, or yell at the top of your voice when you are driving (alone!) in your car. This is useful not only when you are feeling rage, but when you experience a vague discomfort whose source you can't quite locate. Such expression is especially valuable when it's not suitable or possible to express anger to your partner, either because they're not present, or because you don't trust yourself to be appropriate with it.

There are also a variety of exercises that effectively allow energy to move through the body and be released. You might try working with a specialist, such as a Reichian therapist, or someone who does bioenergetic or Lomi work. Many forms of therapy and bodywork specialize in energy release. This is well worth considering if your usual attempts to deal with anger haven't been successful.

When anger is not released it festers. If you use the body to move the energy, what was stagnant becomes a clear, flowing stream. Releasing your anger keeps you from becoming bitter, mean, or contracted into a knot. You honor your vitality while restoring your sense of proportion. You learn that you can be trusted with strong feelings. When anger is present, expressing its energy harmlessly is a blessing for your own health and for the well-being of those around you.

Healthy Anger and Good Boundaries

If you have trouble getting angry, or tend to repress your anger, you will need to learn how to display healthy anger in order to have good boundaries. Healthy anger can be the voice of awakening, proclaiming that something is no longer appropriate for you, that you must say a firm no. If you are not heard when you say it quietly, you learn to convey the message with increasing vigor, until you get through. Here anger can serve as an act of self-love, helping you proclaim what you will not tolerate. This can be a real service to your partner, if they have harmful patterns of unconscious behavior or heavy defenses. At times anger is the only message capable of penetrating such defenses. Your partner may need your fire to wake up.

Once you are comfortable setting clear boundaries, you can learn to do so with an open heart. Setting boundaries lovingly is an art one masters only with practice. In learning when and how to say no, you may discover that it is possible to growl with such grace and love that your partner feels acknowledged and affirmed even as their behavior is being limited.

If you are the kind of person who avoids conflict, the voice of fear may argue that you have no right to do this, that it is wrong to get angry. Such moments are excellent occasions to remind yourself that it is a gift to say no to your partner's expectations when they do not fit yours. It's good to say a resounding no to what would hurt either of you, or divert you from your path. You let both yourself and your partner down when you fail to say no in this fashion.

As was said earlier, we are all climbing the same mountain, but from different directions. Our goal is learning to make clear boundaries with an open heart. Some of us whose hearts may open a little more quickly may need to learn to be a little firmer. Others, more comfortable with making boundaries, need to work on keeping the heart open in the process. In both cases the fruit of the labor is a rare quality of communication in which both parties are equally honored.

Dealing with Your Partner's Anger

One of the most difficult challenges of intimacy is to be present and open to your partner's anger. For many years, when Martha was angry with me, I had a powerful urge either to withdraw or get angry back. Instantly my mind would race to find something she had done that was worse than my own transgression.

When your partner is angry, withdrawal and attack both fail to bring healing. They only prolong the bad feelings. But if you can learn to listen without defense, in a place of pure receiving, you can bring resolution. This is not to say that you are bad, or that your partner's view of the situation has more merit than yours. It is simply to acknowledge that your partner has a right to their feelings. You may learn something of great value from hearing and understanding them.

Being present for your partner's anger is not an easy thing to master. When learning to swim, it helps to practice first in quiet waters before venturing into turbulent seas. Practice being there for your partner when they're mildly upset and their feelings aren't too threatening. Success at this level helps you develop a certain inner muscle, enabling you ultimately to embrace your partner's more powerful feelings as they arise.

Perhaps the single most important factor in becoming comfortable with your partner's anger is your freedom from guilt: the realization of your absolute worthiness. Only when you know your basic goodness will you be able to hold in your mind and heart two ideas that up until now have seldom been able to coexist: My partner is really angry at me, *and* I am okay.

Most of us feel a profound sense of unworthiness. The more your partner gets angry or withholds love, the more it seems to prove that this supremely painful feeling of unworthiness is indeed justified.

Look closely at yourself when your partner is angry at you. You may begin to observe how swiftly their anger triggers defensiveness, a signal that shame or guilt lies beneath. Your guilt is not created by your partner's anger. Already latently present within you, it is stimulated into action by attack. Your partner seems to be saying with their anger that you are unworthy of love, a notion with which your guilt completely acquiesces. It is this feeling of unworthiness alone, rather than your partner's anger, that generates your discomfort.

The more you feel your own worth, imperfections and all, the more you will know in your heart that your partner's anger toward you is not a reflection of who you are. There is no more cause to be defensive or blame them for being angry at you. You have no longer granted them the power to define your worth.

Remember also that when your partner is angry with you and their heart is closed, they are not seeing you in the fullness of your spirit. They are actually angry not with you, but with an image of you that they have manufactured in their mind, an image composed of bits and pieces of the past. Seeing this makes it easier to relax your defenses.

Your partner's anger is likely to convey a two-pronged message: that you did something unskillful, and that you don't deserve love. Believing both, leads to guilt; believing neither, to a defensive state incapable of learning. It is good to disbelieve the second part, while listening without defensiveness to learn if the first part has any truth. If it doesn't feel right, then you can allow your partner their anger, sensing the buried tension and pain they are trying to release.

By letting them express it, as you would a child whom you loved, you can help your partner get over it more quickly. On the other hand, if there is truth in their assertion, you have just learned something of value on your path to greater consciousness.

It takes the courage of a warrior to train yourself to be lovingly present for your partner's anger. It isn't easy work, but it is a profound gift to you both. If, over time, you are willing to hear your partner's anger without defensiveness, your partner will come to trust you at a new level. In addition, you will be forging a vessel that is capable of holding all feelings and processing them completely. Certain kinds of important communication will now be possible for the first time.

When Martha gets fierce with me, a very human part of me may feel uncomfortable. But at another, deeper level I rejoice, because I know what her life would be like if all these negative feelings couldn't be expressed. This awareness considerably softens my discomfort.

When your partner is angry with you, rejoice that they feel safe enough to express all their feelings to you. It is an honor to participate together in this extraordinary healing process.

Challenging the Beliefs That Lead to Anger

So far we have emphasized the importance of avoiding what we have called the Spiritual Mistake, condemning, repressing, or denying anger. It is essential to accept and appropriately express anger, understand its relation to the past, find physical ways of releasing it that do no harm, and learn how to use it for making appropriate boundaries. However, another factor is needed if one is fully to receive all the teachings of anger. We are, in effect, approaching anger from two different directions. Our work is like freeing a stuck car by rocking it from both ends. Thus we now we'll shift our attention to the Psychological Mistake, through which anger is justified and indulged.

It may well be that the bulk of our anger arises out of values, beliefs, and assumptions that simply aren't true. If this is so, there is a real necessity to investigate these false beliefs, the ones that support our getting angry in the first place. Perhaps if we become more conscious, we may release these beliefs and have less need to be angry.

In photography, developing is a process that can be done only in the dark. If a light is turned on, the process is ruined. The mind, too, has processes that cannot proceed in the light of awareness.

For example, notice how often your anger toward your partner can be traced to blaming them for not being sufficiently loving—in other words, for being in their ego. Our ego has the hidden belief that when our partner closes their heart it is "bad" and worthy of condemnation. In our unawareness, we justify the closing of our own heart and get angry at our partner. Such sleight of mind could only go on in the dark. If the light of awareness were turned on, and we could see clearly what we were doing, we would let go of the whole thing with a burst of laughter

Another common hidden belief says that our partner is responsible for our state of mind. We manifest this belief every time we assume they've caused us to feel bad. Those who'll investigate will discover that this is a profound error. Despite appearance to the contrary, we have a complete say in the quality of our consciousness through the way we interpret our experience.

For example, much of our anger comes from feeling powerless. Parents' anger at their children often arises out of such a feeling. Some parents will plead "Please don't do that," over and over, plaintively, until they finally explode in anger when their child repeats the same behavior for the seventeenth time.

If this happens to you, perhaps the Universe is asking you to look closely at the belief that you lack power. If a parent were feeling confident and in control, they could get more and more forceful if the child didn't respond to their request, until they elicited what was required. If you were that parent, you might need to express your fire, but there would be no reason to close your heart.

Look to see whether you feel powerless during fits of anger. If you do, ask yourself if circumstances are really making you powerless, or if the feeling is actually a belief arising out of your fear.

Sarah was angry at her husband Frank for not "letting" her go out more often with her friends. Sarah's fear was actually saying, If I assert my independence it will make Frank really angry. He may hurt me, or even leave me. At the very least, he would show me less love. That would be intolerable, so I will resign myself to staying home, and hold it in my mind that he's kind of a jailer, imprisoning me. Then I can justify being angry at him for denying my freedom.

Frank's behavior, however fear-based and insensitive, was not a cause of Sarah's feeling of limitation or her anger. Sarah's own fear was the cause of both. Without fear, she would have told Frank all her needs, while remaining open to negotiate as an equal.

Righteous Anger

Anger is frequently accompanied by a feeling of righteousness. If you're aware of that feeling, it can serve as a warning signal that you're missing the mark. Saying, "Look at what those awful politicians are doing. How could they be such terrible hypocrites? It really makes me mad!" implies that I am free of the greed, self-centeredness, inconsistency, insensitivity, or whatever inner state motivated their actions. But is this true?

One way of dissolving righteous anger is to become more aware of yourself in daily life, both outwardly and inwardly. Become attentive to the workings of your mind and heart from moment to moment, unflinching and without judgment. If you are also conscious of your words and behavior, you may appreciate the essentially self-centered nature of your ego. The more you become aware of how your ego displays itself through insensitivity to others, unconsciousness, dishonesty, harsh words, judgmental thinking, closed heart, and lack of generosity, the more you realize that your ego is as self-centered, petty, and vain as anyone else's. Egos, including yours, are all the same; they are simply not nice.

To see this clearly forces you into an uncomfortable position. Since you are morally on a par with others, you have to blame either everybody, including yourself, or nobody.

Some religious traditions, such as certain kinds of fundamentalism, lean towards blaming everybody. We are all sinners, they say. Justice requires that self-centeredness deserves the most profound condemnation and punishment, unless those guilty of it repent. To hold this view is to justify anger both toward oneself and toward one's sinful fellow humans. Guilt and judgment become a way of life.

Another viewpoint is possible, which holds that perhaps we are all merely confused, fearful, and in need of healing. Perhaps all this self-centeredness is simply the product of a mind caught up in illusion, flailing about in its ignorance and confusion. If so, all fear-based behavior, including one's own, deserves only a loving response.

If the rational mind were to try to decide between the two alternatives of blame and compassion, convincing arguments might be given and authorities cited for either side. But the limited and conditioned mind hasn't the capacity to discern matters of this nature; it is simply not equipped to do the job. Here the heart must lead the way.

We believe that the heart, when heeded, will tell us that the "outrageous" behavior that's triggered the anger arises from a fearful mind. Healing is needed here, not condemnation. The more you see yourself in daily life as you really are, the more the heart will prompt you to release the judgmental component of your anger. The more you learn how your own fears give rise to imperfections, inconsistencies, and self-centeredness, the greater will be your reluctance to blame your partner for their particular ways of expressing their human imperfections.

Of course you will still get angry, even after you begin to see the truth of all this. But now it will become harder to *justify* it. As your mind begins to puff up with righteousness at your partner's failings, you will find yourself simultaneously becoming aware of your own similar shortcomings, and your righteousness will collapse. It will be easier to see that both you and your partner are not much different from scared children, who deserve only loving guidance and forgiveness for their fear-based behavior. When your anger becomes purified of blame, you will feel it more as a sensation in your body and your mind, and you'll learn how simply to be with it.

No longer supported by the mind's justification, your anger will move another step toward transmuting itself into passion.

Thoughts from Martha

Many women have a harder time than men in being direct with their anger. To a great extent, this comes from their image of themselves as "nice." It's as if they don't feel entitled to be angry. When they do feel anger—as all human beings do—they end up not expressing it at all, or expressing it indirectly, through bickering, sniping, or nagging. When a woman's anger is stifled, she may feel like a victim, as if life is not giving her what she wants. Her husband is not the person she thought she married; her children aren't turning out right; she isn't finding ways to nourish her soul. In extreme cases she may become resigned or bitter.

I know all this intimately: I grew up with it. In our house my father was the designated angry person. My mother didn't feel safe expressing her anger, so she internalized it, and later died of a heart attack. (I suspect there's a connection between women's stifled anger and female illness.) I was brought up to be unfailingly nice, especially around men: cheerful, supportive, accommodating. People thought of me that way, and to a large extent that's how I thought of myself. It took me a long time to learn—largely through my relationship with Don—that I had the normal human complement of anger. Only then, when I became aware of my capacity for anger, did I learn to express and release it.

Today I often see women who remind me of my former self. They may be pleasant and smiling, but there are often key giveaways: a set jaw, furtive eye movements, a certain tenseness in the body. A telltale sign is often the tone of voice. They may believe they are just talking neutrally about their partner, "pointing things out," but the unconscious tone is one of contempt or hostility. In our workshops, we've noticed that for women, the last feeling to be acknowledged is often anger, even when it is apparent to everyone else. These women will willingly express sadness, disappointment, anxiety, frustration—anything but outright anger, which they consider to be a step into dangerous territory.

There may be other reasons for not expressing anger, besides maintaining an image of niceness. Some women, especially mothers raising families at home, feel helplessly dependent on their husbands. They can't afford to rock the boat, or their husbands might react in a volatile way—even leave them. This feeling of being trapped exacerbates the anger and raises the temperature in the pressure cooker that is the relationship.

A woman's unconscious anger (nagging and complaining) or out-of-control anger (ranting and raving) only poisons the atmosphere and pushes her partner even further away. But there's another way for a woman to express anger by simply letting her partner know how his behavior is impacting her, without making him wrong or demeaning him. "There's something you did that bothered me, and it's making me feel angry. I want you to know how I'm feeling." This way of presenting anger often elicits a different response. Many men prefer their partners to express their feelings directly and cleanly, so that they know where they stand. When a woman is able to express her anger in this way she feels empowered, which allows for a new dynamic in the relationship.

I believe anger is meant to be part of a process that results in change. It's part of a woman's fire. When unexpressed, it accumulates and festers, remaining more like a stagnant pool than a flowing stream. It never develops the momentum to explode into useful action. When expressed bravely and cleanly, as a full-bodied No to what isn't working, it can provide useful feedback. Seeing this can be a powerful incentive for a woman to push through the fear that inhibits her around her own anger. If she can understand what that anger is trying to tell her, it can be a useful tool on the path to her wholeness.

CHAPTER 7

The Role of Pain

How We Become Wounded

Few of us grew up in families where it felt emotionally safe to have and express feelings. When we were little, we thought our parents were God, but most were not able to play this role of God in a way that helped us feel our fundamental goodness. Because of their own wounds, those who raised us felt threatened by much of our natural behavior. In response they withheld love when we were crying, angry, sleepless, or any of the many things that made them uncomfortable. We received the message, nonverbally as well as verbally, that these expressions of our humanity were unacceptable. We had it from the Ultimate Authority that there was something fundamentally wrong with us for simply being who we were.

Modern Western culture seems to have special difficulty finding creative responses to the exuberant energy of two-year-olds. Normal two-year-olds are engaging in the natural and healthy practice of differentiating themselves from their parents. "I am ME, not you!" their actions declare. By saying no they're establishing their identities. Unfortunately, this declaration appears threatening to many parents, who haven't learned how to allow a child's feelings while setting appropriate behavioral boundaries, and as a result, much of our wounding occurs around that age.

We learn to feel unsafe in our families. A child is taught to be afraid in many ways, gross and subtle. A tension-filled mother holds her child to her tight body, sometimes with more irritation than love. A confused father, uncomfortable in his role, is emotionally unavailable. Another father becomes ill-tempered and grouchy, unable to deal with a sudden diminution of attention from his overstressed wife. The child's privacy is invaded in a hundred ways, with no regard for his or her dignity. A harsh quality in the parents' tone of voice becomes more frequent. Fault-finding greatly exceeds acknowledgment. In all these ways, parental fear gets transmitted to the child through an unpleasant feeling in the home, teaching them that the Universe is fundamentally an unsafe place to be.

Problems at Birth

Many women of my mother's generation were loving, intelligent people who nevertheless allowed themselves to be taken in by the strange prevailing cultural and medical attitudes toward birth. Go to the hospital and make sure your husband is not involved in the delivery. (We heard a tale, perhaps apocryphal, of one husband who found the only way he could circumvent the stern and rigid hospital rules against being present at the birth of his child was to handcuff himself to his wife and swallow the key!) Drug yourself to avoid any pain, and in the process lose consciousness of the miracle taking place. Then allow your child to be taken away, so that it can spend the next week (a crucial time in its development) mostly without being held or touched. Every once in a while you may pick it up, but don't even think about breast feeding. After you bring it home, hold it for short periods and give it the bottle when the schedule says to, then put it down for four or five hours. Let it cry as much as necessary, otherwise it will become spoiled. Besides, lusty crying is good for its lungs.

It is hard to imagine how a culture could stray so far from anything resembling sanity. It sounds so bizarre to me now, for a mother to allow her own deepest instinct to be overridden by the notion that some professional (generally male) knows better. Yet we are all subject to the powerful pressure of cultural conditioning. How many of us in that circumstance would honestly have had the foresight and wisdom to challenge the prevailing notions?

Infants want so much to be held and caressed with love. Imagine the feeling of a little child being put down and left alone to cry.

Then picture how a father's discomfort can add to the wound. When you are born, your father is proportionally equivalent to being about eighteen feet tall. Gaze up to the top of a two-story building, and imagine a being that enormous looking down on you with anxiety, distaste, or anger. Consider the effect that would have on the psyche of this small being. That small being is you. It is also your partner.

The feelings of fear, guilt, pain, and anger live within, waiting to be healed.

Separation: The Essential Wound

Those who wish to be healed will have no interest in blaming their parents for their pain. The wound that gets passed from generation to generation is nobody's fault. It arises from a primordial misperception in the human consciousness.

When we are born, we feel at one with not only our mother, but with the whole universe. Our mind has not yet developed the concept of being separate and distinct from what is perceived. For an infant, undifferentiated sensation is all that occurs. Then at some early point an ultimately traumatic event takes place: We begin to regard ourselves as separate from the rest of Life, a drop cut off from the ocean. I'd like to suggest that the profound fear resulting from this mistaken perception creates a great inner wound, the primordial source of our human pain. Passed on from parent to child, the wound spreads through the generations like a wave. In our personal psyche it expresses itself as fear, depression, illness, and pain; in the world it manifests as starvation, war, pollution, and exploitation. (It is not necessary to agree with this viewpoint for you and your partner to work together in healing your wounds.)

Only the light of awareness has the power to interrupt this mechanical transmission of the wound. We are here to shine a compassionate light on our childhood wounds, that we may use them in the service of healing ourselves and our world.

Childhood Pain in the Present

Why does intimacy so often arouse such deep and ancient pain? Perhaps it's our choice of partner. We often unconsciously pick an intimate partner who replicates some of our parents' traits. Those with an alcoholic parent often select partners who have alcohol or other drug problems. Those whose parents were emotionally unavailable may choose a similar mate. The unconscious mind is using the relationship to reproduce the conditions of childhood in an attempt to heal the old wounds.

The unhealed pain from your childhood is likely to play a major role in the present dynamic between you and your partner. Virtually everything painful or difficult between you and your partner has some relationship to the childhood wounds of both parties. When your partner acts in some way that you dislike, you may be seeing the manifestation of an old trauma. Those who suffered emotionally as children will often test their partners repeatedly in an attempt to establish whether or not there is emotional safety. Knowing this may not solve everything, but it may elicit more compassion and understanding from the more secure partner.

Exploring the past together can be a fascinating journey. What did it feel like in your home when you were growing up? What made you angry with your parents? What hurt you? What made you scared? Are there periods devoid of memory? Is there any relation between what bothers you now and what went on then?

The exploration can be linked to present-day dynamics. For example, when your pain seems out of proportion to the event that triggers it, which for most people seems to happen a great deal, ask yourself if it feels like an old and familiar feeling. If so, history is impinging on the present, distorting it. Present events, resembling childhood memories, stir up the embers of buried emotions, and the individual experiences transference.

Understanding transference helps you explore old wounds previously hidden in the dark folds of the unconscious mind. You must first experience a feeling in order to release it. The unconscious must become conscious. If in a moment of discomfort you stay quietly with your feeling, it may reveal its message. At times it may take courage to remain with levels of discomfort from which you would normally escape. If you are a warrior, you will sooner or later confront situations that lead you to your major issue.

The feelings that arise from these old wounds can be quite powerful. Yet you can learn to stand outside of them and look at the whole dynamic with spaciousness. If you are totally immersed in your feelings, or you identify with them, it's virtually impossible to get the distance needed for clarity. If you can lift yourself above the battlefield and witness the feelings, then you are no longer a slave to them. You can begin to work with them.

One man we worked with learned this from the seemingly trivial matter of his wife's lateness. Sean found himself feeling extremely hurt every time Margaret failed to show up when she was supposed to. Even when she was only ten minutes late, his feelings would become quite intense. For a while he tried holding them in, which of course didn't ease his pain. Then he allowed himself to feel and express the full force of his pain. This helped at one level, but the intensity was so great that Margaret didn't know quite what to do with it. All she knew was that she couldn't possibly be responsible for such intense suffering on account of being a bit late.

Sean had no bitterness toward Margaret; he didn't feel good about making such a big deal out of something trivial. But he was savvy enough to realize that suppressing his feelings wasn't the answer. After being shown how to put some space around his feelings and inquire into his past, Sean had a revelation. An old memory surfaced. His father frequently used to promise to spend time with him and then not show up, which devastated Sean. He had come to feel there was something fundamentally wrong with him, something that made his father not want to be with him. When Margaret didn't show up on time, it awakened the awful feeling of not really being cared about, of being unlovable.

Sean's insight helped Margaret see how she was not responsible for his pain, but was merely the trigger. Now, with a little distance, she could be of more help to him in his healing process. In addition, she realized that being more conscious and reliable about time would smooth out a rough patch in their relationship.

How Wounds Play Against Each Other

One partner's wound often triggers that of the other, creating one of intimacy's great challenges. A couple we knew had fallen into just such a cycle in which their wounds constantly aggravated each other's.

Joan and Bill were an attractive professional couple in their late forties. Joan was likeable, intense, and a bit driven. Bill provided a balance with a more relaxed energy, though it sometimes seemed to be covering up some unacknowledged fear. They had just gone through another one of their familiar blowouts, and they were becoming weary of the pattern.

One night Bill and Joan both had important phone calls to make. Joan told Bill he could go first. Bill couldn't reach his party; but instead of immediately offering Joan the phone, he proceeded to call someone else, with whom he talked a good bit of time. When Joan realized what had happened, she became enraged at Bill and started yelling at him the minute he hung up. Bill pulled back behind his wall, refusing to hear anything Joan was saying. He felt unfairly attacked for what seemed, at most, a minor infraction.

As so often happened, their conversation quickly escalated. Joan was getting increasingly angry: "You knew I needed to make that call; it was really important. Why couldn't you have just given the phone over as soon as you couldn't reach Fred? I've got better things to do with my time than wait around half the night for you to finish chatting with your buddies. I'm sick and tired of watching you day in and day out take such good care of yourself and act as if I don't exist! I just don't understand you."

Bill looked as if he wanted to leave as quickly as possible. "*You* can't understand? *I'm* the one who can't understand. I fail to see why you continually lash out at me as if I'm some kind of goddamn monster. Look, I admit I blew it, I should have given you the phone, okay? But I didn't know you were on such a tight schedule. So what I did wasn't that bad, and it most certainly didn't warrant your yelling and screaming at me like that. I have to tiptoe around my own house because I never know when to expect one of your tantrums. I don't know if I want to live with someone who attacks me all the time for practically nothing!"

"Practically nothing, is it?" Joan responded, her voice rising half an octave. "That's the trouble with you, you always dismiss my feelings. Every time I try to tell you how I'm feeling you hide behind that damned wall of yours. I might just as well be talking to myself."

And so on . . .

Of course, this is just the kind of exchange that Openhearted Listening is designed to prevent. I asked Joan and Bill if this was typical of their fights and they agreed it was. They both seemed motivated to learn another approach.

Bill agreed to listen first. Just the very fact of entering into the process changed the expression on his face, and his wall seemed to become several shades more transparent. Joan started out from her place of anger, telling him her story, and finishing with the statement that she felt angry for not being taken seriously.

When Bill started to mirror back what Joan said, her face became a bit softer. She wasn't used to having Bill present for her anger. After he mirrored her, Joan had a revelation. She remembered that when she was a child her parents didn't take her seriously. She often felt ignored, as though her needs and wishes were of no importance. Bill's behavior had stirred up her old anger.

That anger now made more sense to Bill. He was able to validate her: "Making that phone call was really important to you. And when I treated it as if it had no significance, it was just like your parents all over again. I was acting as if you didn't matter and your wishes had no value. I can really see how that would make you furious. I'm even beginning to get mad at myself!"

Despite the seriousness of the issue, Joan burst into a broad smile. She felt validated, and the tension between her and Bill was gone. They both understood more clearly how the intense charge behind her anger originated from her past. Now they had clarified an area of special sensitivity where they could both be watchful.

The next time we met, Joan agreed to listen to Bill's feelings. In telling his story, Bill emphasized how scared he felt when Joan suddenly started yelling at him. Then he, too, had his moment of enlightenment. His mother had frequently gotten loud and angry with him, often unfairly. He remembered how as a boy he couldn't understand what he had done that warranted such an assault. When Joan yelled at him after he'd hung up, it was just like being a kid again, receiving a burst of unfair anger for virtually nothing.

It was apparent that they had both become more interested in uncovering the truth than in blaming each other. Now they were in a position to see how each of their wounds contributed to their ongoing conflict. Bill saw how Joan's anger was provoked when he didn't take her seriously. Joan understood why her outbursts scared him, and why he retreated behind his wall to a place of safety. Both their childhood wounds were being activated by the other's behavior, triggering the same fight over and over.

Having reached this level of insight, Joan and Bill each had personal work to do. Joan's task was to let Bill know of her upset without automatically going into attack mode. She needed to stand outside of her feelings, so she could talk about them without being overwhelmed by them. Bill's work was first of all, to become aware of the ways he failed to take Joan seriously, and secondly, to struggle with his tendency to withdraw as soon as he felt uncomfortable. He needed to be willing to listen to Joan's anger without pulling away, even if the anger did sometimes feel unfair. They both needed to be willing to do Openhearted Listening when such situations arose. Joan and Bill began to be more vigilant in identifying their common pattern. An awareness developed that brought a softening and healing of the old wounds.

Responding to Pain: The Two Mistakes

Two mistakes are commonly made in responding to another's pain. The first lacks compassion, while the second lacks perspective. Most of us have a tendency to err in one direction or the other. It's useful for both partners to become familiar with their tendencies, so they may be brought more into balance.

The first mistake is the "on high" response, aloof and devoid of charity. This attitude says that I am not responsible for your pain. You do your thing, I do mine, and if perchance we meet, that's fine. Such a perspective overlooks all the wonderful ways we can be of help to each other. It ignores the rich possibilities for healing inherent in intimacy.

This perspective has often been found in conjunction with the well-quoted New Age idea that says you are responsible for your own reality. In recent times this notion has been misunderstood to mean, "If you are in pain, then you are to blame because you're causing it all yourself, you idiot!" This approach is hardly helpful. Responsibility is not the same as blame, which often implies non-deservingness. Even if your partner is causing themselves pain, they are most certainly in as much need of compassion as anyone. To be a healing force in their life is an opportunity to heal yourself as well.

The second kind of unskillful response to your partner's pain is the opposite: becoming submerged in their drama. In displaying great concern for their situation, believing in the soap opera, treating it as a full-fledged catastrophe, you are contributing to their fear by indulging your own. You are supporting in them the notion that they are in danger.

The inappropriateness of this response can be more easily perceived if you imagine someone greeting your own pain with upset and fear. If someone says "I'm so concerned about you," chances are you would feel annoyance more than anything else. When you fail to appreciate the value that pain might have as a teaching, you have substituted pity for compassion. In your attachment to your partner's process taking a particular form, you have taken on their healing as if the responsibility were yours. Your attitude teaches them that fear is an appropriate response to life's challenges. You have forgotten their safety and your own.

If your partner is caught up in their own pain, your best help is not to become drawn into the vortex. Be aware there is learning going on that neither of you may be able to see at the moment. It is time to trust that your partner is receiving the appropriate teachings.

What is it like to be neither aloof and condescending, nor flustered and caught up in fear? To get a sense, consider how you would respond to a child who has just had a nightmare. On the one hand, you wouldn't scoff at the child for being afraid, or deliver a pedantic lecture about the unreality of dreams. On the other hand, you wouldn't whip up their fear level by getting dramatically upset about the content of their dream. Instead, you might simply hug the child, acknowledging that from their perspective the pain was very real. At the same time, your relaxed manner and body language would convey to them in a tangible way that they were in no danger.

A feeling of safety is the most healing gift you can confer upon a frightened child. It is also the most worthwhile message you can convey to your partner when they are in pain. By displaying compassion for their pain without negating it through some lofty spiritual ideal, you also communicate a deep sense that all is well. It is imparted through your smile, your touch, your tone of voice and the look in your eyes. The transmission of the feeling of safety depends on your own sense of having a safe place. If you can do that, your manner will heal more than any words can.

Should the Past Be Released?

What happens when a painful and traumatic event from earlier in the relationship interferes with the present? Conrad and Anna came to one of our workshops with a classic dilemma. Many years ago, Conrad had been unfaithful to Anna. She had been so devastated that she was unable to let go of her hurt and anger. Whenever Anna was really upset with Conrad she would bring up the incident, obviously feeling that at some level she had not found resolution. Conrad, who had apologized sincerely on several occasions, was now asking Anna to stop repeatedly bringing up the past, and start living in the present.

Both were in touch with a certain truth. It was natural for Anna to want understanding, to be released from her hurt and anger. Nevertheless, she needed to see that playing the wounded victim, making her partner the villain, could never bring the resolution she craved. She needed to convey to Conrad that while she may have strong feelings, she did not want to use them to attack him every time she got upset with him, but was willing to work on releasing these feelings and forgiving him.

It was equally natural for Conrad to want to be forgiven for his mistake, to escape the shadow of the past. Nevertheless, he needed to realize that emotionally charged issues require patience, persistence, and a great deal of listening without defensiveness. He needed to convey to Anna that he had room for all her feelings, that he knew some of her issues might require a long time to resolve, and that he was willing to remain patiently with her feelings to the best of his ability.

It helped for Anna to bring up her pain at the workshop in a conscious way. Asking Conrad to do Openhearted Listening, she focused on her feeling, avoiding attack and blame. As he listened non-defensively she found that deeper layers could now safely emerge. Conrad was able to validate her feelings at a new level, and they both took a powerful step towards healing a major issue. Although she still didn't feel complete, she saw the wisdom of letting it go for a period, rather than bringing it up repeatedly whenever she felt hurt or angry. Instead they agreed to work together on building up the trust level in other areas of the relationship, and come back to this problem at a later time.

Keeping the Wound Clean

Psychological wounds are similar to physical injuries. A minor miracle takes place in the daily healing of a simple cut. The process, which seems to be directed by a powerful intelligence within, occurs naturally as long as you keep the wound clean. Healing is impaired if you allow dirt into the wound.

A natural psychological healing process takes place if you learn to keep the wound free of impurities—the blame and judgment which pervade our daily consciousness. Being harsh with yourself or your partner, either for being in pain or for responding to it unskillfully, is like pouring dirt on the wound. Given the prevalence of such judgment it's no wonder that our emotional wounds so often fail to heal. The process would be greatly facilitated if partners could learn how to keep their wounds clean through acts of love.

The heart is open until the mind closes it. Keeping the wound clean entails a willingness not to believe in all the mind's reasons for closing the heart, for harboring judgment, resentment, and non-forgiveness. It means having the courage simply to be with pain, your own or your partner's, without moving away from it. It means trusting that an inner intelligence, without interference, can heal the heart.

Stanley and Eve, an attractive young couple, appeared at our workshop one day. He was jovial in manner, with a full beard and overalls. She had long hair, a tasteful skirt and blouse, and a more serious air. When they began doing Openhearted Listening it became apparent they had unconsciously been allowing dirt into their wounds.

Eve's difficulty centered around Stanley's behavior toward Tracy, their two-year-old daughter. He had the habit of suddenly grabbing her and tossing her up in the air abruptly. Eve felt Stanley, even though his intention was pure, was being insensitive, treating Tracy too much like a thing. This evoked some disagreeable memories from Eve's childhood, where she was similarly treated. She took her mothering seriously, and felt some disapproval toward Stanley for not showing more responsibility.

Stanley was equally bothered by a habit of Eve's. When he was with her, she would often turn her attention abruptly away and focus on their daughter, without realizing its impact on him. It felt to Stanley as if Eve regarded Tracy as more important than he was. This evoked in him an old wound, too: As the youngest child in his family, he had often felt dismissed or taken lightly. Hurt of this kind often turns into judgment. Stanley ended up resenting Eve for being too uptight about her mothering, too concerned about the child and not enough about him.

The more Stanley judged Eve for not giving him enough attention, the more she reacted by turning that attention elsewhere. And when Eve judged Stanley for not being a more conscious parent, he closed his ears to the notion that there might be something thoughtless in his behavior.

When Eve and Stanley saw what they had been doing, each understood what was needed. Stanley told Eve that he was willing to look at ways he might be more sensitive toward their daughter. Eve told Stanley that she was willing to look at ways she could be more considerate toward him. Both had begun to cleanse their wounds so that they could begin to heal.

Being Lovingly Present for Yourself

Helping each other to heal will have significance only if each of you is also working to heal yourself. Although the way your wounds express themselves may vary, the work is the same for all. Simply put, you learn to be lovingly present for yourself in the midst of your pain. This may represent one of the greatest of all challenges.

You may be struggling with a feeling of loss and emptiness in your heart, from being emotionally abandoned as a child by parents unable to nurture you. Your old attitude might have been that you weren't loved as you deserved or needed to be, and thus were permanently scarred emotionally. But it's possible to consider these same facts in a different way. Since you weren't loved as you deserved to be, you learned from your pain the immense importance of loving attention. As a result, you are now especially willing to love and be loved.

If you feel sad and deprived, consider this your signal that the injured child within you needs support. Take it as your cue to do what is really nurturing for yourself. If you feel surges of anger at your parents, realize that this does not mean they are worthy of blame, but rather that your inner fire is engaged in burning up the old misguided patterns. You may find in yourself the true parent you have always wanted.

Every committed love has its own discipline. As you undertake the discipline of being fully present for your pain, every instance in which you feel shadowed by old hurt will be experienced as a call to your deeper heart. The wounded child will at last receive the loving attention they have so deeply craved.

What Do I Need from My Partner?

Once you begin attending to your own wounds, enlisting the aid of your partner will have a different quality, since you're no longer seeing them as being responsible for your difficulties. You're no longer demanding their help, you're inviting it. Your partner can serve in a useful capacity, especially if you have some sense of what would be helpful when your wound is displaying itself.

Many people, especially men, believe that being in pain automatically requires shutting down and becoming emotionally unavailable. This needn't be the case, even if your history asserts that to be open is to be unsafe. It does, however, take a special kind of courage to be open to your partner when you are hurting.

When you are feeling your familiar wound, when you are feeling hurt, angry, or withdrawn, ask yourself what would be the most healing way for your partner to respond. What possible behavior on their part would increase your feeling of safety?

By making observations over time, you will begin to sense what might help. At times you will require a wider berth and need to be left alone. Other times you might allow yourself to be coaxed out of it like a young child. Sometimes you may simply need to be heard, perhaps through Openhearted Listening. On other occasions, lightness and humor may be helpful. Experience will teach you what works.

There are times when a special kind of reassurance may be needed. Jim and Kathy were going through a difficult time financially. Jim had quit his hardware business, finding it personally unfulfilling. Kathy had chosen not to enter the workplace in order to take care of their four children. While their financial reserves became increasingly depleted, Jim ventured halfheartedly into a few projects, none of which was successful. As their bank account neared zero, Kathy showed signs of stress. Her normally pleasant manner gave way to increasing testiness. In fact, many of Jim's mannerisms, which she had previously tolerated, now became irritating, and she was snapping at him and the children with greater frequency.

When Kathy told Jim that she was distressed about running out of money, Jim replied that this was a time for trust, that everything would work out if she could just let go of her fear. True perhaps, but not the most skillful rejoinder for Kathy, whose irritability only increased whenever she heard such "spiritual" advice. Something was decidedly missing for her in Jim's response.

As a child, Kathy had often overheard her parents engaging in anxious conversations about their financial worries. The little girl's natural insecurity was now reawakened by her current situation. What Kathy needed most was a strong, reassuring presence, a bottom-line feeling of safety.

Jim's first task was to listen to Kathy's fear of running out of money, play it back to her, and validate it. But he also needed to reassure her of his commitment to his family. He was able to tell Kathy that he took full responsibility for seeing that the family's basic needs were provided for. When Kathy heard this, and felt Jim's sincerity, something in her was able to relax deeply. Her manner toward Jim softened, and family dynamics improved.

Both partners can become allies to help the wounded partner find the needed reassurance. The wounded partner can put forth the kind of reassurance they most need for their healing. The other partner can offer their willingness to provide it, and perhaps specific suggestions as well. Learning how to comfort a partner's wound skillfully is an art that can be fine-tuned over the years. (Remember that one's partner's feelings must be validated before one offers reassurance.)

One of the most effective forms of reassurance doesn't involve words. Sometimes your partner's wound is so great, their perception so clouded over, that their mind is completely confused. At such times words have limited use. When I am in this state, Martha will hold me like a child, with my head on her breast, which allows me to sink more deeply into my feelings. We begin in silence. After feeling more relaxed and safe, I may begin to talk about my feelings. Being held in this fashion can be a powerful aid in uncovering old hurts.

Educating Your Partner About Your Needs

Once self-scrutiny shows you what you most need for healing, you can begin to educate your partner about it. Inform them that when you become distant (or you nag, whine, get angry, or start to lecture), your scared child needs something from them. If you can, be specific about your need. Partners may be able to help each other explore these areas.

Our friend George was able to do this with his wife, Teri. One night Teri suddenly became sullen and withdrawn after dinner. George had just suggested inviting some new friends to come along on the hike they were planning. This seemed a perfectly innocent proposal to George, who was taken aback by her unexpected withdrawal. He pulled back as well, and they went to bed on distant terms.

The next day, George decided to try a different approach. He began by asking Teri how he could be of help when she withdrew. In this case Teri first needed for George to hear her feelings. It turned out that she had perceived George to be overly interested in outside activities and friendships, to the exclusion of their own intimacy. At last, when they had finally scheduled some time alone, George had wanted to dilute the intimacy by including others. Teri's little girl had felt hurt from want of attention, fearful she would never receive it. She responded by sulking and pulling away.

Because of George's interest in her feelings, she could now get in touch with and share what had been unconscious the night before. Once she was heard, Teri realized what she needed. She needed to know that George was interested in spending more intimate time together. George was glad to give her this reassurance, and they both experienced a healing.

Two common ways of handling pain, neither of which are very skillful, are either complaining, or being resolutely stoic. The latter is more often the strategy employed by men, who learn when they are young that expressing their feelings does not bring the hoped-for love. Women often find stoicism difficult to be around. In fact, the majority of women at our workshops say they wish their partners would talk more about painful feelings. Men, on the other hand, have a hard time accepting a woman's need to complain. (These are broad generalizations, of course.)

Neither stoicism nor complaining creates a comfortable environment. Only the conscious expression of feelings, while putting some space around them, does that. Martha and I sometimes employ something we call "conscious complaining." We introduce our feelings by informing the other that we are in a grumpy mood and need to get rid of some emotional baggage. We then ask the other if they would be willing to listen to our complaining self. With such a preface, we find each other's lists of grievances far easier to abide.

It's always worth discovering what's needed for your partner's healing. You don't necessarily have to give them what they want, but know that when you do, you are healing yourself as well. If you both take the trouble to educate yourselves and each other, you can become increasingly skillful at responding when your partner is confused and afraid.

Martha's responses to my wounds are often effective because they speak to the part of me that lies deep beneath the surface disturbance. Of course her ego sometimes gets hooked, but she relates with increasing frequency to my essence instead of to my ego. She takes me seriously without believing the story my fear has created. With room in her heart for me to be going through whatever I am feeling, she is able to smile lovingly at me in a way that lets me know that, despite appearances to the contrary, I am indeed safe. Every time I receive this gift, I am freshly in awe of the miracle of healing.

Being at Peace with Your Own Pain

Those at ease with their pain convey true safety. But most of us feel discomfort when we see our partner hurting. What is it that makes being lovingly present for their pain so difficult? What is the nature of the work that will allow us to accept another's pain with grace and ease?

The main key to feeling more comfortable with your partner's pain is to be at peace with your own. There is no magic formula for attaining this capacity quickly. It is the result of your willingness, over time, to resist the temptation to run from discomfort. You are continually faced with the seduction of escaping unpleasant feelings through drugs, overeating, sex, entertainment, work, fantasy, rationalization, or mindless pleasure. The more you resist or flee from your pain, the more strongly entrenched it becomes, and the less likely you are to be able to receive its teaching.

When you resist pain, it can feel quite unpleasant. Yet by itself, pain does not have that much force. It need not feel so terribly uncomfortable, if you welcome it with an open heart. The worst experiences are more often the consequence of resisting pain than of the primary feeling of pain itself. Even though pain is by its nature an unwelcome guest, you can learn to move compassionately into it rather than fearfully away from it. When you are at home with your own darkness, you can be far more helpful to your partner in their suffering.

Consider how you develop the capacity to be compassionate toward the suffering of others. Empathy for another's sorrow is not possible without having first experienced your own pain. If your life had been a smooth and comfortable ride, it is unlikely you would have your present level of caring. The purpose of pain in your life has been to teach you to open your heart where it had been closed, so that suffering may be transmuted into compassion.

Once you've accepted the value of the role that pain has played in your life, you can perhaps allow that your partner's suffering is serving them in a similar way. We are not recommending the unskillful use of a kind of "spiritual" perspective to create an indifference to another's sorrow. It is possible to feel compassion for their suffering while at the same time not view the pain as something regrettable. If your partner is in pain, remind yourself that to be in pain is not the same as to be in danger. Being in touch with their safety, as well as yours, will allow you to convey the message: Pain is not to be feared, but to be held in love.

Freedom from the Need to Fix It

When children witness their parents' distress, whether through alcohol, depression, violence, or an unhappy marriage, the children will often feel personally responsible for the parents' misery. This can contribute to a strong feeling of guilt.

We tend to do the same with our partner. But being at ease in the presence of your partner's pain will free you from the need to make it go away. Observe yourself carefully when your partner is unhappy or unloving, and see if there isn't some part of you that blames yourself. Perhaps, like many, you harbor the belief that your partner's unhappiness is a reflection of your own inadequacy. If only you were a better partner, lover, provider, if only you were more attractive, interesting, decent . . . your partner would find your relationship sufficient to keep them perpetually satisfied. Your shortcomings, you think, are the source of their suffering.

If you have taken on this unhealthy responsibility to keep your partner happy, then every instance of their being unhappy serves as an unpleasant reminder of your inadequacy. Who would want to be around such a reminder? In fact, you may become downright annoyed at your partner for being in pain and thereby making you so uncomfortable. You may lash out at them, or you may close down to protect yourself from feeling yet more uncomfortable. If they could just be happy, you could relax and feel good about yourself.

From this urgency to escape your own discomfort, you may try everything you know to get your partner to feel better. It may seem like you are motivated by compassion for their suffering, but your efforts are laced with fear and have a different flavor from true compassion. Such attempts don't feel genuine to your partner, for actions arising out of guilt are not healing. With every failure to alleviate their suffering, you feel more guilty and resentful of them. You have entered into a painful vicious circle.

Men especially are conditioned to react to their partner's pain by problem solving. Instead of simply being lovingly present for a woman's feelings, they often suggest either some action she ought to take, or a more enlightened way of regarding the situation. Such advice tends to sound glib, and the woman doesn't feel heard. (Of course, women can fall into this pattern as well.)

A few things may help in letting go of the need to fix it:

- When you are hurting, observe closely how inappropriate, and even annoying, it can feel when someone offers advice before truly hearing your feelings.
- See with clarity who is responsible for whose state of mind. If you suspect that your partner does not cause your feelings, then it should follow that you have not caused theirs. To the extent that you truly see this, you'll be freed from the false belief that it's up to you to make them happy.
- Work to free yourself from your own feelings of unworthiness. The more you are in touch with your basic goodness, the more you can be in the presence of your partner's pain

without stimulating your feelings of guilt. Remind yourself that your partner is in pain *and* you are all right. Although this sounds simple, it takes real work to create a feeling of worthiness independent of your partner's seeming well-being.

As the two of you learn to accept all painful feelings, trusting in the safety that lies underneath, you can create a spaciousness around the suffering. This allows the intelligence of love to heal what has been hurt.

Where Does Hurt Originate?

Although at one level the unskillful behavior of our parents and others has wounded us, this is not the entire picture. The notion that someone else is responsible for our present pain deserves to be seriously challenged.

True intimacy requires that, at least some of the time, I have soft, flexible boundaries—that I be vulnerable. Most of us carry around the assumption that exposing our vulnerability allows us to be easily hurt. If I believe that you are potentially capable of causing me pain, I am going to relate to you with a certain wariness. If I feel that I need to protect myself from your hurting me further, I will try to make myself invulnerable by hardening my defenses. Common sense seems to say that this gesture will keep me safe. This would be true if my current psychological pain can really be caused by someone else. But what if the source of this pain comes from my own mind? If that is so, then a psychological defense against another is unnecessary.

One of the hallmarks of a spiritual relationship is its challenge of the usual assumptions about common sense. By way of engaging that challenge, I'd like to suggest that as an adult, you—not your parents or your partner—are the source of your present hurt, which arises from your feeling of unworthiness.

It was natural as a child to believe the messages that your parents conveyed about your unworthiness. Since you hadn't the mental equipment to challenge these messages, they were in effect a given for your tender psyche, and thus could be said to have produced your wounds.

But these wounds do not persist in the present because of what happened in the past. You perpetuate their presence by accepting now the messages of unworthiness that your parents or others long ago inculcated in your young mind. It is not the past that's now wounding you, but rather your present acceptance of an old conditioning that has no more relevance. Though you may have once accepted your parents' negative image of yourself, your continued belief in that image now represents a choice—one you have the power to remake.

If you accept your parents' (or anyone else's) evaluation of your worth, you are giving them the power to define who you are. As an adult, it may at last be time to take this power back. You no longer have any need to accept anyone else's opinion of who you are and what your worth is. When you reclaim this natural right to define your own worth, you cease being a victim of the past.

A similar shift is needed with your partner. To the extent that you let them define your worth, you are severely limiting your capacity for intimacy. The fear of being hurt will dominate your mind and condition your behavior. It is virtually impossible to be yourself, to act from your essence, if a major part of you is hanging back protecting itself from the felt danger of an unfavorable evaluation from your partner. Is it your partner's behavior that hurts you, as common sense seems to dictate, or is it your own feeling of unworthiness?

It is easy to assume that your partner's accusation caused your bad feelings. If you sound an E near a guitar, the guitar's E strings will vibrate in resonance. Similarly, if your partner accuses you of being bad, your feeling of unworthiness resonates to their accusation. But if you were feeling comfortable in yourself while they attacked you, there would be nothing within to resonate, and therefore no source of hurt. A frightened child is crying for help, and you are safe.

You may, however, take a close look to see if you might learn something about yourself from your partner's accusation. Perhaps their attack was triggered by unconscious or unskillful behavior on your part. Feeling good about yourself doesn't mean you are free of imperfections, or you have nothing to learn. But it does mean you've no need to lacerate yourself when you find you have erred.

If you can refrain from tormenting yourself, you may be able to accept what is true in your partner's communication, which is usually no more than the fact that your behavior was unskillful. At the same time, you will reject the false notion that you are a bad person for having erred and deserve censure. In so doing you will not feel hurt, even though you have been attacked, although you may feel a momentary and perfectly healthy remorse over having contributed to pain. The feeling is often accompanied by gratitude for having learned something valuable.

The Two Perspectives of Hurt

Feeling hurt by the way others treat us is such a common occurrence that we may well ask if it isn't simply a normal reaction to life. Feeling hurt is a normal reaction, which we wish both to embrace and transcend. This requires holding together two separate views of hurt. The first view accepts and takes seriously both your partner's hurt and your own. You can learn to hold the hurt lovingly, do Openhearted Listening around it, and investigate how you can be of help in healing it. This helps avoid the Spiritual Mistake, the view from "on high."

In the second view, we are interested in going beyond the sense of victimhood that arises from fear, avoiding the Psychological Mistake. A clearer, less fear-based view tells you that as an adult, you cannot be psychologically hurt by another. To realize this is to challenge, any time you feel hurt, the notion that your partner did it to you. It is sometimes difficult to hold both views of hurt together in your mind. But doing so is essential, if you wish to go beyond the traditional limitations of the ego while remaining genuine in your human feelings.

The radical notion that it is you who hurt yourself alters your concept of forgiveness. It is not surprising that the ego, loving to play at being "spiritual," will take even the idea of forgiveness and distort it for its own purpose. How does the ego "forgive?" First it feels injured, victimized, righteously indignant at what has been done to it. Then it pulls itself up and proclaims grandly that it has been hurt, but it will forgive. There is a patronizing quality in this, a subtle attempt to make oneself feel superior and another feel guilty.

A moment of honesty shows that as long as one remains in this hurt posture, one has not really forgiven. But with a different perspective, you see that no one else has hurt you, and therefore there's nothing to forgive. Herein lies true forgiveness. As a couple, you have the opportunity to practice this mind-altering shift in perspective every day. One of the great gifts to bestow upon your partner is to let them know that they are innocent of ever having hurt you. Nothing can be more valuable to your mutual healing.

Thoughts from Martha

Intense pain is often what brings couples to our workshops. We have many opportunities to hear about their distress, and how it keeps the love from flowing. Each partner has their story of how the other has hurt or offended them. Sometimes they have enough insight to trace the hurt back to their childhood, to some wound that they suffered at the hands of an insensitive or troubled parent. They can explore their childhood, they can look closely at all the ways they interact with their partner, they can become familiar with all the complexities of modern psychology, and this can help peripherally. But quite commonly they're unable to move beyond this hurt.

This approach is limited because it comes out of the same thought system that produced pain in the first place. To end my pain fully, I have to go to another level, beyond the rational mind. The key lies in understanding the basis of all pain: the illusion that we are separated from the Source of All Life. All our specific instances of hurt are only tiny instances of a single enormous hurt. As long as we remain at this level, we are dealing merely with the little branches and stems of a central root.

This is why, when I'm working with couples who are lost in their conflicting stories, I often encourage them to start by turning away from their pain-producing thoughts, which tend to create agitation, confusion, and paralysis. In such cases, it always helps to be in touch with the breath. I ask the partners to breathe slowly and consciously from a soft abdomen; this tends to slow the mind down. I may ask them to visualize a peaceful scene, or to connect with some inner place of compassion, far from the territory of their issues. When the biochemistry has settled down, it is time to invite in "the witness"—the part of the soul that stands outside and observes the pain without being caught up in it. Watching one's pain, seeing how it originates in the mind, helps us understand the most important truth of all about pain: that it is self-created.

It takes a while to understand this. We generally look on pain as being caused by something or someone outside of us: a spouse, a parent, or circumstances. This makes it seem like the pain is beyond our control. But I believe that all pain comes from us not being connected to the Source of Love. When we open ourselves to that Source— and we can, at any time—our relationship to pain changes; it ceases to have such a hold on us. We see how the suffering that feels forced on us really comes from our refusal to open our hearts.. When we get caught up in the drama, we are forgetting our connection to the love and safety that surrounds us at all times. Our major work is to remember that connection. The only pain is forgetting.

Though pain is hardly a welcome guest, I can be grateful when it's strong enough to provoke a crisis. For many people, it takes an acute level of pain to turn the ship around. People at this level of suffering may be ripe for a real opportunity. Intense pain throws us off kilter because we believe in its ultimate danger. But through patience, *gentleness toward oneself, and a willingness to question assumptions, that belief can be undone. Painful events are then no longer tragedies, but merely temporary discomforts that lead to greater blessings. As difficulties present themselves, one can begin to say, "No big deal, I can handle this." When the lessons of pain are fully learned, it can be a remarkably effective teacher.*

PART II:

Working on Yourself

In the first half of this book, we have focused on how two people can bring greater understanding and compassion to their mutual interaction. However, if the intimacy is to flourish, the partners must also become interested in their inner landscapes, bringing the same qualities of understanding and compassion to themselves. Without this exploration, intimacy will quickly stir up the embers of buried issues—unconscious patterns that breed painfully repetitive and unsatisfying habits of relating.

This private inner work is like a tree with two major branches. They are not totally distinct entities, for at the base the branches are connected. But for the sake of understanding, it may help to regard them separately.

The first branch is the journey toward greater consciousness. This journey requires learning how to observe the outer and inner landscape without the usual mind chatter, without history or interpretation. When the mind's confusion dies down it becomes spacious and clear. In the light of such awareness, the pain-producing patterns of thinking and acting may be dissolved, enabling both partners to interact with more grace. Chapters 8 and 9 explore how this quality can be encouraged in daily life.

The second branch of the tree involves learning how to release the blockages to love. Understanding the mechanisms of fear and guilt—the hidden assumptions that create judgment of self and others—allows us to move toward this goal. Chapters 10 through 12 bring us to the ultimate challenge of relationship, toward which all our work has been leading: the opening of the closed heart.

CHAPTER 8

Mindfulness

The Importance of Awareness

In order to be in direct contact with the fullness of this moment, the mind, with its almost continual stream of thought, has to become still. If your mind is full of thought when you are looking at a beautiful sunset, you are not really receiving the splendor of the moment. The same is true if you are listening to a piece of music, or looking into your beloved's eyes. Thinking keeps you from awareness of what is actually taking place.

We move through the day with our mind almost continually occupied. We ruminate about money, sex, relationship, work, and a thousand trivial items. While we are thus preoccupied with our thoughts, we are living like a person in a dream: walking through life in an unconscious and mechanical state. Within this dream, we create conflict in our mind, in our home, and in the world. Those who sense the relationship between this unconsciousness and the problems in their life will naturally become interested in waking up. A key to this awakening is awareness.

It is possible to work alone and with your partner toward a more spiritual life without being directly interested in the work of awareness. But we feel its exploration will help create a more conscious and loving relationship in a number of ways.

Releasing us from our conditioning—We all have conditioned attitudes and habits, passed through generations from parent to child, that interfere with the feeling and expression of love with our partner. To become free of these reactive patterns requires that we develop the capacity to step outside of them and see ourselves unflinchingly and without distortion. This necessitates freedom from self-justification (denial of our imperfections) or self-condemnation (guilt). Living with awareness helps us see ourselves with clarity.

Particularly when we feel emotionally overwhelmed, it is important that we detach ourselves from the melodrama of our relationship and simply witness what is happening. There are times when our efforts to change things only make matters worse, because we do not have enough clarity to see what is really going on. These are the occasions to take a step back—to breathe, allow, and watch— and to refrain from becoming further entangled. The ability to let go of our habitual response is central to a conscious life. Awareness lovingly instructs us in these ways.

Becoming comfortable with difficult feelings—When darker feelings are denied or repressed, they don't go away. Unexpressed negativity tends to fester, and to create additional pain through its indirect expression. For negative feelings to serve their proper function, we must connect with them more fully. Learning the lessons that fear and pain have to teach us requires developing the elusive quality of equanimity. When we no longer cling to what is pleasant and stop resisting what is unpleasant, we develop the courage and strength to stay with what is disturbing without running away. What had previously been below the threshold of our conscious mind can be brought into focus. Awareness hones these capacities.

Seeing our flaws clearly—To be aware means, among other things, to become deeply intimate with our own self-centeredness. Only then do we begin to see the great extent to which we participate in the very flaws for which we judge others. Being mindful in daily life brings into clear focus the essential sameness of all egos: our own, our partner's, and everyone else's. We are released from feeling "better" than our partner or others, and from the righteousness that mars our perspective.

Living in the present—Awareness allows us to be more present for the fullness of this very moment. Much of our existence is spent with the uncomfortable sense that we are passing time, waiting for the curtain to rise on our *real* life, which will commence as soon as we find the right relationship, a secure situation, or some other ideal circumstance.

This attitude has an unfortunate consequence. The present moment, instead of being sufficient unto itself, is treated as a mere step to the future, in which we place all our hopes. In the meantime, longing for the onset of our true existence, we amuse ourselves the best we can, while life passes us by.

Awareness reminds us, as often as necessary, that the significance of living lies right here in this moment. It will never be other than *now*. The effect on our intimacy is profound. Since real contact with our partner depends on our full presence in the moment, the practice of mindfulness allows us to explore at new levels what it means to be truly intimate.

Connecting with our deepest truth—When the mind stops its chatter, there comes an inner silence, essential to receptivity from our deepest core. Only with the ceasing of thought do we become sensitive to prompting from the quiet wisdom within, which knows far more than the rational mind.

If you try to eat soup with a fork, you experience difficulty. The thinking, discriminating mind is like a fork. It can probe, it can pull apart, it can analyze, but it cannot contain. This is the spoon's function, which is more like the intuitive part of your mind. It is not a question of choosing between them, but of using each quality of our intelligence where it can serve us most fully.

Our intellect is best used for practical matters. Although it is an exquisite instrument, when it gets involved in trying to wrestle with the deeper issues of life, it is completely out of its domain. Only when the rational mind is silent can we be receptive to a truth that lies beyond self-deception. Awareness can be a gateway to an entirely new dimension, one in which things are not what they seem, and the Universe is recognized as safe and loving.

Freedom from Judgment

The most pervasive and stubborn obstacle to connecting with our deeper truth is the tendency to judge whatever we encounter as either good or bad. Virtually all our perceptions get filtered through this judgment, which occurs both consciously and unconsciously. The mind, which is constantly evaluating according to its prejudices, prevents the direct seeing of things as they are. Hung-jen, the Fifth Patriarch of the Ch'an Buddhist tradition, said, "The Perfect Way knows no difficulty, except that it avoids all preference."

This truth is also acknowledged in the biblical story of the Garden of Eden. Mankind's stay in the simple beauty of paradise is ended by the eating of the apple from the tree of the knowledge of good and evil. Although discernment has its place in daily life, the mind must learn how to function without passing judgment, if it is to find the freedom it so powerfully craves. Teachings of every tradition attempt in their own fashion to depict this truth.

In watching the parade of outer and inner events without judgment, a quality arises which has been traditionally called the "witness." In this state, there are no opinions about the rightness or wrongness, goodness or badness, of what is perceived. There are no beliefs and values, nor is there a need to analyze. The mind is empty and spacious, and regards with equanimity all that occurs as part of the passing show.

Once you have developed the capacity of the witness, you are no longer merely a pawn in life's game. You can choose where, when, and how you will invest yourself in your relationship. You are free to live a caring, passionate, deeply involved existence without the fear of drowning in your own feelings, or of being consumed by the relationship.

Furthermore, the witness plays a crucial role in the release of uncomfortable feelings. Trying directly to get rid of disturbing feelings is a mistake. Resistance, however subtle, guarantees that the feelings will be strengthened, and in this way we perpetuate what we most dislike. If you are experiencing something unpleasant, it's not possible to let go of it until you first acknowledge it, embrace its existence, and allow yourself to feel it fully.

Change occurs not from your attempts to change, but from the pure light of understanding. It requires finding a part of yourself that can stand outside emotions, fears, beliefs, judgments, or desires. The witness is simply aware that these emotions are taking place and is able to embrace anger, pain, and fear. Your feelings are simple facts, to be greeted in an absolutely choiceless fashion, neither clinging nor resisting. Only then comes the understanding that leads to release.

Releasing the Image of Ourselves

In addition to letting go of judgment, a clear vision requires that the mind release its images from the past. When we regard something through an image, a symbol, or a name, we don't see it as it really is. Try looking at the mysterious being we call a cat without the word "cat" appearing in your mind. You may catch a glimpse of something far more interesting when you don't have the symbolic word in your head.

An even more challenging test is to look into the eyes of your partner without the intrusion of the past. You may see them in a new way. Whatever you regard through an image will limit your perception to an interpretation, rather than to what is actually taking place.

This is equally true when the object of your attention is your self. Through the years, we have built up an image of ourselves, positive and negative, which we have a vested interest in maintaining. For example, many of us like to carry the image of ourselves as basically decent and kind. Whenever we have a stirring of dark feelings, our nice-person image is profoundly threatened. In order to protect the sanctity of this frozen image, we develop inner mechanisms of denial that prevent these negative feelings from reaching our conscious awareness. As a result, our vision of ourselves becomes seriously distorted.

On the other hand, if we carry an image of ourselves as fundamentally unloving, selfish, cynical, or emotionally crippled, we may feel too threatened to let ourselves feel the genuine love that lies beneath these defenses.

Any image you have of yourself, whether positive or negative, will distort what you see. Therefore, your self-image is an extremely important subject for investigation. First, become aware of the image, without making the fact of it bad or wrong. Then witness the image and stop identifying it as yourself. As you begin to see this image as just one more occurrence in your mind, rather than as some kind of absolute truth about who you are, the image will lose its all-consuming hold over you.

Experiencing Awareness

To perceive without judgment, to let go of the images of the past, is to see a different way. If you would like to explore this state of mindfulness, start this instant to be aware of the feeling of your body. Now include your breathing in your awareness. Notice how this causes your consciousness to be more centered in the present moment.

When the mind has quieted down, your awareness, which began with your breath and body, can broaden to encompass sights, sounds, and smells. Explore these without letting the mind rush to define what is going on. Notice how pure listening brings a quality of quiet alertness, especially when you listen to the silence between the sounds.

After remaining for a while in this state, broaden the awareness to include inner events: thoughts, feelings, fears, desires, likes and dislikes. Perceive how the distinction between the outer and the inner is actually just a creation of thought. Note that thought is the basic obstacle in being aware.

Tune in to the totality of what is going on in this very moment without judging, analyzing, or interpreting it. No longer are you greeting the present with the past. In this state of mindfulness, or awareness, you are open to learn a great deal about yourself.

Meditation

What you have undertaken is meditation. Meditation is an ancient spiritual resource, a means by which you can close the doors to the expectations of the world, the incessant cravings of the restless mind, and turn within to the Source of Life. It is the quality of mind that observes life in silence, without judging. It is also an inquiry into the essential nature of the one who watches: the "me," or the self.

Meditation is also a very practical discipline. It is helpful to set a time aside for being quiet because this permits your energies to harmonize, and a spacious quality of consciousness to emerge. We feel there is great value in spending time each day in such a state. In fact, when Martha and I begin our day in this fashion (our usual practice), we notice ourselves to be more conscious and in tune for the rest of the day. When we do it together, we unite our energies. If both partners meditate together on a regular basis, they are likely to find a new blessing entering their life.

Techniques abound to raise your energy, to bring quietness, focus, and balance. You may find value in experimenting with such tools. Concentration on the breath, or a word or phrase, can help focus the mind. Seclusion, fasting, sensory deprivation, or other self-imposed forms of austerity can sometimes intensify the depth of your experience.

However, meditation is not merely sitting in a certain position or applying a particular technique. Techniques are only ways of

Don't Respond to the Ego

When your partner is hurting, you may be tempted to relate to their ego (the fearful, self-centered part of their mind) as if it should be reasoned with. However, there is no value in arguing with the ego at its own level, trying to convince it of its errors. This just serves to strengthen the ego and grant it greater reality. Your opposition demonstrates your tacit acceptance of the whole distorted thought system upon which it is based. There is no need to oppose what is unreal.

Rather than reacting to the voice of fear, respond instead to the spirit underneath the ego. Be like an X-ray, which passes through the flesh as if it weren't there and goes right to the bone.

It takes wisdom to see beyond the content of your partner's negativity. If the content is obviously insane, it's relatively easy to offer compassion. If your partner were sick and delirious and claimed that you had just landed from a spaceship as part of an alien plot against them, it would be possible to distance yourself from the message because it would be so palpably false. You could respond instead to the pain behind the attack. But if, because of their pain, your partner denigrates you by asserting something that you secretly suspect to be true—something that touches on your feeling of unworthiness—it hits closer to home. This is black-belt work.

When your partner seems to be rejecting you, it takes some tuning in to determine their true need. Train yourself to slow down. Listen closely, the way you would to a young child who is telling you to go away. When my son was younger, during times of upset he would sometimes put out a surface message that told me to leave him alone. There were times when it was plain that he didn't want me near him, and I respected that. But there were other times when I could tell that he really wanted me to coax him out of it. The trick is to discern the subtle difference between the real "no" and the "no" that's a "yes." Listen carefully to the nuances of nonverbal communication. Then you won't take your partner's seeming rejection as their ultimate truth.

focusing energy and quieting the mind. The exploration of consciousness beyond the limitations of the ego is far too deep and subtle an activity to be reduced to mere technique.

What does it mean to function without a "me," a self, an ego, a center? In daily life, the mind behaves as if this ego were an absolute reality. Most thoughts, as well as fears and desires, revolve around it. All efforts to control one's environment and find security arises from this center. All friction and conflict stem from the entity that calls itself "me." Fear is the essence of this "me." Wherever there is pain, anger, confusion, conflict, at the center of it all is the "me." An old German poem says,

> "Wherever I go
> I go too
> And spoil everything."

Is it possible for this ego to come to an end? Can consciousness free itself from the illusion of the separate self? Can it function in an entirely different mode, without the conflict, fear, and pain associated with this center? Meditation is a way to explore this fundamental issue without any preconceived notions, through deep and silent inquiry into the nature of one's true identity.

Is there a "me" meditating? If so, who is he/she? If not, what is going on here? How does one inquire? Who is asking? Who or what is going to answer? A bit of investigation will soon reveal that if you employ thought to explore new territory, all you will get is a mind playing around uselessly within the framework of what it already knows. A mind that turns to itself will sooner or later come to see that thought will not go very far, and that another mode of inquiry is needed. There is no need, however, to make an *effort* to silence your thoughts in pursuit of a quiet mind. True silence comes when the mind ceases all pursuit, when it stops trying to grab hold, figure out, nail down, and control.

Even concentration, however useful it is for finding quiet at the start, can be seen as an effort of the self because it involves control. It takes effort to exclude whatever you are not concentrating on. Any concentration of energy around a privileged point is still an expression of the self. The same is true if there is a goal. If you make a non-judging mind into an objective, then of course you begin to judge how much you are judging. That process simply tightens the knot in your heart. With any goal, however subtle, meditation becomes but another activity of the self.

An ending is needed to all goals, thoughts, judgments, and images. If the mind makes an effort to direct the investigation, that effort still arises out of the "me." Freedom from the "me," then, requires no effort, no control, no choice or preference. There can be no plan, no preconceived path, no technique or strategy.

What remains? If all activities of the "me" cease, all that remains is pure awareness. If you have gone this far, you can explore whether there is a self—a meditator who is meditating, a watcher who is watching—or whether there is just what is happening—ever changing, yet always in the "now." You may discover that without the belief in the one who is meditating, all conflict will come to an end.

What happens to time in such a state? Without thought, where are the past and the future? They are seen as nothing other than the content of present thought. In a state of mindfulness, time comes to an end, and one remains in the eternal now. Without thought bouncing back and forth from the past to the future, where is the "me"? It is seen as an image from the past, having no more reality than a dream. A state without time is also without the "me." All that remains is the eternal now.

Perhaps meditation had begun as simply another activity of the "me." But now the seemingly separate self that got into this out of its own ambition or despair begins to connect with something vaster than itself. No longer can identity be defined so tightly, so imperviously, so rigidly. Consciousness, having let go of its images and self-conceptions, is now available to learn its true nature.

The Meditative State in Daily Life

It is relatively easy to practice being aware while sitting undisturbed on a cushion. Many who have developed this capacity, however, find that their prized equanimity evaporates with alarming rapidity when they are faced with an upset partner. Perhaps this is a message that mindfulness needs to expand to include every aspect of life, including our emotional habits and responses under a variety of circumstances.

Once you have learned to become quiet when there is no distraction, you may then find yourself being more frequently in a mindful state when you are taking a walk, driving your car, or doing the dishes. Then, perhaps, you might be able to maintain mindfulness in the midst of relationship. Continued practice may allow you to remain centered during a mildly upsetting moment. Finally, even when a moment of conflict explodes unannounced, you may find yourself responding consciously, rather than being totally reactive. Such moments are a great encouragement on your path to freedom.

Thoughts from Martha

Don and I approach mindfulness from two different directions, each linked to a different style of meditation practice. Don's approach to meditation is to use the mind as a sharply attuned instrument of awareness. His method is that of investigation, being with whatever "is" in the moment, simply observing its nature without commentary or judgment. It's like shining a powerful, radiant crystal light on experience, especially on the unconscious thoughts and beliefs that limit us. This method brings wonderful clarity and insight, and I've learned both to appreciate the way Don uses it, and to use it myself.

My own practice has a somewhat different quality. I approach my inner world through the medium of devotion, reaching out in love and gratitude to the Source of All Being. I believe there is a magnet of love pulling us all Home, into the embrace of what I see as the feminine aspect of God, or Divine Mother. Through prayer, through my heart singing to God, and especially through meditation, I awaken my deeper consciousness, my remembrance of my Divine heritage. Whenever I am in communion with this reality, I become part of a vast One-ness, complete and joyful.

There was a time when Don and I saw these different paths as divergent. I confess, when I started on mine, I thought of it as somehow better, more complete—as though Don's path were missing something. I even tried to convince him to change, to move closer to my way. Of course my implied judgment of his path as somehow inferior hardly won him over. The irony is that our efforts at meditation—intended to bring us both peace and harmony—were in fact creating a small, nagging tension in our relationship.

We can laugh about this now, since it's clear to both of us that our paths are not opposed at all, but complementary. In a way they represent dual poles: the male and the female, inquiry and surrender, the austere and the passionate, the skeptical and the faithful, wisdom and love. They are simply different aspects of the universal aspiration for wholeness. Now that we see this truth clearly, our paths have become mutually enriching. Each of us has learned tremendously from the other, and neither of us would wish it otherwise. The message to other couples is that they don't need to be in lock-step spiritually, that all paths converge ultimately at the apex of truth and love.

A question that I'm sometimes asked is: If meditation means being without choice, fully accepting of what is, how do I reconcile my reaching out in devotion to embrace the Divine Spirit? I can only say that for me, the yearning for the Divine is part of "what is." It is my deepest reality. My daily thoughts, so used to being engaged with the business of the world, need a great jolt of commitment and devotion to allow me to rise above "the dream" and into a land of inspiration and love. When I align my thoughts with the reality of my intimate, primary relationship with the Divine—thoughts that reflect love, peace, and joy—I feel connected to my soul. When my thoughts fall out of that harmony, I go back and choose, once again, the thoughts that keep me buoyant. I choose these thoughts over and over, from moment to moment. It is my way of being in the present. In a sense, I train my consciousness to go to thoughts that breed happiness, because those thoughts are more reflective of truth.

For me, this is mindfulness. *Often I pause in what I am doing during the day, whether it's gardening, washing the dishes, or preparing for a session with a client, and offer up a prayer, attuning my thoughts to the Divine or simply saying, "Divine Mother, I love you." This practice shifts my whole consciousness into the loving present. It allows me to feel, through a deep surrender, how vast, time-less, spaceless, and blissful my soul is, and to put the love of the whole universe into each little thing I do.*

To me it seems simple. I feel no need to analyze, interpret, or under-stand. I just need to remember to offer and receive love in this moment. It is a gesture that never fails to bring me Home.

CHAPTER 9

Energy Leaks and Discipline

What Are Energy Leaks?

G. I. Gurdjieff likened humans to great balloons that have a constant supply of air being pumped into them. But these balloons remain only partially full due to a number of leaks. Our leaks are holes through which available energy flows out and gets wasted. This needless drainage keeps us from feeling fully alive and operating at maximum potential. It also keeps us from having the energy and focus to be aware.

We all have our own unique forms of leakage, generally a few major holes interspersed with a larger number of minor ones. Typical leaks might be too much alcohol, poor eating habits, lack of exercise, insufficient sleep, stressful work, stressful marriage, low self-esteem, frequent self-criticism, too much mindless entertainment, unprocessed emotional toxicity, lack of real meaning in daily activities, and so on.

Plugging the leaks increases available energy. Every time a leak is plugged, our balloon inflates, and we feel more alive. Any significant transformation must take into account one's own individual pattern of leaks. It makes little sense to put effort into plugging relatively minor leaks when energy is rushing out through a major one. To a person smoking two packs a day, eating organic rice is not likely to contribute much in the way of improved energy or health. But whatever the pattern of our leaks, our intimacy will suffer until both partners become familiar with their leaks and develop effective ways of dealing with them.

Agitation and Dullness

Energy leaks not only detract from the amount of energy, they also detract from its quality. We were designed to function optimally with a feeling of vitality and a quiet, calm energy. For most of us, energy leaks lead to an absence of either calmness or vitality. The first produces agitation, the second produces dullness. Both are imbalances that intensify the difficulty of living together consciously.

Agitation is a continual fidgeting, physical and mental, that sends us racing ahead of our breath. We lean forward into the future with nervous energy. We are decidedly uncomfortable when there is nothing to distract us. Our restless mind endlessly searches the future and past for comfort and pleasure. Agitation means being stressfully on the go; it is ambition, hedonism, tension, and release. Agitation is rock music, neon lights, rush hour traffic, too much coffee, the need for a drink. In such a state, one finds it virtually impossible to stop and savor the show. Agitation is endemic among the young, and is often found more in urban dwellers. The natural bent of agitation is to seek further agitation until at last we weary ourselves and become dull. Tiring of our own nervous energy, we overeat, drink too much, or do something else to bring ourselves down, which leads to dullness.

Dullness, the opposite of vitality, is another feeling we all know. It is marked by the low energy that comes after overindulgence. We are able to function, but the spark of creativity is missing. Dullness is the escape from pain into mindlessness, avoiding the intensity of the moment, with the predictable consequence of feeling less alive. Dullness is watching too much TV. It is Muzak. It is boring, repetitive work. It is too much alcohol or tranquilizers. It is a body lacking exercise, staying indoors too much. It is comfortable, shopworn opinions, repetitive discussions about other people's affairs. Many of us, as we get older, begin to slide imperceptibly into dullness, which becomes the space we inhabit.

Sometimes, getting bored with dullness, we may begin again seeking out some pleasure that we hope will bring back the feeling of aliveness. Generally, all it brings is the return to agitation. For many of us, this pendulum swing between agitation and dullness is the only quality of energy we know. When we have energy, it is scattered or nervous. When we are calm, there is little life force behind it. Seldom do we notice how both of these common states help us escape reality by rendering us insensitive.

We make ourselves insensitive because we wish to avoid feeling uncomfortable. A sensitive being will feel everything completely, pleasant or otherwise. Becoming insensitive is a classic strategy to soften the edge of uneasiness. In the process, the capacity to be mindful is seriously curtailed.

The Sources of Agitation and Dullness

It is not difficult to discover the more obvious sources of insensitivity. Agitation is the result of too much input or nervous animation. Watch the state of mind after any hectic activity. You will probably have difficulty being quiet, unless you have become exhausted. Too much loud or inharmonious music brings agitation. The media, with its overwrought pacing and excessive violence, jangles the nervous system. Constant talk, movement, disturbance, and worry are agitating, as are too much stress or change. Excessive sweets create a jumpy mind. And, of course, the misuse of certain drugs, notably caffeine, cocaine, and amphetamines, help create a chronically agitated state.

Dullness is just as easy to trace. One of its chief sources is overeating. Not getting enough exercise is another, as is too much mindless entertainment. Overuse of drugs can also dull the system, some immediately (barbiturates and tranquilizers, for example), and others later.

Habitual patterns of thought and behavior bring dullness. Just as too much change breeds agitation, too much unbroken routine fosters dullness. Dullness can be an early warning for disease and premature aging. And finally, a most tragic source of dullness is a fundamental lack of interest in one's work, or the absence of meaning in one's life.

In resigning ourselves to living between the twin poles of agitation and dullness, we have forgotten their original purpose, which is to provide feedback when the system is out of balance. A balanced person, neither agitated nor dull, has an abundance of energy, like a fine, well-tuned engine in neutral. Calm and centered, the energy springs instantly to life when there is challenge, returning to quiet when the challenge is over. The system is alert, at peace with itself, harmonious, and capable of real creativity.

Without realizing it, we long for this balance. We desire both vitality (the absence of dullness) and peace (the absence of agitation). The difficulty comes from misreading the feedback that tells us when we're out of balance.

Listening to Feedback

At every moment, our system, like all of life, self-corrects disharmony by sending itself messages about its state. The function of these messages is to alert the organism to action whenever it's out of balance. This follows a principle similar to that of a thermostat. When the temperature goes beyond certain limits, the mechanism is designed to turn itself on or off, in order to get back within the desired range. The process is called "feedback," and it plays a vital role in living harmoniously. When we feel thirsty or cold, it means the body is sending a message to the mind to pay attention. If we listen properly to this feedback, we take some action, such as drinking water or putting on a sweater. This brings the system back into balance.

While we are normally aware of the grosser forms of feedback, we have not been educated to appreciate the nuances of more subtle varieties. Agitation and dullness are often not recognized as indicators of imbalance. When these states arise, we try to escape from their discomfort. We would do better to listen carefully to what they tell us about our lifestyle, habits, or recent behavior. When we feel dull, we often counteract it with caffeine or sugar. When we are agitated, we reach for a drink. These ways of tinkering with our nervous system may seem effective in the short run, but sooner or later they brings us to the opposite extreme. Nature has designed our little discomforts as an efficient way of getting our attention. Because we haven't learned this lesson, our traditional responses to agitation and dullness tend to create more of the same.

We ignore these early warnings to our peril. For example, a man may disregard a feeling of chronic tiredness, frequent colds, or waking up dispirited. In the next stage, the feedback becomes more intense. The man may now get pneumonia, or perhaps become involved in a minor accident—again, nature's way of asking him to pay attention. If the second level of feedback goes unheeded, the volume gets turned even higher. The next stage might be a heart attack, cancer, or a serious accident.

Disharmony always gives signals. If we learn the art of listening to our feedback, lessons don't have to be so painful. But when pain does come, it can be a blessing in disguise, because it has the capacity to shake us loose from habits we need to release. The crisis stage is often the result of a long-term refusal to change.

Energy Leaks and Total Diet

A relationship that breaks free from the prison of the past requires awareness. You can't do the work of transformation while you are unconscious. But by their very nature, agitation and dullness both make being conscious quite arduous. When you are moving fast, it's hard to appreciate the scenery; when the mind is racing, it's difficult to be in touch with what's happening. But it's similarly difficult to be tuned in when the mind is dull, because alertness requires energy. When you are agitated or dull you simply forget to be conscious. Both these states can be seen as hindrances to a conscious relationship.

It's worth investigating how to transform these qualities. The key is in learning to plug your energy leaks. And the first step in doing that is to become aware of your total diet.

This process is just what the name implies. The quality of your energy is affected by the raw material you take in, just as the quality of a plant is influenced by the nature of the soil. And the raw material you absorb involves a great deal more than merely the food you eat. You also eat with your senses, your mind, and your heart. Your total diet has many aspects:

- quality and amount of food
- drugs
- air
- relationships
- sleep
- variety and balance of activities
- sex
- order or disorder at home
- time alone or in contact with nature
- entertainment
- music
- reading materials

It may seem strange at first to consider the sights and sounds of the world as food. But consider the total effect on your being if you spend a week in the mountains, taking in the air, the vast and inspiring panorama, the rustle of the wind against a backdrop of deep silence. This is nourishment of the highest quality, satisfying and healing.

Now consider on the other hand a week spent in a clamorous office or a factory, in rush-hour traffic, smoky bars, or a chaotic home—a week filled with blaring music, TV, loud voices, radio commercials, relational dissonance. Just as the body functions less efficiently on junk food, so the mind is bogged down and polluted by unharmonious sense impressions. Everything we take in gets digested and turned into consciousness, whose quality reflects the nature of the input.

If you want to begin changing the quality of your consciousness, take a careful look at your total diet. There are total diets that inspire more awareness, and those that allow forgetting. If you and your partner are serious about leading a more conscious life together, you may want to review your total diet for a typical week and ask yourselves if it is in alignment with your deepest purpose.

Some Common Energy Leaks

Most people have developed their own personal assortment of self-destructive habits, ways of not being true to themselves. It is not our interest to pass judgment on these habits, but rather to examine their effect on consciousness. Here are some of the habits that frequently result in energy leaks. (Note the significant overlap between these and the traditional escapes from intimacy described in Chapter 5.)

Incessant activity—Many don't know what it feels like to have their organism running healthily, because it is overheated from ceaseless movement. Other than when we are exhausted, we rarely halt activity altogether. Indeed, the thought rarely even occurs to us. Too seldom do we sit under a tree and watch the clouds, or quietly nourish ourselves with the ever-changing music of a stream. Many of us would plug a significant energy leak if we balanced our doing with more being.

There is a rhythm between the outward and the inward flow, between making contact with others and resting, between expressing yourself and withdrawing. When your energy moves according to this natural rhythm, both action and rest are restorative.

Poor eating habits—Many of us simply eat too much. For others, the problem lies in the quality of nourishment. Food that has been refined and devitalized has had many nutrients drained from it. Your being responds to the wholesomeness of the food you eat.

Addictions—This is a vast topic. Besides food and obvious chemical substances, there are many other activities and behavioral patterns that can fall into this category: sex, overstimulation, emotional crises, depression, and so forth.

Addiction to alcohol and other drugs, a highly prevalent phenomenon, is beyond the scope of this book. If you suspect this addiction is an energy leak in your life, try doing without it for one month. If it proves really difficult, there's a good chance you have a problem, in which case outside help may be called for. If your partner has a problem, we recommend getting help of your own, perhaps through counseling or through an organization such as Al-Anon.

Addictions interfere with our natural feedback mechanisms. For example, if you are addicted to caffeine, you will interpret the feeling of tiredness (actually the body's call for rest) as signaling a need for more caffeine. Also, with caffeine, you get used to a much higher level of tension in the nervous system, which then becomes your normal way of feeling. Many households, unaware of the role caffeine can play in the emotional climate, have become accustomed to low-level irritability as a standard background hum.

It's interesting to note the frequent connection between caffeine and alcohol use. Regular use of caffeine strains the nervous system, so that by the latter part of the day, one craves to soften the harsh edges. Alcohol is one way of accomplishing this, since for some it does balance out the irritability (if you like alcohol, caffeine may increase your craving for that drug). The next day, the system is further dulled and depleted, and desires yet more caffeine to stay alert. This in turn produces more craving for alcohol, and so on. Some substitute sugar for caffeine, which can have a similar reaction. A remarkable number of us are caught up in this cycle.

Entertainment, too, can be a major addiction. Activities such as watching movies or TV aren't necessarily in themselves energy leaks; the problem is their misuse. There's no harm in consciously balancing your focused intensity by relaxing with a detective story, a TV program, or a ball game. But if you use these things to avoid other areas of life, then you invite serious energy leaks.

Lack of rest—Not too many people these days get regular, high-quality sleep. What makes this difficult to recognize as an energy leak is that moderate sleep deprivation doesn't always show up as fatigue. Instead, the symptoms are often similar to those of excess caffeine use: irritability, depression, and a ragged nervous system. We become so used to these symptoms that we don't suspect they might be signaling a need for change. For some, an hour or two more of sleep each night might bring back a peace they have long forgotten.

Lack of proper exercise—The body contributes far more than we realize to the totality of how we feel. Many of us get used to a body that feels deadened, not realizing how much it affects the quality of our consciousness. When the body lacks vitality, the mind becomes dull, often without us realizing it.

Lack of exercise, like other energy leaks, can be a self-perpetuating habit. Feeling uncomfortable with a sluggish body, one attempts to energize it with various stimulants. After the initial boost, the system crashes and is left further depleted. In this state, exercise is even more distasteful. The resulting inactivity completes the vicious circle.

To break out of this arduous cycle, think of pushing a stuck car. A great burst of energy is required to get it going, but once the car is moving, a much lighter push will keep it in motion. Breaking free of sloth is similar.

If you wish to step out of the prison of dullness, bring your physical energy more to life. Stretch, move, dance, and free your body so you can more fully liberate the vitality within you. Just as you cannot easily play beautiful music through a clogged instrument, it is difficult to feel joy when your body's needs have been dishonored.

Poor breathing—Emotions and breathing have an interesting relationship. Positive emotions are associated with deep, regular, and slower breathing; negative ones, with breathing that's shallow, irregular, and faster. When your emotions change, your breathing is affected. But it works equally the other way: Changing your breathing has a significant effect on your emotions.

The first way to change your breathing is simply to become aware of it. The second is to soften your diaphragm. The predominant features of breathing associated with feelings of freedom, peace, and joy are a soft belly and a relaxed diaphragm. The belly expands on inhale while the chest remains relatively steady. Try consciously breathing in this fashion, sitting or lying for a few minutes, doing nothing but being aware of your breath. In this position, you may find it harder to hold on to difficult feelings. Experiment with it and you will come to appreciate the powerful effect that conscious breathing can have on your emotional state.

Lack of touch—The need to be touched is most obvious with babies (and the young of other animals), but it is equally present in the rest of us. Lack of touch deprives us of a basic nutrient.

For touch to be nourishing, it needs to be loving and conscious. (Sexual touch can be, though it often isn't.) Massage is an excellent way of offering this gift. Even five or ten minutes of massaging the head, neck, shoulders, feet, back, or any other place that calls for attention, can fill an extremely important gap.

Many older people cease to receive touch, much to their detriment. Learning the value of touch now may help you and your partner to continue enjoying it as you get older.

Repression of feelings—Unexpressed feelings have a habit of turning in on themselves. They become disease, depression, fatigue, hostility, sexual shutdown, passive-aggressive behavior, or emotional paralysis. When the feelings are not engaged, they tend to atrophy; this tends to reduce one's vitality in almost every area.

Stressful relationships—These can be among the most powerful and prevalent energy leaks. We hope this book will be of help.

Alienation from nature—It is useful to recognize the feeling we get when we have been indoors too much. For us, it is a musty, stuffy feeling in the mind, a bit like being in a dank, ill-lit prison. Its symptoms are easily relieved by spending time outdoors, away from the clamor. Nothing brings balance and perspective to a troubled heart more surely than allowing nature's harmony to enter and heal.

Lack of solitude—We bring so much more to our intimacy when we take time to be alone. A by-product of our addiction to activity is our perpetual engagement with others. Our connections with others are important, yet many of us in the modern world get swept up into a life of nervous, agitated energy. The result is a profound imbalance. When we leave ourselves no respite from company, we allow a major source of nourishment to dry up. Drinking at the fountain of silence occurs most often when we are alone.

Not doing what we love—Were we not designed to get up in the morning with passion for what the day brings? The notion of "work" that most of us have is a strange one, antithetical to the natural rhythms of life. So many of us accept long hours of doing what we don't really care for. Even when not technically working, we often neglect the things that truly nourish us. When we step back to take a broader look, we may find we are no longer living according to our true priorities.

If life has lost its passion, perhaps your spirit is asking you to rediscover your true needs. If you take time to renew your spirit, you will be better able to distinguish true needs from counterfeit ones. What you never truly wanted will never satisfy in any quantity.

We feel it's especially important for women to find ways of nourishing themselves outside the relationship. (This doesn't mean sexually!) By so doing, they help dissolve the resentment that may arise from perpetually giving and caretaking. In addition, they will be lightening the pressure their partners may feel to keep them happy and contented. It is not selfish to make time for what truly replenishes your spirit. On the contrary, it is an act of rejuvenation that liberates you to more effective action.

Resistance—This is a fundamental energy leak, arising from the very way our minds operate. When we inwardly oppose what is happening, we freeze energy that could otherwise be in circulation, diminishing our basic aliveness. Discomfort in daily life arises far more from our resistance than from the circumstances we are resisting.

The phenomenon takes many forms, but it always involves a sense that things should be other than what they are. This feeling—so pervasive in our consciousness—produces a tightening of both mind and body. Our fear that the future won't unfold the way we wish is often accompanied by an anxious effort to control. We resist our partner's behavior, the state of our health, our moods and feelings, our financial fortunes, and, in general, whatever isn't going the way we prefer. This tendency is so deeply rooted in the human condition, that learning acceptance has been a major theme in the world's great spiritual teachings.

The thought process—This is the ultimate energy leak. It is so much the ocean we swim in that it may not seem anything special. But as we have seen from the preceding chapter, a great waste of energy occurs from fearful thinking.

Eliminating Energy Leaks

Taking care of energy leaks will increase and harmonize your energy. It will also nourish the spiritual side of your intimacy by creating conditions for greater awareness of your interactions.

The way two people start the day can set the tone for both their levels of consciousness. The tradition of pouring a cup of coffee and sinking into the newspaper leads in one direction. A different way might be for the two of you to start the day by reading something together, something that reminds you of the perspectives you'd both like to carry through your day. Meditating together, even if for a short while, is another way of encouraging conscious priorities. The conclusion of your day also deserves attention, for it determines the kind of energy you carry into your sleep.

Take time every day to allow the agitation of daily life to settle. It helps to meditate, do yoga, or practice any discipline that balances and harmonizes your energy. Share your common interest in becoming more conscious, more loving. Talk about your successes as well as your struggles, and acknowledge each other for the work you have been doing. Open yourselves frequently to what your deeper wisdom would have you know on your path.

Stay in touch with nature on a regular basis. If possible, take frequent walks in beautiful places together. Keep the body sensitive in whatever ways you can. Tack up reminders in your home. It helps to form alliances with others who are also trying to awaken. Meet with other couples who are trying to be conscious. Remind each other lovingly of what is important and what isn't. Support and encourage each other in activities that foster greater aliveness and awareness.

The Fruits of Yoga

One activity in particular has been a great blessing for Martha and me in nurturing sensitivity of mind and body during the past thirty-five years. Shortly before meeting Martha, I had discovered hatha, or physical yoga, and shared the practice with her. At thirty-two, I was beginning to feel the first signs of aging. Here was something that I could tell would have a profound effect upon the way the body aged. Within a few short weeks of starting yoga, I could already feel a noticeable difference in the way my body felt and moved.

The feeling is difficult to put into words, for I had never felt it before. I felt younger, but without the nervous energy I was accustomed to. I felt more like a wild animal moving with grace. I breathed deeper, more slowly. My posture became naturally more erect. I felt more alert and energized, yet more relaxed. When I sat down, an instantaneous tranquility would often come over me.

Besides transforming the way I felt, yoga also taught me an important lesson about how to respond to tightness, whether physical or mental. Traditionally, one either does battle with tightness or ignores it. Neither is effective. To fight against tightness is resistance, which only serves to increase the tightness. But ignoring it is an equally inadequate response, since tightness is a message from the system to do something.

Without an appropriate response to tightness, the body ages without grace. Most people stay away from the tight areas of their bodies, the places where the muscles are becoming unnaturally rigid. As a result, the body begins to close in on itself. With age, the range of movement becomes increasingly limited, the tissues tighten up, and there is a diminishing of energy flow to the various organs, bringing slow atrophy. We generally think of this as normal aging.

Yoga showed me what it means neither to battle tightness nor to ignore it, but to use a the third alternative of experimenting with it consciously. Shortly after beginning yoga, I learned that its essence involves what I call playing the edge.

The "edge" is a degree of stretch that lies somewhere between comfort and pain. When stretching brings pain, one has gone beyond the edge. When stretching is totally easy and comfortable, it hasn't yet approached the edge. The postures of yoga serve as highly refined tools for exploring the nature of the body's limits. When explored consciously, they can open up long-held areas of tightness.

Yoga is a deep leverage for change whose practice explores the nature of blocked energy and allows us to come into direct contact with the nature of resistance in the body, so that we can actually feel the blocks. Working with these blocks in intimate and subtle ways helps the body to begin breaking out of confining patterns. Slowly but surely, by repeatedly going to the edge and staying there, the edge begins to move.

This proved remarkably true in my case. Postures that appeared impossible at first, yielded over time to an almost miraculous loosening of the tissues. The edges moved further and further back with little apparent effort on my part, though I did allow myself to linger as consciously as possible in places of intensity. I came to see that the quality of my yoga depends not on how flexible I am, but rather on the quality of attention I bring to playing my edge.

Playing the edge involves finding a creative balance between the polarities of control and surrender, safety and adventure. The capacity for focused attention is thus refined. Using one's own body as a teacher, one changes the relationship with one's body so one is no longer alienated from it. The body can actually become more finely tuned as it ages.

Over time, I have found that the concept of playing the edge goes well beyond the physical. It applies to much of what we've talked about in this book. Hatha yoga is like entering the narrow end of a funnel: It widens into unsuspected areas, bestowing its blessings everywhere.

Discipline and Freedom

The word "discipline" has been often used to mean an attempt to force yourself to do something you would rather not be doing. But "discipline," which comes from the Latin word for "instruction" or "knowledge," can have a very different meaning in adult life, one that is essential to learning.

One part of us longs for the quiet, pristine order that flows from the life of spirit. It wearies of being driven by cravings and compulsions that are not really in our best interest. But another part insists on a passionate encounter with life through the senses, refusing to destroy passion through ruthless ascetic measures. This part of us generally has the upper hand. It wishes to satisfy desires in the moment, whenever and wherever they occur. We're feeling a bit down, so we light a cigarette, pour a drink, or head for the refrigerator. It's easy, and for the moment it works.

There is no inherent reason, really, why we shouldn't do whatever we feel like in the moment. Allowing ourselves to succumb to immediate gratification whenever we want seems, superficially, to bring us freedom. In fact, the opposite is true. Doing whatever we desire in the moment makes us a veritable slave to our cravings. Following the consequences alertly over time will show us clearly where our different desires lead, what kind of experiences they produce. Some cravings lead to energy leaks, others to greater harmony.

Seeing this, my deeper wisdom may decide that life would be more interesting and fulfilling if I were to eliminate certain unwholesome habits. But if I indulge myself in the so-called freedom to do whatever I want, whenever I want, my capacity to say no to life-denying habits is lost to me. In fact, I am caught in a rather limited sphere of behavior. Therefore true freedom requires discipline. It lies in having the capacity, in the interest of a greater good, to say no to the behaviors that no longer serve me.

The capacity for discipline is essential to eliminating energy leaks. The same universal force that urges every being toward greater aliveness and creativity is now urging you to stop doing the things that may bring immediate gratification but in the long run actually cause you to become deadened and mechanical. True discipline is not the forbidding of any particular behavior, but the capacity to listen to your deeper wisdom for guidance.

Identify the biggest (or at least the most obvious) energy leak in your life, whether it's food, drugs, lack of exercise, too much activity, mindless entertainment, or something else. Changing just that one thing often begins a chain reaction that spreads into every area of your life.

Real magic is possible when a couple explores what it would be like to get rid of energy leaks. Any kind of discipline you create with your partner will bring more consciousness into your lives. To practice that discipline together is more enjoyable. Through your mutual support, you can create structures that eliminate or lessen some of the more energy-draining aspects of your life. If you're not sure where to begin, take a few moments together, go within, and ask your deeper wisdom what areas of your life would benefit from change. With serious attention to the answers that emerge, the feeling in your home can undergo a major transformation in a surprisingly short time.

Thoughts from Martha

When Don and I first met in Alaska, we had a sense that we were pulling away from the world we had been raised in. It seemed as though that culture as a whole was designed to distract us from our real purpose in life: waking up from the dream and finding our deepest selves. We both strongly suspected that there was more to life than just eating, sleeping, working, socializing, and entertaining ourselves. And so we set out to create a different life, one with fewer distractions, one with more spaciousness and silence both within and without.

We still want that, deeply. But our path, like that of so many others, eventually led us back into the world of work, family, and relationships. And to live in this world, especially in the America of the twenty-first century, is a challenge. Our culture puts great pressure on us to expend our energy outwards: buying things, working hard to pay for them, entertaining ourselves restlessly. None of this is inherently bad. But we do tend to become addicted to the frenetic lifestyle entailed in our pleasures. At worst, such a lifestyle fills us with stress and a sense of meaninglessness, and even at best, it fails to satisfy our deepest yearnings.

It's interesting to me that so many thoughtful people are similarly discontent, feeling trapped, suspecting life has another dimension. They speak wistfully of what it might be like if their pace were slower and more spacious. Many don't consider the possibility that such a life could be theirs if they began making a few different choices—ones that are more attuned to their inner being.

We've found that such choices are indeed possible. It takes a little awareness and discipline, but nothing beyond the range of ordinary people in ordinary circumstances. The key is not trying to make too many changes at once—that is usually doomed to fail—but to experiment in small ways with manageable chunks. It could mean seeing what it would be like to put the TV away for a few weeks, avoiding certain heavy or unhealthy foods for a time, or trying to stay home one evening a week instead of going out. It could mean going to fewer social gatherings and taking more walks. Or—this is how small it could be—trying to sit still for just five minutes at a time. Our lives are more pliable than we realize. There's plenty of room in everyone's life for experiments. It's always fascinating to see where experimentation leads, and none of it has to be grim or burdensome: It can all be done—it is best done—in a spirit of play.

Central to it all, in my mind, is the need for space. This means less distraction, more room for what's essential. Without space in your life, there's no way to get in touch with what's going on inside, where your soul is trying to speak to you. The busier the life, the greater the need for time set apart from it: periods of meditation, quiet communion with one's partner and with nature, longer intervals away from daily life in order to renew and fortify the spirit. This brings the inspiration and energy needed to maintain a life of integrity and joy. The biggest obstacle is the way we dissipate energy.

What is all this dissipating energy meant to do instead? That's the interesting question. We are all granted a certain amount of intelligence, life force, and creativity. Surely this was designed to be harnessed for our ultimate freedom. I believe this involves learning how to collect and focus much of the energy that normally gets wasted in the fruitless outer and inner fidgeting we call energy leaks.

I can't imagine a life without the regular injections of inspiration, quiet, and refuge that come from a different dimension. Some of the most nourishing and invigorating moments in my life are those that Don and I spend just sitting still together, opening our hearts, and absorbing the inner Presence.

Moments like those have convinced me that perhaps the biggest energy leak is not taking the time to regularly connect with the Source of Life. When I fail to do this, I become inwardly sloppy, more prone to nagging or complaining. I fall prey to my time-worn habit of failing to see Don's divine nature, and instead tend to focus on his flaws. The ups and downs of our daily life and relationship assume an undue proportion and throw me off balance. However, in the midst of confusion, a moment of remembrance, often prompted by meditation, shifts everything. I appreciate and love Don as a unique, individual soul, and my life is more centered.

Don and I find ourselves simplifying our lives as we get older. We occasionally take a whole or half day to spend in silence, allowing the energy consumed by talking and being busy to flow back into our core.

Releasing our largest energy leaks has not felt to us like a restriction, but rather an expansion, a commitment to moving at last toward our ultimate Home.

CHAPTER 10

Fear

What Is Ego?

Most people who observe themselves with any honesty will perceive fundamental aspects of themselves with which they're not comfortable, aspects they would like to change. Yet those who attempt this change inevitably find major obstacles. For change to occur, it is necessary to be intimate with these obstacles, and respectful of their strength. Where are the obstacles to be found?

Our own personal set of obstacles can be found within a certain layer of our mind. Consider our consciousness as being divided into three layers. The first is the outer layer that is our superficial personality, our conditioned mind, caught in the dream and laced with fear, but usually claiming it wants peace and love. The third or deepest layer is in the heart of our being, shining brightly with our true nature, which is nothing but love. The real challenge lies in the second, or middle layer, which is the great obstacle to change. Herein dwell the more elusive regions of our darkness, the core of our painful dream, our forgetting. Here are found the hidden, twisted threads of fear and guilt, which have an energy and influence greater than the outer layer. Because the middle layer is not conscious under normal circumstances, it is more insidious in blocking us from the direct experience of our innermost core. For any real change in our life to happen, we must take this unconscious layer seriously into account. As long as it isn't dealt with, we make a prison of it.

Gurdjieff once said that the single most important step in getting out of prison is first to recognize that you are in prison. Our prison is whatever keeps us from feeling our birthright of love and joy. We call it the "ego." We are not using the word here in the Freudian sense. Rather, we are employing it to stand for a part of the mind that we have created. The ego believes itself separate, cut off from the whole; it is therefore always in fear, incapable of love. One highly important step in attaining freedom lies in learning to recognize when we are caught in one of the ego's many forms.

The ego is a belief about who we are, arising out of an elemental misperception. Somewhere along the way, the mind came to the conclusion that it was separate from the whole, like a wave that believed itself separate from the ocean. From this single thought has emerged the entire world as we perceive it. Ego, the seemingly separate entity, lies at its center. In this perception my "self" appears to be a body, cut off from other selves, isolated from the Source of All Life. This ego, like everything in the world of form, faces the certainty sooner or later of ceasing to exist. The wave, forgetting it is part of the ocean, fears breaking on shore as the ultimate catastrophe.

The ego is the source of all the conflict and pain in our relationship, for it does not coexist with love. When ego is present, fear is the basis of consciousness, and there are problems. When love is present, there may be challenges and obstacles, but when there's no fear, there are no problems. In a way, this greatly simplifies things. Two partners, instead of confronting a great variety of problems in their intimacy, now address a single challenge: the challenge of ego. To be sure, that challenge is formidable, since it is deeply rooted, persistent, and frequently intense.

Wherever ego is found, fear lurks. Since ego is terrified of coming to an end, fear pervades its activities. Most of its responses to fear breed more fear. Release from this entanglement entails learning a different response to fear.

Fear Has Many Forms

Fear is part of the human journey, just as winter and darkness are part of the cycle of nature. It presents a precious opportunity to mature into one's full intelligence.

Nothing affects the quality of my life more significantly than the way I respond to fear. Fear displays itself incessantly in many forms throughout the day, as I relate with my partner, read the newspaper, watch TV, or interact with others, and especially as I encounter the chatter of my own mind.

Fear is a single tree with many branches: boredom, dullness, depression, illness, anxiety, pain, hurt, anger, blame, guilt, conflict, violence, worry. Like the branches that extend far from the trunk of the tree, these elements always partake of the essential quality of fear: an unhealthy tightening of mind and body, which prevents the awareness of love. Whenever love appears absent, you can be sure that fear is present.

If things are going badly, fear announces that they will never get better. The pain I'm feeling now will never go away, and it's hopeless. If things are going well, fear reminds me that it won't last, things will get worse. I'll lose my health, my relationship, my money, my job, or my good mood. Fear makes sure I never win.

Should Fear Be Our Teacher?

Lurking a few inches under the surface, fear waits to spring. It enters in the dark and promises, quite persuasively, to keep us safe. Although it goes against all reason to think that fear could keep us safe, we believe its promises. We carry layers of armor in our muscles because we feel the need for protection. In our minds we worry obsessively, cling to the past, try to control the uncontrollable future, and resist the present, seeking in vain to find a sense of security. At the emotional level, we also erect defenses for our seeming safety by closing the heart. The very mechanism we've created to protect ourselves serves to keep us from the awareness of love.

Day and night the overheated mind remains in a state of stress, contracted against the threat perceived in virtually everything. The apprehension of danger lurks in the behavior of our partner, in someone being unkind to us, in the prospect of getting older, in our work, our pleasure, our finances, our body. But no matter how adroitly we juggle our images, the threat seems unrelenting.

a fresh opportunity to choose love, to bring the light where dark-ness was, to open the heart where the heart had been closed. Choosing love is a simple gesture, ever available. It is always the same, regardless of the content.

It is a continual challenge to recognize fear in all its guises. A dis-tinct feeling occurs whenever fear seeks a place in the mind to take root and multiply. It is helpful to recognize this feeling in your body, your thinking, and your heart, as quickly as it arises. Know that this is the same voice of fear you have been believing all your life.

Fear is a poor teacher. Look where listening to it has brought us all. Consider rejecting its teaching and listen to a different teacher. Fear is cagey enough to masquerade as love, and frequently does. However, fear can always be recognized by its mode of operation. Even disguised as love, fear resists and fights, blames and judges. Fear also thrives when I reason with it, even when I fight against it, for to do either is still to accept its premise that my danger is real. Everything I do based on that premise encourages more fear. To meet fear at its own level is a great mistake.

Love does not resist, having no need to fight against fear, any more than light has to fight against darkness. Love simply shines forth, dissolving fear in its light. Love embraces the whole content of experience, pleasant or painful. Such a love lives in a place beyond the dualism of good and bad, neither clinging to the former nor resisting the latter.

Each moment that I encounter fear, I am granted the freedom to respond with yes or no. When I say yes, I am willing for this moment to be whatever it is. I am willing for my partner to have their fear or anger. I am willing for them to show me no love. I am willing to allow my own contracted feelings in response to that. I am willing for my reaction to my partner's behavior to be imper-fect. I am willing to trust the process that led us to this point. My willingness to say yes to this moment is the voice of love in action.

The moment and place where I make the decision to choose

We have taken on the habit of listening to fear because it prom-ises us something we desperately want. In myths, the devil is attrac-tive, smart, and believable. Fear is wily, and knows how to sound ever so reasonable. Indeed, there is a tiny germ of truth in fear's message, which it uses in its appeal. When the body is in genuine danger, fear plays a useful role as a call to pay close attention or to take immediate action. But other than physical danger, do we really have anything to fear? It's an interesting question. Either psycholog-ical fear is real and justified, or it is an interpretation based on an illusion.

Walking at twilight, I see a coiled rope on the ground and think it's a rattlesnake. Although my fear is palpably real, it exists because of a mistake. I am afraid, but not actually in danger. Our work is to find out if the vast majority of our fear is of this nature.

Skepticism and Faith

Despite the fact that the intellect has lately come to have a bad rep-utation in some spiritual circles, it can be a vital tool in the great task of confronting fear. Normally the mind serves and perpetuates fear by its unquestioning faith in the reality of things as they seem to be. Here is where it needs to become a little more skeptical.

Skepticism has a place in the service of spirit. It asks us to chal-lenge our most cherished beliefs, particularly the ones that tell us we are in danger. There may be reason to distrust the seemingly obvious premise of fear, so deeply ingrained in human conscious-ness. If we sense the truth of this, a vigilance arises that makes us suspicious every time fear tells us we need to defend, blame, or worry.

Although they seem to be opposites, skepticism and faith are joined at the core. They are both necessary in deciding how we shall respond to the world. We are faced with two diametrically opposed belief systems about the essence of life. One says that we are in danger, the other says that we are safe. To doubt one is to believe the other. Even those who see themselves as having no faith, in fact have a great deal of faith. The conditioned mind, skeptical of the notion that we are in fact safe, has faith in the "obvious." It believes that things are as they seem, the universe is an unsafe place, and all the defenses of fear are necessary to remain secure. Our own fear level is proof of our faith in this belief.

In the awakening mind things are reversed, for it is highly skeptical of the obvious. It challenges the notion that we are a body doomed to die, in danger everywhere, and with continual need to defend ourselves. The awakening mind has glimpses of its true safety. If some of the light shining from deep within manages to filter through the thick clouds of forgetting and enters our consciousness, we call it faith. The faith of the awakening mind rests on skepticism toward the perception of psychological danger.

The ego's central belief is that I am not safe. When I envision relationship as a spiritual path, I am trying to use every difficult situation to illuminate this crucial issue. Since intimacy is a particularly fertile field for perceiving danger, I am given endless opportunities to challenge this belief. Whenever I get upset at my partner, whenever I withdraw or go numb, I have a fine opportunity to explore my feeling of being threatened. I might typically feel threatened when my partner frowns at me, withdraws from me, uses a certain tone of voice, gets angry at me, isn't in tune with me sexually, doesn't remember to keep agreements, seems unsupportive, fails to hear my truth, and so on. Fear casts its shadow over my inner world, insisting firmly that it isn't safe to love.

Here is the question continually confronted by the spiritually oriented relationship: Is the threat genuine? If we were truly threatened, fear, with all its protective defenses, would be an appropriate response. But if the feeling of threat is based on a false belief, then we are thinking like a classic paranoid, frightened by a threat that exists only in our mind. One way to define the work of a spiritual relationship is this: to explore together the notion that we are not a threat to each other—that in fact, no threat exists.

Greeting Fear Lovingly

If the feeling of threat is only one interpretation of reality, then there must be an alternative. Fear's voice is not the only available teacher.

Although I may not be able to prevent fear from arising in my mind, I do have a choice of whether or not I accept it as my teacher. There is another teacher within, which we call "the voice of loving truth," or the Greater Wisdom. Never far from my awareness, its quiet voice remains largely unheard through the clamorous static of the fearful mind. This other teacher lets me know, any time I stop to ask, that I am now, and have always been, safe. But if I am entrenched in the habit of believing fear, I seldom ask myself what love is saying right now.

The voice of love is available even to a mind with a fearful content. The content is the changing flow of outer and inner events. The sun is shining, there is the sound of a bird in the distance, there is a pain in my knee, a feeling of low energy, a thought about food, a vague feeling of sadness, and so on. All this is content. Each moment of my life I have a choice about my fundamental posture toward the content, the way I hold it. We may call this posture or attitude the "context." I can greet the content with the context of a fundamental no, believing fear and resisting the content. However, I also have the opportunity to say yes as context, embracing the content with love. This is especially useful whenever I am confronted with fear, because if I am aware, then the fear becomes merely content. I neither deny nor repress the fear, but hold it with an embracing yes. Fear is the content, but the context is love.

What does this feel like in practice? If you are aware of fear, feel it in its purity, abandoning the thoughts that normally accompany it. Breathe deeply with a soft belly for a few breaths. Then soften around the fear, the same way you might soften your muscles around a hypodermic needle to change the experience of pain into mere sensation. This is a mental softening, as if you were rounding the fear in love. Each moment of life, each now, you have

either fear or love is usually unconscious. However, I cannot alter my decision unless I am aware of making it. Therefore, in learning to choose love, I need to learn how to be conscious of the moment and place where I make my decision.

I once became aware of such a moment when I slipped on the ice and landed quite ungracefully, the wind knocked out of me. There was a moment's pause, and then I burst unexpectedly into laughter. Just prior to the laughter, I remembered a split second of choice, a moment of truth, where I saw how I could either get really upset or laugh. I made a choice in that instant, one that felt somehow healthier.

I wish to develop this awareness more globally. The instant before I get upset with my partner, I make such a choice, probably unconsciously. I want to become aware of making that choice, so that next time I can make a different choice. I want to learn better what I've grown to suspect: at bottom it is *all* my choice. I want to make use of as many negative moments as possible to practice seeing how and why I make the choice, and then choosing differently. I will receive many opportunities, particularly with my partner.

Words can only go so far in describing the inner gesture of making the other choice, the choice of saying yes to fear. By practicing this gesture, I may find that the quality of my negative experience changes, sometimes dramatically. Whenever I greet fear with love, that very love becomes my reality. Every time I consciously lift myself above the battleground, I learn afresh that the way out of conflict is instantaneous.

By making this gesture as often as needed, I begin to suspect that the entire thought system by which I have led my life is untrue to its very core. Fear is a false teacher. To ward off fear, I have put great energy into striving for security, pleasure, or power. Clearly none of these has brought me what I truly want, and none ever will. It becomes increasingly evident that only love will bring the satisfaction I crave.

A powerful force is set in motion when a couple unites to confront fear head-on. Realizing that they have been listening for a lifetime to the voice of fear, they now combine their wisdom, reminding themselves as often as possible to listen to the voice of love. Whoever is more conscious can take the lead.

The Real Source of Discomfort

While living in Alaska, I once bought a parcel of semiremote land with a friend. We hastily erected a six-by-nine- foot sauna in which we spent the intense, frigid, mostly dark Fairbanks winter, while we built a larger cabin. It was quite an experience in intimacy!

One morning I awoke bathed in sweat, uncomfortably roasting in the overheated room. My housemate was fiddling with the wood stove. "Findlay," I yelled, "for God's sake turn that thing down and open the door. It must be a hundred degrees in here!"

Findlay turned to me and quietly murmured something about how he thought it might be nice to start the morning with a sauna. Then a strange thing happened. All of a sudden the heat, which was getting more intense by the moment, totally lost its uncomfortable quality and transformed itself magically into the friendly warmth of a sauna. I was impressed by this event, and thought about it for a long time afterwards. The same physical sensation of intense heat was experienced first as a sticky-hot, undesirable intrusion, and then suddenly as a warm, friendly sensation. If someone had asked me then about the source of my discomfort, I would have had no doubt that it lay in the physical sensation of too much heat. Yet, a moment later, the word "sauna" served to trigger a powerful change in my experience. Although perception filtered through a symbol can interfere with direct experience, in this case "sauna," standing for something desirable, allowed me to let go of my resistance to the heat. Suddenly I had given myself permission to enjoy what I had previously hated.

The meaning of this was clear. The source of my discomfort was not, as I had assumed, the simple experience of heat. Rather, it lay in the mind through which the experience got interpreted. A simple shift in perspective changed everything.

Whenever we are disturbed, we usually believe that the disturbed feeling has been created by circumstances. In intimacy, we almost always assume that we're upset because of our partner's imperfections. A major shift occurs when we begin to question the true source of our feelings.

We are not upset for the reasons that we think. We believe we are troubled with our partner because of the fact that they spoke angrily or accusingly to us. In truth, we are upset over our own interpretation of our partner's actions. Through the filter of the conditioned mind, we interpret our partner's unfair anger at us to mean that we are threatened. The discomfort we experience over this perceived threat suggests that we are seeing through a distorted lens. Our uneasiness invites us to challenge the inner posture with which we have greeted the disturbing event.

Underneath the seemingly disparate circumstances, our moments of upset actually have a monotonous similarity. He did that, she said this, which means I am unsafe. So when my partner acts unlovingly, I interpret it to mean that I am in danger.

I know I am making such an interpretation by the contracted feeling in my body and the change of energy. I know this from the black thoughts in my mind, the way I blame my partner and close my heart to them, my defensiveness, my feelings of being hurt and rejected. None of these reactions are possible when I am feeling truly safe.

I have often, when the person at the checkout counter scowled at me, left the store feeling a little bit worse than before. When a friend seems unsupportive, I feel as though my being is threatened. When Martha complains about my lack of consideration over something, I shrink inwardly. In clear moments, I perceive these interpretations as mistakes made by a confused mind. It is becoming plain that 99.9 percent of the pain and discomfort that I feel in my adult life results from similarly mistaken interpretations. My feeling of continual threat exists in the absence of any real danger. The same is true for my partner.

Perhaps this is why, in walking down the street, you don't see many adults who seem to be enjoying themselves. Most of us move through our lives more or less continually overstressed. We feel tension not only from the pressure of having to get things done, but even more from our fearful interpretation of the events in our life, including the behavior of our partner.

Whenever Martha and I investigate our own negativity, we are always led to the truth that things are not what they seem. The mind is mistaken in believing both that we are unsafe, and that our pain is caused externally. Neither my partner nor events cause my suffering. It is caused by my mind alone. More specifically, it comes from the part of my mind I call my "ego." I may, however, still have appropriate grounds for asking my partner to change their behavior or to listen to my feelings.

Is the Ego Real?

This ego, which plays such a dominant role in the life of the relationship, seems so dense, so solid. It might seem strange to ask whether it is in fact real. Nevertheless, the continual challenging of the ego's reality serves to erode its hold. Moments of clarity may appear, glimpses of truth that show us the ego has the same reality as a child's nightmare. The nightmare is real to the child when it's happening, and yet there isn't the slightest substance to it.

What would it mean in practical life if the ego weren't real? We respond to something that isn't real in a very different way. Think of the countless times you may have reacted to your partner's ego with attack and defense, as if you were genuinely threatened. But if ego isn't real, you can't be threatened, and therefore require no defense.

In every fearful occasion lies an opportunity to uncover and challenge the belief that ego is real. If your ego isn't real, there is no need to be hard on yourself for seeming to have one. Its unreality means it can be no bigger, smaller, better, or worse than anyone else's, though it is in the nature of the ego to condemn itself, and other egos as well. The most shameful places are remarkably similar in everyone.

How does the mind come to grasp that the ego isn't real? Some of the practices we have discussed in this book give a clue. If you do Openhearted Listening with persistence, you may learn that it's possible to step out of the ego with a peculiar kind of inner gesture. When you let go of the ego, it is not vanquished, like a deadly enemy. It simply isn't there anymore, just as darkness simply isn't there when light comes. The light of love, always present at your core, is available to shine away the darkness of the ego.

After frequently observing something that appears dense and solid evaporate in an instant, you may begin to sense, with growing assurance, that the ego's darkness can disappear in the light of love. The ego is a dream that ends in a moment of awakening. The chance to end it is offered by life every moment of now.

True intimacy cannot exist between two egos, but it can take place when two people are interested in waking up from the dream. Every time our partner relates to us from their ego, we have an opportunity to practice stepping out of our own ego by seeing theirs as not real. At such times, our partner is giving us a gift. They are offering us the possibility to feel love again, by changing the way we regard them.

We are not our egos. Belief in the ego's reality has persisted for thousands of years only because it is not sufficiently challenged. Imagine the powerful force for change if both members of a couple were intent on challenging the reality of the ego every time it arose.

Getting into the Darkness Together

From an airplane, you can observe that an east-flowing river is actually flowing north, south, east and west as it loops around at various points. If you are floating down the river, even though its basic direction is east, it's going to look some of the time as if you are going west.

Similarly, you can expect that as intimacy increases there will be times when the relationship feels as if it has regressed. It will seem more negative, crazy, intensely dark, and uncomfortable than it has ever been. This can actually be a healthy sign, signaling the creation of sufficient safety and trust for your deeper layers of repressed fear, pain, and anger to emerge.

During times of difficulty, whoever is the more conscious in the moment can act as the beacon. In a healthy relationship it will switch back and forth. The one holding the light can remind the other that we have asked for pockets of unconsciousness and fear to come to the surface, so that they're seen compassionately for what they are and released. The more intense the negativity, the closer we are to the core of the illusion. Instead of using this situation to blame each other, we can use it to investigate what's really going on.

As our trust increased, Martha and I went through periods, often lasting weeks, where our disharmony was more intense. It seemed as if every little thing could trigger volcanic anger. At times we began to think something was terribly wrong. We felt literally insane. Our east-flowing river was looping west, and displaying some challenging rapids to boot. But we would always emerge from the darkness with our love intact. And, of course, in the flow of our relationship there were also long periods when the river was smooth and easy, when it was effortless to be loving.

We came to accept this as a natural rhythm, because we now had the tools to respond effectively to the darkness. We could now resolve difficulties in minutes rather than days. Even while our egos were displaying themselves at their most raw and disturbing, we were able more often to love ourselves. In the midst of the most intense craziness, we realized that we were discharging our most corrosive inner toxins.

Martha and I have always kept in our heart the possibility that we could create a life together infused continually with the presence of love. It may not be realistic at present to expect to feel love uninterruptedly. But it is possible to become increasingly aware of fear's presence. And when you become conscious of fear, the next important step is to release your defenses.

Thoughts from Martha

Elizabeth Kubler-Ross, a pioneer in the death-and-dying movement, who sat at the bedsides of thousands of dying people, made an interesting statement about fear. She said that by far, the greatest number of people nearing the end of their life were not afraid of dying. What they feared most was not having fully lived—to which I would add, not having fully loved. What has prevented me from loving fully has been fear. The more that I deal with fear in myself, the more I'm able to create an atmosphere of safety for others to heal their own fear.

Couples usually come to our workshops carrying a lot of fear, which intrudes on their capacity to love and keeps their relationship stuck. Let's say an individual in a workshop has become stirred up emotionally by what's happening. They've reverted to survival mode: trying to protect some position or opinion, or avoid facing some awful-seeming truth about themselves that they've been avoiding. Fear has taken over. I might ask them to step back, close their eyes, and locate a safe haven within. It may be basking in a parent's loving smile, or recalling a physical location where they once felt peaceful, or it might be a spiritual feeling of harmony with creation. I ask them to consider the possibility that contact with a deeper, abiding peace is still there, that it is always there, safe and loving. Access to this peace and safety is found only in the present. Some would call it the place of the Soul, the part of us that knows we are not separate and isolated, but part of the One.

When people are able to do this, the fear may still be there, but it is softer and less dominating. The safety surrounding their fear is larger than the fear itself. This allows them to be aware of their fear without identifying with it. They can then come back to the anxiety-provoking situation and have a fresh opportunity to deal with it, or they can move on to something else, but they are no longer stuck. Fear is no longer calling the shots.

I'm not necessarily without fear myself at such times—nor do I have to be. Fear is naturally contagious. When someone in a workshop brings up a challenging issue, I sometimes think, Uh-oh, how are we going to deal with this? Their fear is so palpable that my own fear starts resonating with it. Before I can help them work with their fear, I need to contact my own place of safety. I do this by going inward and by asking for help in prayer. In response, my own fear diminishes, and I am guided how to proceed. No matter how daunting my fear, the next step is always apparent.

It's the same in my own life. Fears come and go, no one can stop them. One that pops up in me from time to time is the fear that Don will die prematurely and I'll be left alone (not surprisingly, this tends to happen when I see him eating something that doesn't seem healthy, or driving too fast). I have to take a deep breath and contact the loving Divine Presence within me. She whispers, "My child, you are loved whether Don is in his body or not. You are loved by him, but also by my all-embracing Love. Breathe into your fear, relax your whole body, and remember that you are safe, held deeply in my embrace no matter what."

One thing that is pivotal to me in doing this is my own meditation practice. All I need for my fear to soften is the willingness to become quiet and receptive. Here is where I have direct experience that I am not struggling alone, that I am supported on all fronts, and that healing love and peace are available at every instant.

A further lessening of my fear occurs when I look back on my life with some perspective. I see that the fears driving my most extreme crises were not well founded. I often feared I would not survive this or that event, yet I would emerge intact, perhaps a bit battle-scarred, but invariably stronger. There's no reason to believe any of my current difficulties will prove different.

I've learned a lot from fear. For years, I treated it as an enemy, an alien presence needing to be eradicated. This was never helpful; indeed, it only tightened the knot inside me. Only when I learned not to be afraid of my fear did I begin to feel free from its grip. I came to see the fearful part of me as the unknowing terror of a small, innocent child. I could be both that child, and the Divine Loving Presence, embracing the child and all her fears with a tender and unconditional love. Whenever I remember I am held in that way, fear has no power over me.

CHAPTER 11

Defenses and Guilt

The Many Forms of Defensiveness

Eliminating defensiveness is one of the great tasks of intimacy. Defensiveness prevents love and communication from flowing between partners. Openhearted Listening can temporarily end defensiveness when something difficult is discussed. We now turn our attention in more detail to the cause of defensiveness, and the possibility for its transcendence.

You have possibly noticed that when your partner regards you critically, you tend to shut it out. Defensiveness is swift and automatic. It can be prompted not only by criticism, but by virtually any expression of fear, anger, or pain from your partner. In fact it can be triggered by anything your ego interprets as a threat. You may even respond defensively to your partner's happiness and success.

Because defensiveness takes many forms, it pays to become familiar with your own favorite versions. Defensiveness often takes the form of attack, or puts up a thick wall, sulking or withdrawing. Many defend through denial. Others justify their behavior. We may defend by inflating ourselves with grandiosity. Defense can use a strategy of distraction, or evasion—not being fully present. We may dismiss our partner, sometimes with humor. We may defend by moving from our true feelings into our intellect, analyzing, lecturing, or arguing. Some partners will burst dramatically into anger or tears so they don't have to listen. Some defend by seeming to agree with their partner, and then proceeding as usual. Whatever its form, defensiveness lies behind most failed attempts at communication.

Your body can be a very useful source of information about the presence of defensiveness. Frequent physical indicators of defensiveness include constricted breathing, contraction around your eyes or in the muscles of your face, a tightness in the belly, abnormal posture, a brittle or higher-pitched quality in your voice, hunched shoulders.

Two Defensive Parents

Gina and Mark were an attractive young couple who were having repeated arguments, ostensibly about the children. Gina had a real charge in her voice as she described how Mark favored Seth, their older child, over Rachel.

> "What really bothers me is you seem totally unaware of the effect you're having on Rachel. When you come into the room you smile at Seth, you pick him up, you treat him like he's the greatest thing in the world. In the meantime, Rachel just sits there waiting for some attention. The poor thing probably thinks her father doesn't even love her. I've asked you repeatedly to stop playing favorites, and you just don't seem to get it! Last night I saw the same thing happen after you got home from work."
>
> Mark shot back, "Look, I'm not so crazy about the way you show the kids love. Your idea of love is to let them do whatever they want. From what I've seen, you don't know how to say no to either of them. They just walk all over you. I was watching you yesterday when Rachel was taking so long to get dressed, and you just couldn't seem to put your foot down. Kids need firmness, not a wishy-washy parent."

Gina, who had actually been trying hard to be more firm, was bothered by the way Mark, instead of acknowledging her efforts, often pounced whenever she slipped up. She had another level of annoyance in her voice as she responded:

"I'm not perfect, okay? But why can't you ever see my moments of success? It just infuriates me that you only notice what's wrong. You never recognize that I've been working hard to get a handle on discipline. Why can't you at least acknowledge my efforts?" She burst into tears.

Mark waited with a stony face for her to stop crying. Finally he said in a hurt tone, "Well I feel exactly the same way! You've told me many times about what you saw as my favoritism, and believe it or not, I've tried! I've been trying real hard to show more affection to Rachel and treat the kids more equally, but you never seem to notice. All you do is jump on me when I forget. It feels like you're gleeful every time you see me make a mistake."

Here is one of the most common patterns of discord. Gina and Mark each felt unacknowledged by their partner for trying to improve. Those who have worked hard to behave more consciously know how infuriating it can be when their partner notices only their failures and neglects to appreciate their moments of success.

To let go of their defenses, Gina and Mark practiced doing Openhearted Listening, where each one heard and validated the other's anger. Neither of them found great difficulty in validating the other's feelings, because each had experienced what it felt like not to be appreciated. Being validated allowed them for the first time to release their defenses.

Now Mark could say to Gina, "I honestly see myself as working hard toward treating the children equally; but I'm sure there are times that I slip up. I give you permission to give me a signal if you think I'm being unfair. I promise to take an honest look at what I'm doing in the moment. And I'd love it if you were to acknowledge the work I've done in that direction."

Gina thanked Mark and responded, "I know within myself how much work I've done on limit-setting with the children.

I'm aware that I have a ways to go. If you see me getting lax, I give you permission to let me know, and I *will* take a look at what's going on. I also truly believe that if you look closely you'll see that I'm improving." Mark smiled and nodded.

With their defenses dissolved, Gina and Mark could take pleasure in acknowledging the work the other had done. They had become allies in bringing about what they both wanted, which was to give their children the very best.

The Source of Defensiveness

Defenses are not just responses to particular events. At a deeper level they represent the elaborate psychological structures, carefully honed since childhood, with which we greet the world. When as young children we begin the healthy and natural process of individuating, we also erect a psychological barrier. The barrier arises from our belief that safety lies in being the way others wish us to be. This is at the core of our false personality, which inhibits true intimacy by covering over who we really are.

Most of what we present to the world and perceive of each other is this shell of personality. Various pictures may be painted on the shell, attractive or otherwise. In proportion to its thickness, the shell prevents contact and intimacy. Encounters with other adults are often unfulfilling because the exchange has occurred not between two beings, but between their shells. Relationship is satisfying only when the essences meet. The process of becoming intimate involves the dissolving of this personality shell. For this to occur, we need to trace defensiveness to its ultimate source.

Defenses occur only when you are feeling bad about yourself. When you are feeling good about yourself, there is no need for defense. If someone criticizes you in an area in which you feel secure, check to see if you aren't relatively free of defensiveness. You may examine what is said, in order to see if it has any validity, and if it does, you have learned something of value. Defensiveness increases as you come upon self-doubt and unworthiness. The very area where you are most intent on proving your innocence is often the place where you feel the most guilt. The more you defend, the more you're convinced there's something wrong with you, and the less safe you feel.

Your capacity for intimacy will depend on whether you accept these unwieldy defensive structures as necessary, or whether you challenge their very foundation. If you find you are being defensive, there's no need to castigate yourself. Instead, shift your attention lovingly to your inner state and see if you can ascertain what's causing it.

It's a blessing every time you're able to release yourself from the chronic need to explain or defend. Sometimes it's enough just to say, "I am sorry, I blew it. I was unconscious and wasn't aware of my impact upon you at the time. I was wrapped up in my own emotional reaction. Please forgive me."

Your feeling of safety does not lie in more effective defenses. Rather, it lies in seeing your absolute worthiness, which includes all of your imperfections. An innocent mind has no need of defenses.

Defenses and Boundaries

When it's suggested that defenses aren't necessary, fear may rush in to tell us that without our defenses, we'll be a victim of our partner's behavior—that they will walk all over us. The only safety, fear says, lies in keeping our defenses vigilantly in place.

Everyone who has gone beyond the romantic state of intimacy has had to confront this paradox. On the one hand, the mind holds tightly to the seemingly reasonable belief that we can't survive without defenses. On the other hand, it seems equally apparent that defenses destroy intimacy. How can we remain safe and still have an intimate relationship? How can we open ourselves to another and still retain our individual integrity? The answer lies in the distinction between defenses and boundaries.

We all have likes, preferences, and needs, from which arise the necessity to set healthy and appropriate boundaries with others as to what we will and won't tolerate. Loving and honoring ourselves will naturally give rise to such boundaries. Out of respect for myself, for example, I may not wish to remain long in the presence of someone who is trying to hurt me. In leaving, I am making an appropriate boundary arising from self-love.

Defenses, which are fear's way of trying to keep us safe, may superficially resemble loving boundaries, but they feel quite different. Defenses use the excuse of self-protection to close the heart. They manifest an underlying hostility. They involve contraction, resistance, a shutting down. In lessening our feeling of love, they tend to trigger much the same in our partner.

Unfortunately, we have learned since childhood to equate setting limits with closing the heart, having associated the need for boundaries with anxiety. In addition, many of us seldom experienced loving boundaries when we were young. Therefore we don't know how to make boundaries while keeping our heart open.

There are two common ways to miss the mark. Some, in order not to seem closed-hearted, avoid making clear boundaries altogether. This gives other people undue power, making the individual feel like a victim of the insensitive or inappropriate behavior of others. Then there are those who make boundaries easily, but close their hearts while doing so. This breeds another kind of resentment.

The two mistakes can be clearly observed in parenting. The first mistake is made by the permissive parent, the second, by the authoritarian parent. One has trouble making boundaries, the other makes them harshly. Neither alternative is effective; neither feels good to either the child or the adult. Judging from the prevalence of ineffective parenting, it appears that the art of making loving boundaries is a difficult one to learn.

And yet learning this art is critically necessary to intimacy. Some of us, in moments of skillful parenting, know what it feels like to create loving boundaries. It is worthwhile to summon those experiences to mind. And it is worth exploring together those resentful areas in your relationship where loving boundaries might replace fear's defenses.

Wanting More Space

For many couples, the boundary issue is particularly poignant when one person wants more contact and the other wants more space. Aaron and Shauna were such a couple. Aaron valued his privacy, and frequently put up a cold and unfriendly barrier when Shauna wanted to be close. Shauna experienced this as rejection, which made her feel bad about herself, as well as upset with Aaron.

Aaron had a different view. He told us that he often felt smothered, pushed by Shauna into being closer than he wished to be at the moment. Whenever he felt the need to be alone, he found it hard to express that to Shauna in a way that didn't hurt her feelings.

This is a common source of pain in intimacy. One reaches out for more contact, and the other, feeling pressured, pulls back. Repeated quarrels and bad feelings are the frequent outcome. Is there a more conscious way of handling the situation?

There is if we better understand our true desires. One kind of desire in relationship centers on getting our own needs met. We want the other to be there for us, to satisfy some personal impulse, or perhaps simply to leave us alone. But there's also a different kind of desire. This is our desire for our partner to do what *they* want, for them to be happy, for them to have everything they need.

For the relationship to feel harmonious, the two kinds of desires have to be in balance. If you tend to over-please, you risk losing your integrity and disrespecting yourself. You will likely end up resenting your partner. On the other hand, if you are without a sense in your heart of another's needs, you miss out on the richness and joy of unconditional giving. The fulfillment of your petty individual needs will feel rather empty. A successful relationship will find the proper equilibrium.

Aaron didn't want Shauna to be the sole arbiter of when they would be intimate. He wanted to be his own person and set his own limits. Such a desire for self-determination is perfectly healthy. But in being his own person, Aaron has no need to put up defenses, to be critical of Shauna or push her away. He can be his own person within the relationship.

The way Aaron withdrew triggered Shauna's feeling of a frightened little girl. Perhaps it reminded her of how her mother or father were not emotionally available when she really needed them. Of course that would leave an imprint. Aaron now had an opportunity to show his partner a level of respect she had never before received, by making his boundaries with an open heart.

What kept Aaron from making gracious boundaries was guilt. When Shauna blamed him for not being available, he felt responsible for her pain. Naturally, he reacted with guilt. This reaction caused him to pull back even more, and become even less able to help. Shauna felt even more abandoned, and responded by pulling even more intensely on him. A classic vicious circle had asserted itself.

The painful dynamic was interrupted when Aaron, for the first time, declined the temptation to feel guilty. Instead, he remained comfortable with the fact that he wasn't as available as Shauna would like him to be, even perhaps as *he* would like to be. Now, feeling more at peace with himself, Aaron gave a different response.

He told her on that occasion that he was feeling withdrawn and was unable to be present. He emphasized that he wasn't abandoning her in his heart or trying to hurt her. He simply needed time to be with himself. He also made a point of letting her know that he valued his closeness to her, and would soon be available again.

From that point on, freed from guilt, Aaron could now be both responsible and fair in coming upon the right balance between his own and his partner's needs. Sometimes he was able to go off in peace, clear about his need, and able to relax. Because his needs were now being fulfilled, he found other occasions when something in Shauna called forth to him. He was surprised to find his overwhelming urge for solitude dissipating.

Shauna found Aaron's new response more reassuring. Now it was easier for her to locate the courage to face her fear of aloneness. At last she could begin to release the belief that her safety and worthiness required his willingness to relate. Whenever Aaron declined the invitation to be with her, she saw she could find within herself the affirmation she had been seeking from outside. Because she was now willing to allow Aaron the expression of his own personal need, something in him was able to trust her further, and he felt closer to her. Each began getting more of what they most deeply wanted, and together they were moving toward freedom.

Unworthiness Casts Its Shadow

Like Aaron and Shauna, most of us feel rather bad about ourselves. The consequences of this guilt are immense. Besides experiencing specific instances of guilt for having committed "bad" acts, the mind is pervaded with a more general, all-encompassing feeling of unworthiness. This feeling has many names: inadequacy, self-doubt or self-hatred, feeling like a failure, unworthiness, a sense that one's life is steeped in sin. It is associated with powerful feelings of shame. Other quite natural human feelings, such as sadness, disappointment, or frustration, can become unbearable when laced with such guilt.

Those who feel unworthy don't respect themselves. They send forth the message, largely unconscious, that they are not worthy of being honored. Others hear and believe this message, and oblige by withholding respect. In fact, others will tend to offer you respect in proportion to how much you respect yourself. Depending on the extent to which you harbor the feeling of unworthiness, it will be difficult both to give and to receive love.

The feeling of unworthiness also darkens our lives through self-sabotage. Those who feel guilty tend to undermine themselves through illness, depression, addictions, accidents, destructive relationships, alienation of others, or self-induced scarcity and discomfort. The guilt underlying these forms of suffering is an extraordinarily pervasive phenomenon. The more relationship difficulties Martha and I witness, the more convinced we are that a sense of unworthiness is the source of virtually all relationship problems.

Letting Our Partner Define Our Worth

When you were little, your sense of worth came naturally from your parents. Now that you are an adult, it would be interesting to ask yourself if you still allow your sense of worth to be defined by others. Do you give your partner, your parents, your friends, your boss, or some outside opinion or teaching the power to define whether or not you are worthy?

Most of us do. If your partner or parent is critical, you may feel compressed into a small space, conforming to their negative picture of you. If you become defensive, it suggests that you believe there's truth to their accusation, a thing worth defending against. In either case, you give the other the power to define your worth.

Perhaps it's time to take back this power. Your response to unloving behavior would be transformed if you knew for certain that the other's evaluation of your worth was irrelevant. If you felt truly good about yourself, another's harshness would be seen as their own cry for help, stemming from their own feeling of unworthiness. Such attempts would elicit compassion rather than guilt.

It is essential that we learn to open our hearts to ourselves, to honor and respect ourselves in the midst of our humanness. Yet most of us seem quite far from that level of inner peace. Is there a path to knowing our basic worthiness?

Unsuccessful Ways of Dispelling Guilt

There are several common strategies for dispelling guilt that don't work. Letting go of them is a step toward compassion for oneself.

Creating ideals—The first strategy for feeling better about ourselves is to create ideals, which we believe will prove our worth if we live up to them. Ideals can include making money; being successful at work or in the community; being attractive, healthy, youthful looking, or well-disciplined. They can include living up to spiritual norms such as kindness, morality, or nonviolence, having pure thoughts and feelings, or doing good deeds. Many ideals can be found around our intimacy, such as having an exciting sex life, a happy partner, or—and remember that anything can become an ideal—a fulfilling, harmonious relationship.

Although we hope to lessen our feeling of unworthiness by living up to these ideals, what actually happens is the reverse. The ideal is the "should," which we hold up continually against what actually is, the way we truly are. Invariably we find ourselves wanting. Every time we fail to live up to our ideals, our level of guilt increases. In fact, we are never able to satisfy our ideals for long. Even if we should for a moment, the mind swiftly reestablishes our unworthiness by setting fresh ideals that are beyond our capacity to achieve.

Many who have not succeeded in living up to their ideals think of themselves as failures. What a merciless and painful label to give oneself.

Imagine having two children. One is successful at school, popular, attractive, confident of his future. The other gets bad marks, is socially clumsy and unpopular, totally confused about the direction of his life, and has pimples. Couldn't you imagine loving the second one, in the midst of his or her unhappiness, just as much as the first? You would scarcely want to use the word "failure" to describe a lost and confused child. The very word comes from an unloving place in our being. "Failure" could actually be considered a secular term for "sinner," since it carries the same condemnatory connotation.

Living up to ideals cannot possibly succeed in eradicating primordial guilt. If we feel unworthy in the core of our being, no change at the level of mere behavior can touch that place.

Seeking approval—Another method of trying to expel the feeling of unworthiness is to find a partner who will approve of us continually. In this, we're actually asking for the unconditional and continuous positive regard that we didn't get from our parents when we were infants. The worse we feel about ourselves, the more we demand that our partner disagree with our self-evaluation, in effect, by showing us nothing but love. They are not allowed to be human and display their own childhood wounds. This strategy leads into a morass, for love must be freely given. If your partner demands to be continually loved, you will tend to shut down in the face of this demand. The more you yourself demand to be loved, the more you will blame your partner for not loving you enough, and the more unloving both of you will become.

Feeling superior—The third strategy is to find a person or persons to whom we can feel superior. Our ego hopes that by finding others lacking, we will establish our greater excellence and thereby rid ourselves of inadequacy.

Strangely, it is often our partner whom we elect to play this role. Many, when they complain about their relationship, attribute its failure to their partner's shortcomings. Because judging our partner seems to soften the pain around our own unworthiness, our mind may become quite vigilant and skillful in noticing our partner's errors and flaws. This may offer us a crude pleasure on the surface, but at the depths it brings no satisfaction. Like drinking salt water to quench your thirst, the more you judge, the more unloving you become, and the worse you feel about yourself. The burden of guilt is lightened instead by releasing judgments, both of yourself and of your partner.

Since these common attempts to eradicate guilt are destined to fail, we are interested to find what does help. A way to begin is by exploring two very different inner voices.

Guilt and Conscience

Learning to walk necessitates falling down; it's a natural part of the process. Learning to mature also requires "falling down" a great many times. Being at peace with oneself depends on one's attitude toward the inevitable tumbles.

One perspective regards these mistakes as unfortunate and

regrettable occurrences. With this outlook, the awareness of my failings will elicit guilt. The voice of guilt asserts that without feeling really bad about myself, I have no way to correct my mistakes. Without guilt, it says, I would become immoral, drown in chaos, or repeat the same mistakes endlessly.

But another voice within offers a different perspective toward my failings. This is the voice of conscience, which responds to my mistakes in a far more compassionate and effective way. The difference lies in the spirit from which these voices emanate. Guilt, arising from fear and confusion, attacks like a harsh parent: "Dammit, you fool, look at you! There you go again!" Most of us have an inner parent that frequently talks to us that way.

As a child, when your parents blamed you harshly, it likely left you with little desire to please. You may have even repeated the undesired behavior in a retaliatory spirit. The same is true when your inner parent is harsh with you. When you are guilty you tend to repeat the unwanted behavior. Although guilt tells you self-condemnation is necessary to keep you from mistakes, the truth is quite the contrary. You are far more capable of releasing an undesired behavior if you are first able to love yourself in the midst of it.

An entirely different inner guide is available, kind and effective. Conscience sees your imperfections as an invitation to loving attention. When you replace guilt with conscience, you are able to regard your failing with a clear, unflinching glance, uncontaminated with blame. Conscience kindly points out when you make a mistake, always with love and respect, and urges you to try something different next time.

True conscience has nothing to do with obeying the transient customs of society. Rather, it is a recognition of moral integrity, arising from the same depths where truth and beauty are seen. Conscience, being grounded in truth, is ultimately loving. Because it is loving, it actually succeeds, unlike guilt, in correcting mistakes.

Being a Loving Parent to Yourself

Becoming a father helped me discover the quality of being loving while pointing out mistakes. When my young son was misbehaving, it was possible to see his behavior as the result of confusion or pain. The same fear-based behavior in an adult might have led me to close my heart. But with my own child, it wasn't hard to make the firm boundaries necessary to prevent him from destroying property and hurting himself or others. In the act of making these boundaries, I found I could say no to his behavior, while at the same time saying yes to his being. He could still feel my love.

Within me, too, is a scared, confused little boy, who sulks, lashes out, or acts inappropriately. When I am behaving in ways that Martha doesn't like, it's usually the hurt little boy in me acting. He, too, needs a loving parent. The way I am when I'm being a good parent can be my model for responding to my own mistakes. I can learn to open my heart to myself when I am socially ungraceful, when I overindulge, when I fail at something, when I close my heart, when I display the ten thousand imperfections that are part of being fully human.

Whenever I feel genuine compassion for myself, I have a natural interest in bringing more harmony into every aspect of my life. I notice mistakes and correct them spontaneously. But I do so with honor and respect for the maker of the mistakes. And in so doing, I find that there is a far greater tendency not to repeat them. Children who are lovingly corrected will more likely want to please their parent.

Moving Out of Self-Judgment

Developing this quality of honor and respect for yourself requires going beyond some powerfully entrenched conditioning. It is not a simplistic process that you can learn from a few rudimentary exercises in self-esteem. It takes focused attention on a regular basis.

Each day brings many incidents that provide opportunities for you to turn against yourself. It happens very quickly. The harsh critic in you arises, taking over the mind so rapidly that you don't even know it's happened. All your efforts to escape seem to trap you more tightly.

The moment you become aware that you've been judging yourself is a moment of great opportunity. It's relatively easy to love yourself when you are functioning well. But when you've done something you dislike, something unskillful, you have a chance to alter the self-feeding cycle of negativity.

When you are about to enter the old pattern of judging yourself, you can think instead: Because I hurt my partner, ate too much, did a poor job parenting, closed my heart (or whatever it was), I am presented with an opening for change. I could easily move into self-judgment in the usual way. But I know from my own experience the pain that results, how pointless and unnecessary it is. Therefore I hereby choose not to react in this way. You have stopped perceiving the voice of guilt as the truth, and now accept it as the point of focus for your work on yourself.

Every time you have an occasion to belittle yourself, you have at that very same moment a choice not to do so. You have the chance instead to affirm your power to deal with all situations out of love and respect for yourself. Every time you decline an opportunity to be harsh with yourself, you deepen your connection to the spring of innocence at the center of your being.

What happens when you find yourself forgetting, engaging in the old pattern of self-blame? This will happen; the old life-denying patterns take time to undo. When you notice it happening, you are bringing the unconscious, mechanical quality of self-blame into the light of awareness, where it may be dissolved. Vigilance and persistence are required to continue noticing, to unhook the sense of self from that quality of blame.

Feeling bad about feeling bad is the trap. You are not asked to be perfect. Instead, you break the chain by refraining from judging yourself even when your self-esteem has faltered. A lack of self-esteem is not a sin. There is no finer expression of self-love than to see with forgiveness when you are not loving and accepting yourself.

Life gives us a gift that perhaps we have not yet fully appreciated: the permission to make as many mistakes as we need to. In the value system dominated by guilt, mistakes are considered grounds for self-hatred. But love warmly accepts our seeming imperfections, rejoicing in the opportunities they provide.

Those who have truly accepted their own shortcomings have no reason to pass judgment on others. Every time you forgive yourself for not living up to the standards you have created for yourself, you are also forgiving every other human being who has displayed a similar failing. Feeling better about yourself will allow you to be more gracious toward your partner's imperfections. Now it will be easier to take another step forward by releasing your judgments, and opening your heart more fully to the one you have come here to love.

Thoughts from Martha

It's amazing how deeply the guilt runs in all of us. My earliest memory is one of feeling guilty for being born. Even as an infant, I could sense how overwhelmed my mother felt, having to contend already with my very active and assertive fourteen-month-old brother. My little heart sank at the prospect of being an additional burden. And so, very early in my life, I learned not to make waves in the family. I tiptoed around feeling apologetic for being alive. Growing up, I dealt with my guilt by being unfailingly "nice." I was the peacemaker in the family, the dutiful daughter who did what people expected, the student who worked hard in school to conceal her dyslexic handicap. So apprehensive was I about offending anyone with my behavior, that what I really wished most was to be invisible.

When Don and I first met, I thought, Phew, what a relief. Here was someone who loved me—proof that my fear of being unworthy was unfounded. But of course the proof was valid only as long as Don continued to show me love all the time. To make sure that would happen, I now had to be unfailingly "nice" with him, too: to be an appeaser, a harmonizer, to never rock the boat—no matter what I was feeling. As long as Don was loving, I could manage it. But when I started to feel interruptions in his love, I began reverting to my "unworthiness" tapes. I began resenting Don for putting me face-to-face with my own demons. Since he was experiencing very much the same thing, we began resenting each other. The downward spiral had begun.

None of this was apparent at the start. Our time in Alaska was relatively peaceful and stress-free. When we moved to California, had a child, embarked on earning a living, and began relating to a lot of high-intensity people, it really stirred the pot. I could no longer mask or stuff down my anger. When I tried to suppress it, it came out sideways. When I did express it, I felt guilty for having behaved badly. It became harder to ignore the discontent: It felt like the bottom had dropped out of our love. I had already been through a divorce, and worried that maybe this wasn't going to work either. Both of us were feeling despair and hopelessness. Seven years into our relationship, we came agonizingly close to splitting up.

In retrospect, I see that this painful period was not only inevitable, but indispensable. A toxin was erupting, coming to the surface where it could be released. Don and I saw that we had been placing our faith in the false assumption that each of us could count on the other to make us feel all right about ourselves. This unquestioned assumption lies at the heart of why so many relationships fail to flourish.

Once we realized this, we had more room for each other's humanness. It took the pressure off, lightening our burden considerably. For me, this means I no longer have to be perfect. I can, for example, blow up at Don without feeling guilty. My anger is no longer a seething volcano, but merely a momentary letting off of steam, which I know will pass quickly. Ironically, because it feels okay to be human, I get upset less often and less intensely. We don't stop loving each other every time one of us gets a little annoyed. Most important, we're willing to hear each other's feelings, and have well-tested methods for doing so. Because I have faith that I will be heard when I have negative feelings—even if I don't express them in the best way—I feel relaxed about sharing them completely. This actually makes it far easier to put them out in a respectful manner. The spiral has turned back upward.

When my son was born, I cried, remembering my own birth, feeling the poignancy of an immense consciousness incarnated in a tiny body. His utter innocence was so apparent. Why not extend that to myself as well? As I continue meditating and challenging my unconscious beliefs, the feeling of unworthiness softens and recedes. I begin to realize that the little collection of atoms I call my personal human life is really part of a vast Ocean of Spirit. Forgetting this, believing I am a separate, vulnerable being, is what allows in all my unconscious guilt. Every time my soul becomes aware of my divine heritage, I leave guilt behind, and am free.

CHAPTER 12

Opening the Heart: The Greatest Challenge

Is Judgment Necessary?

In moving through life, it is necessary to make many evaluations: Being here would serve me better than being there, this food is not good for my body, this car is not good for my pocketbook. We call this "discrimination," an essential faculty for living in the world.

Judgment is something quite different, involving the closing of the heart. From birth, we are exposed to judgment of ourselves and others as a standard accompaniment to every aspect of our lives. Judging others has a comfortable and familiar quality, tempting us to indulge frequently for the pure pleasure of it.

We expend a vast amount of energy judging ourselves and others, particularly for fear-based behavior. We judge others for their anger, their self-centeredness, their insensitivity, their inconsistency, their greed. All are things for which we also judge ourselves.

Closing the heart may also manifest as failing to see the unique beauty of another. When the heart is truly open, there is a natural sense of appreciation for others, even while being aware of their imperfections. An early warning sign of the heart's closing is the loss of appreciation. Even though you may not be consciously aware of judging your partner, lack of appreciation dampens the love and the flow of energy between you.

Are we saying judgment is bad? How is one to regard the more extreme forms of inhumanity and violence? How is one to regard Hitler, or a serial killer? At a more immediate level, how is one to regard the insensitive behavior of one's partner? Do I need to close my heart when my partner doesn't keep agreements, or isn't tuned into my needs, or gets angry at me unfairly, or treats me insensitively? How is one to respond, in short, when confronted with another's fear?

My own fear presents its case with convincing logic and consummate skill. It asserts that I need judgment to move through the world. If I have a problem with my partner, my discomfort is due to their behavior. In order to remain safe, I must close my heart to them. And yet a basic obstacle to the harmony of our relationship is the judgment that we develop toward each other. No relationship can flourish in the midst of such mutual harshness.

My deeper wisdom has a different perspective. If my heart were truly open to my partner at this moment, would there really be a problem? Perhaps the "problem" really lies in the fact that my heart is closed. If so, there is only one solution.

Responses arising from a closed heart perpetuate fear. They never fail to create further pain and division. The pain in the human consciousness is in urgent need of healing. Judgment doesn't heal; it perpetuates the very quality that it's judging. We need to respond to fear-based behavior without succumbing to our own fear. Yet—and this is a core issue—it is important to avoid setting up non-judgment as an ideal. Many couples have their most acrimonious debates over who is being the more judgmental. When we idealize the quality of non-judgment, such absurdities are the inevitable outcome.

Ideals Versus Vision

Ideals elicit harshness and blame. Whenever I hold an ideal, I cannot help but compare my behavior or another's to that ideal. If my ideal is non-judgment, I am going to judge anyone I find being judgmental. Using a harsh means to attain a gentle end, my ego is blind to its pretense of spirituality. Fear is once again masquerading as love.

Ego loves to play in spiritual realms, to usurp every important spiritual truth and use it for its own ends. This gives rise to all the forms of spiritual seeking by which we attack others for their wrong beliefs and practices. In the name of spirituality we condemn those who do not follow our particular path.

A fundamentalist preacher I once heard interviewed on a radio talk show informed the audience that a large number of them would end up in perpetual hell for not living up to the precepts of his religion. After he'd gone on for some time about this, the interviewer, seemingly a little dismayed, offered a fantasy. He pictured a poor sinner dying and going up to the Heavenly Gate, where he is confronted by a stern, awesome God. The sinner is asked if he's lived his life according to the correct teachings. The sinner, an honest sort of fellow for all his backsliding, admits that he hasn't. At this point the Lord's severe countenance softens. He smiles and says, "Ahh, that's all right, come on in anyway." Perhaps more of this quality of forgiveness is needed with our partner.

There is a difference between an ideal and a vision. Holding an ideal often leads to the closing of the heart in the service of open-heartedness—an obvious contradiction. But a vision operates in a different way. When I remember an ideal, I tend to berate myself for not having lived up to it in the past. When I remember a vision, I have the opportunity to practice it now.

To have a vision of living non-judgmentally means that I have seen the beauty of it, and deeply wish to live with my heart open. When I become aware that I have closed my heart, I don't close it further by blaming myself. Rather, I look within to see the fear that has closed my heart, and offer myself forgiveness for being afraid.

Ideals place change in the future. A vision of a changed heart allows change to occur in the present. Loving means are necessary to a loving end. With an open heart as a vision, I practice opening my heart to the best of my ability now, as often as I remember, with no distinction regarding content.

The Source of Judgment

Why do certain people annoy us, while we overlook others' flaws? The imperfections we react to in others remind us, in however disguised a form, of what we have not forgiven in ourselves. Others become a mirror, showing us a disconcerting reflection of ourselves.

If you want to know where your spiritual work lies, focus on the people whom you judge the most, the ones who exist beyond the outer limits of your compassion. They may be individuals or groups: your partner, your parents, former lovers, present and former friends, bosses, or teachers; or perhaps certain politicians, sports figures, celebrities, or famous villains of history. Sometimes you judge personality traits such as aggressiveness, passivity, or dishonesty. Sometimes your judgment will extend to whole classes of people: right-wing conservatives, "bleeding heart" liberals, yuppies, spouse abusers, child abusers, serial murderers, hypocrites, victims, hippies, rednecks, "the establishment," the military, macho men, wimps, feminists, pro-choicers, anti-abortionists, incompetent doctors, sleazy lawyers, politicians, proponents of other religions . . . the list is endless. Do you recognize anyone? We all have our favorite judgments, which we defend with vigor.

Interestingly enough, we often judge our partner the most. We have many reasons, but perhaps the fundamental one is that they are not loving us in the way our ego demands. Ego doubts their love, first of all because in their humanness they are unable to love us with continuous unconditional perfection; and second, because their love does not always express itself according to our image of what loving behavior should look like. Of course, they judge us similarly for not loving them in the way they want.

Once the original, basic judgment of our partner is in place, we find ourselves looking for—and finding—a great many little things for which to judge them. Their habits and human imperfections, once easy to overlook, start unaccountably to annoy us. Sometimes our partner can scarcely do anything right. Traits we would forgive in a good friend are suddenly less tolerable in our partner. The bramble bush of judgment, spreading outward, can take up a great deal of space in a relationship, ultimately crowding out the love.

I am in a relationship with a powerful, independent woman who doesn't always hold my views or want the same things as I do. In working out her issues, she sometimes displays her human imperfections, which has given me many opportunities to watch my heart close. Sometimes I have justified this closing to myself; at other times I have wished fervently that it were otherwise. But my desire for an open heart does not automatically make it so. Obviously, something more is needed.

The Motive for Eliminating Judgment

The motive for opening the heart has traditionally come from an external authority, such as a religious or spiritual teacher or teaching. Virtually every religion tells us to love, be kind, and forgive. If we succeed, we are promised future rewards in this life or another. If we fail, we can expect punishment. But apparently rewards, punishments, and commandments don't seem to have much effect on the deeply rooted habit of judgment. Even strong exhortations to open the heart have little impact. The heart seems to close on its own, without our volition. Heavily rooted conditioning is not going to disappear without some major inner change.

Our heart is more likely to open when our motivation comes from within. Such motivation arises quite naturally when we suspect the immense level of pain that comes, both to us and to those in our lives, from living with a closed heart.

To be in the presence of someone with a closed heart can be painful enough, but to harbor it in oneself may be the closest thing we know to Hell. I need not believe in the traditional religious concept of Hell to experience it in this life. Hell is the world I inhabit when my heart is closed.

In the world of the closed heart, I get sidetracked into thinking that my happiness comes from having a bank account, a certain lifestyle, a good relationship, good sex, an attractive or healthy body, a fine home, respect from others, and so on. But when I take an honest look at how I have fared after achieving what I had so ardently coveted, I find the hoped-for state of undisturbed satisfaction turning rapidly into the usual gnawing discontent.

Nothing in the material world brings any lasting contentment. All the possessions, experiences, pleasures, and successes that I have fervently hoped would relieve my pain are but ineffective consolation prizes, sooner or later leaving the heart empty. All my striving for security, pleasure, or power has taken me down a path that leads nowhere. I begin to realize that the largely unconscious value system by which I have lived my life is false to its core.

To experience the motivation for altering my inner world requires first that I feel a powerful distaste for the Hell of my closed heart, and next that I harness this aversion in the service of my release. The Hell is not merely private. The discomfort I feel when my loving relationship turns into hostility or bitterness is related to my feeling when I read about painful and violent conflicts in troubled areas of the world. The conflicts in my relationship are made of the same stuff as war among nations.

My distaste for all this pain and conflict can lead me to the passionate search for a better way. I must have an earnest persistence, the kind that won't stop when it meets with obstacles. If I have the intention, I will receive the perfect teachers, examples, experiences, insights—whatever I need.

The return of Heaven comes only when the closed heart opens. As I get older, it becomes increasingly plain that the only thing I really want, the only thing that will bring me peace, is to feel love. Whenever I meet my fear with love, whenever I forgive by releasing my ego, there is a joy that has nothing to do with outer conditions or with the surface fluctuations of my emotional life.

Our hearts have not on the whole been very open. Our parents could not teach us how to open them, nor could our places of worship, elders, schools, or culture. Nor, in most cases, has intimate relationship taught us the secret. How then can we learn, together with our partner, to make that elusive transformation from a closed heart to an open one?

Opening the Closed Heart

The formidable task of opening the heart requires a major inner shift. Simple formulas or mechanical exercises don't suffice for this level of transformation. Nevertheless, a few guidelines may hint at the direction to be followed.

Work on forgiving yourself—Your attitude toward your partner is a direct reflection of your attitude toward yourself. Self-blame projects outwards as judgment, while forgiveness of yourself softens your responses to others. If you want to love your partner more unconditionally, nothing is more important than working to release your feelings of unworthiness.

Accept your closed heart—Paradoxically, a major key to opening the heart is accepting its being closed. When your heart is contracted, the temptation to deprecate yourself is strong. But fighting against an undesired trait merely serves to strengthen it. And turning against yourself when your heart has hardened toward others only causes you to resent them for triggering this feeling. It is easy to get caught up in an endless pattern of blame.

When your heart is closed to your partner, it does not mean you have stopped loving, though you may be out of touch with your love. It may mean you are not immediately available for certain kinds of interactions. But what a burden to feel obligated to be open to your partner all the time!

The truth is, you cannot open your heart by an act of will. The heart has its own rhythms of expansion and contraction. When it is expansive it may seem to be fed by a richly flowing river. Other times, the river feels sluggish, unmoving. At such times it takes true discipline to stay present and loving toward yourself.

Your partner will do a thousand and one things that elicit your judgment, ranging from major offenses to the merest glance or tone of voice. Become familiar with these triggering mechanisms, and acknowledge them. The pain of your closed heart is trying to tell you something important that you haven't yet learned. Your healing will be impeded if you make yourself wrong for judging. By accepting yourself, ego and all, you make it easier to become conscious of your judgments. This is an indispensable step on the way to releasing them. Such acceptance allows you to relax inwardly enough to be able to shift attention from the judgment itself to the mind that is judging. When you explore this mind, you will begin to see its own pain, fear, and confusion.

Stand outside your judgments—Once your judgments are acknowledged, the next step is to put some space around them, to cease identifying with them. To identify with a feeling means to be caught up in it. The feeling so dominates you that there's no place to stand outside and be aware of it. Listen to people arguing about politics, and observe what it is like to be identified with being right. To stop identifying with a feeling means to find an inner place from which to observe it, a place which is itself not part of the feeling. It is important to be aware that you are having feelings, while neither justifying nor condemning them.

See yourself with honesty—Awareness of oneself has immense power. Because it touches your core, it can transform more deeply than trying to live up to ideals. An honest look at yourself, the one who judges, will begin to weaken the belief structure that, through the years, has supported all the judgments.

If at the dinner table you knock over a glass of water, it would be hard to feel righteous toward your partner for their carelessness if they did the same thing a moment later. Most of the things for which we blame our partner are things we do as well, though perhaps in altered form.

It can be painfully revealing to see that you participate in those very qualities you judge. If you judge your partner for being self-centered, can you honestly say you are not that way? If you judge them for not listening, consider whether you yourself always listen. If you judge them for being insensitive or greedy, take a look at your own level of sensitivity or greed. Perhaps you judge your partner for not taking your needs more fully into account. Do you always do that much for them? If you judge people for being unloving, you are probably not confronting the great irony of closing your heart because someone else has closed theirs. In the act of judging people for being in their ego, you are taking yourself to that same place.

Look into your heart when you become aware of judging someone. See whether or not it feels genuinely good to be judging. Pay attention to the hidden assumptions of moral superiority that underlie the judgment. Observe how you're feeling about yourself. Perhaps you'll become aware of the feeling of inadequacy that drives the judgment. Instead of trying to change the content of your judgmental thoughts, shift your attention to your painful feeling of unworthiness. Now you are addressing the root cause of the judging.

As you observe yourself in this fashion over time, it becomes increasingly hard to support your judgments with your intellect. Before self-examination, you not only passed judgment, but justified it as well. Now there is a useful separation between your emotions and your intellect: The latter no longer supports the former in its delusion. When you cease believing in the righteousness of your judgments, an inner circuit is broken. You are in the peculiar position of harboring feelings whose basis you have come to doubt. A process of erosion is taking place. The voice of fear, challenged to its very core, is no longer the only force operating within the mind. Through persistence in the process, you may find the habit of judgment beginning to lose its hold.

See difficult behavior as a call for help—Think for a moment about your partner, when they are behaving in a way you find distasteful. See if it's possible to perceive their behavior as an expression of fear and pain. Out of that fear they are being aggressive, withdrawn, dishonest, self-centered, inappropriate, or dismissive.

Consider that your partner was in that moment simply a hurt, frightened child, in need only of compassion. Of course your compassion allows you to make firm boundaries when needed. But it does not allow you to close your heart.

Take this a step further. Imagine that your partner and you are allies in a scenario you are creating together. Both of you are seeking a teaching that will release obstacles to the expression of your love. Every time your partner acts unlovingly, you are presented with that teaching. If you're able to see their actions as a call for help, rather than a threat, and respond accordingly, you have been graced with additional love into your life. Through your more loving response, something in both of you is healed.

The temptation exists to hold in your mind an image of your partner in their fearful state, to believe that their ego is who they are. Yet whatever feeling you hold toward them tends to bring out that very quality in them. Whenever you think about your partner, try to look beyond the surface manifestation of fear and penetrate right through to the core of who they really are. See them as a being of divine origin, who may be momentarily caught up in confusion and fear, but who therefore deserves only compassion.

It doesn't really matter if you have forgotten this perspective for a few minutes or months or decades. At this moment you have an opportunity to release the past. It's been just as tough for your partner as it's been for you. They have gone through just as much pain and fear as you have. Like you, they are doing the best they can. Each moment of pain is an opportunity to find compassion for both of you for all the suffering inherent in the whole process.

The fearful mind continually suggests that it is not safe to love, that there is good cause to close the heart. But for Martha and me, in our moments of clarity, one truth stands out above all: We are not in danger from our partner's ego. The only thing that feels threatened is our own ego.

There is never any justification for closing our heart to our partner.

One of the great challenges of my life, and of my relationship with Martha, is taking this idea and actually putting it into practice.

If Martha snaps at me, my main interest is to avoid the temptation to withdraw or attack, and instead to see that she is in pain and fear, to which the only appropriate response is compassion.

If you have tried, you know that this is a most difficult challenge. Learning to open the heart when it wants to close has been the most arduous lesson of my life. Although the ideas and practices outlined above have been helpful in softening the rough edges, there have been times when things between Martha and me became so filled with hostility that we hadn't the personal resources to cope. When it becomes that murky and confusing, the usual tools and techniques may seem insufficient.

Asking for Help

At such times there is a resource available, a Greater Wisdom, that operates at a totally different level from the limited ego mind. This resource is accessible at any time for the asking. Native Americans call it the Great Spirit; the Christian tradition calls it the Holy Spirit. This Greater Wisdom lives within each being, knowing the truth of every situation. It can be appreciated only through direct experience.

At the physical level, the Greater Wisdom functions quite efficiently underneath conscious awareness, providing with inspiring precision the trillions of biochemical responses necessary to digest our food, nourish our cells, move our muscles, and heal our wounds. At the mental level, this same wisdom is available to guide, comfort, and inspire us, and to help us move toward harmony and peace.

When a couple is at an impasse or in a serious argument, resolution may seem impossibly difficult. Each person is locked fiercely into their own position. Neither wants to let go, despite the obvious pain involved. Whenever Martha and I are mired in such a place that feels beyond our power to escape, we make use of the Greater Wisdom and ask for help. We find that when we do, help invariably arrives.

The only difficulty lies in getting to the point where we're willing to ask. The magnitude of this challenge should not be underestimated. When I am so completely enmeshed with Martha in an angry, blaming state, my ego has absolutely no interest in love, peace, or resolution. Ego most decidedly prefers to be right, even at the cost of remaining miserable. Asking for help, which is tantamount to surrender, is the last thing in the world it wants.

If my entire being were imprisoned in this view, there would indeed be no hope. But buried deep within, there's a place untouched by ego, remaining sane and clear enough to suspect the ego's view of the situation is untrue. A small fragment of my awareness is willing to be released from the ego's stranglehold, willing to step outside the painful prison of attack and defense. Somewhere within dwells a little bit of willingness to see by a different light.

When I'm holding tightly to my pain, the most difficult task is locating the 1 percent of my being that's willing to let go. It sometimes takes a supreme effort to find that willingness. The other 99 percent is loud, insistent, and convinced there is no perspective but its own. However, this is not a struggle between the two. Nothing is ever accomplished by fighting against the ego. What does the fighting is only another aspect of the ego. The only worthwhile struggle lies in locating the willingness to abandon the battlefield. The inner act by which one finds this little willingness cannot really be described in words, but is worth learning, for in it lies release from suffering.

If one of you has been able to locate the little willingness not to be in the ego, they can request that their partner join in asking for help. Pause for a moment to get in touch with the part of you that's willing to do that much. Whoever first suggested it might ask the Greater Wisdom (in whatever vocabulary is suitable) to help the two of you release your limited perspective and see the situation through different eyes.

Sit together for a while in silence. Let go for an instant your entire history, whether it be a minute or twenty years. Experience together a moment where thought and conflict have ceased, where the mind is empty and receptive to what lies beyond its chattering.

It's as if this were the only instant that ever existed, a timeless moment. It doesn't matter if the cave has been dark for ten thousand years; if you light a match, the cave is now lit, and the duration of its previous darkness is irrelevant.

This silent asking can bring a miraculous shift. In one second, the endlessly complex tangle of despair and blame can be transformed, the ancient darkness wiped away, and a blessing allowed to take its place. No matter how much pain and confusion you have created together, it can all evaporate in a single instant of love.

There is great beauty every time you perform this fundamental spiritual gesture. Through it you keep learning anew that all healing takes place *now*, and that it does so with an ease unconnected to your degree of pain.

I once heard an interview with a man who had successfully freed himself from a major heroin addiction. The interviewer was impressed: "It must have taken a heroic effort to overcome such a powerful addition. How long did it take you to kick the habit?"

The former addict instantly replied, "Oh, about one second."

On many an occasion Martha and I have invited the Greater Wisdom when it felt beyond our capacity to free ourselves from our toxicity. Healing has always graced us, no matter how seemingly hopeless the situation. The very intention to receive help aligns us with something greater than our limited minds. The actual resolution may take various forms. Sometimes one or both of us will receive a revelation that allows us to see the situation in a fresh light. We may talk about it anew in a wholly different way. At other times Martha and I have only to look up and find each other smiling. The clouds have simply parted, and it's over. The truth may arrive wordlessly; it may come in different guises. But it always comes.

Summarizing

To open the closed heart one first focuses on oneself: releasing feelings of unworthiness, accepting that the heart is closed, putting space around judgments, and seeing oneself clearly and honestly.

The next step focuses the same clear light on the object of judgment, seeing that person with compassion. The final step is turning to an energy beyond the limited confines of the mind, inviting it in to perform its healing. Though I describe these as "steps," they are not necessarily a linear progression. The work can be done in all areas simultaneously.

It's not that this process will immediately bring an end to all judgment. The mind's habit of closing the heart is tenacious, and the ego will persist in its ancient ways. You will doubtless stumble on the path many times. Nonetheless, change eventually begins, perhaps at first scarcely noticeable. Something alters. A new vigilance persists under the surface, one that quickly spots the old habits as they arise, and in whose light they quietly dissolve. Primitive patterns of attack and defense don't have a chance to take hold the way they once did. The slightest tightening in the body, negative thought, or closing of the heart sets off a warning signal, an invitation to investigate the attitude behind the contraction.

A miracle takes place when two people dedicate their relationship to the sanctified task of opening the closed heart. An extraordinary process is begun that goes far beyond what is possible for one person. Once you set foot on this path, the universe will grace you with creative ways to see things differently, to release weary habits, to reinterpret in a new light what happens between you and your partner. It will send you tests, difficulties, and obstacles of the highest order. But you will also receive many encouraging and satisfying reminders that you are on a path in harmony with the highest good for all.

Thoughts from Martha

I'd like to return to the message of hope that I began with. The opening of the heart—which Don and I have talked about throughout this book as being the key element in the work of relationship—can seem at times almost impossibly difficult. It's very common for couples to become discouraged at some point. "Other people may be able to do this," they may say, "but we can't. Our relationship is too much of a mess." When resentment has built up sufficiently, partners may feel they no longer even have any interest in forgiving each other. It's all come to seem a hopeless morass.

We can assure you that this feeling is not only common, but well-nigh universal. Virtually all couples experience this hopelessness at one time or another. When they do, I wish I could play them a video of Don and me from our past. I wish I could show them the horrendous fights we used to have, when we wouldn't talk to each other for days. I know that if they could see the extent of our venom and hostility, most of them would say "Wow, these people are worse off than we are."

It was our very agony that produced a change. We didn't have half the tools and resources that are available today—therapy, books, workshops. All we had was our misery, and the feeling that something different had to happen. That was enough. We saw the only thing that did make a difference was to open our closed hearts. Once we saw this, we had no choice but to follow that path.

We've seen many couples who believe they lack the sophistication to do this work. I want to put my arms around them and reassure them. We've seen couples from every social or educational background, from blue-collar workers to high-level professionals. No one has an edge, no matter what category, profession, educational background, or spiritual tradition they come from. I've seen people who are therapists them-selves struggle with the basics, while less psychologically schooled people "get it" right away.

Learning to open the heart is not a subject like history or physics. It's an inner gesture that comes from seeing plainly where the closed heart leads, and demanding something different for oneself: I don't know how I'm going to learn this, but I intend to. I want it with all my heart and soul. Literally anyone with such an intention can do it. Here is the beginning of change.

When you do embark on this path, the content of the issues doesn't really matter, nor does the intensity of built-up resentment and pain. It takes no time to discharge the whole of it; it can all happen in an instant. If one can say "I want to release all this old pain," and really mean it, it can be gone in that moment. You may have a choice whether to invite it back in the next instant, but at that moment, it's truly gone. I've seen couples after being stuck for years break free from their pattern in a thirty-second exchange. Such moments can shift the whole course of a relationship.

Often the only factor preventing change is the simple belief that I can't open my heart to my partner as long as they're behaving a certain way. A woman client recently explained to us why she couldn't open her heart to her husband: He was drinking too much, he wasn't relating to her and the children, he wasn't earning enough money. How could she open her heart to that? What she came to see is that whether her heart is open or closed is not up to her husband; it's up to her. She controls her heart valve. When she gives away that control, she becomes helpless, and real change becomes virtually impossible.

The truth is, although the mind will say it's not safe to love, there's never a good reason to keep the heart closed. The mind is no judge of the heart's domain. Letting it overrule the heart is like giving control to a disturbed child. Whatever happens, I always have the power to turn the dial to a more loving part of my being. When I notice a judgment of Don—say because he let the grass grow so long that the mower couldn't handle it and shut down—I ask myself: Do I have room for Don to make mistakes? Is he supposed to have it all together? Or is he, like me, a work in progress? Can I look upon his mistakes as a mother appreciates her child, recognizing his foibles, even being frustrated by them, but still loving his being?

Having gone to the depths, Don and I contend that if we can open our hearts, anyone can. We're not in a special category; whoever has the desire can follow this path. If your desire doesn't feel strong enough, pray for it to strengthen. There is always light behind the dark clouds, if you're willing to look for it. And as Don and I know from experience, a little willingness is all it takes.

About the Authors

Don Rosenthal was born in 1938 and grew up near New York City. After college, he began a career as a musician, playing the bassoon in major symphony orchestras and chamber groups. In 1963 he gave up that profession to move to Alaska, where he worked as a fisherman, bartender, and teacher, and embarked on a lifelong spiritual journey. It was there that he met Martha, whom he married in 1971. They built a cabin in a remote area and for several years lived a quiet life of inner exploration. In 1978, obeying an impulse to return to the world, they moved to the coast of California, where Don trained at the Tomales Institute of Psychotherapy under Robert Hall, graduating in 1986. He and Martha had a son, Aram, now grown, whom they homeschooled. In 1990 they moved to rural northern Vermont, where Don continued the counseling work he had begun in California. Since arriving in Vermont, Don and Martha have led over a hundred workshops on intimate relationship, mostly in their home but throughout the country and in Europe as well. In addition Don counsels couples and individuals privately, employing psychotherapy as a means of spiritual investigation. He is at work on a second book, about the challenges and mysteries of the inner life.

Martha Rosenthal was born in 1943 and grew up in Oregon. After graduating college she taught elementary school in Massachusetts, Germany, and Alaska. She left teaching to live in a small cabin on the Alaskan seacoast, where she serendipitously encountered Don. In their first years together they shared a life of outward simplicity coupled with intensive yoga and meditation practice. Following their move to California, Martha studied body and energy work, and developed a private practice emphasizing the union of physical and spiritual elements. With the birth of their son, Aram, in 1982 she began to devote more time to her family, while at the same time she and Don began to work together in the area of relationship. After the move to Vermont, Martha returned often to Alaska, where she led contemplative wilderness retreats for women. In Vermont Martha coleads couples workshops with Don, for which she generally provides the culinary and inn-keeping amenities. She also leads women's meditation retreats—an outgrowth of her own meditation practice—and assists individuals, couples, and families in applying spiritual perspective to their lives. She and Don live in a 600-acre land co-op where they garden, keep house, and maintain their home as a workshop and retreat facility.

Awakening Together
Workshops

---

with
Don and Martha Rosenthal

Don and Martha offer weekends for couples based on the principles enunciated in this book. They also offer private retreats for individual couples. For more information, including a current schedule, call (802) 439-6769, or e-mail couples@sover.net. Information is also contained on The Heartwork Center Web site, reachable at either www.heartworkcenter.org or www.awakeningtogether.org.

The Heartwork Center is a nonprofit education and retreat center founded on the principles of Don and Martha's work. Located on six hundred rural Vermont acres, it aims to provide couples with the resources for cultivating harmonious intimacy. These include workshops, conferences, and other educational offerings, as well as private couples retreats. For information consult The Heartwork Center Web site (www.heartworkcenter.org), call (802) 439-5324, or e-mail lostm@sover.net.